Imagining
Lahore

HAROON KHALID

Imagining
Lahore

THE CITY THAT IS,
THE CITY THAT WAS

PENGUIN
VIKING

An imprint of Penguin Random House

VIKING

USA | Canada | UK | Ireland | Australia
New Zealand | India | South Africa | China | Singapore

Viking is part of the Penguin Random House group of companies
whose addresses can be found at global.penguinrandomhouse.com

Published by Penguin Random House India Pvt. Ltd
4th Floor, Capital Tower 1, MG Road,
Gurugram 122 002, Haryana, India

First published in Viking by Penguin Random House India 2018

Map of Lahore courtesy of the Office for Conservation
and Community Outreach; illustrated by Aqib Taj

10 9 8 7 6 5 4 3 2

The views and opinions expressed in this book are the author's own and the
facts are as reported by him which have been verified to the extent possible,
and the publishers are not in any way liable for the same.

ISBN 9780670089994

Typeset in Adobe Garamond Pro by Manipal Digital Systems, Manipal
Printed at Replika Press Pvt. Ltd, India

www.penguin.co.in

MIX
Paper from
responsible sources
FSC® C016779

This is a legitimate digitally printed version of the book and therefore might not
have certain extra finishing on the cover.

*To Soha, Zarrar, Abeeha, Kabir, Raem, Reyah and Arya
for making this world a much more beautiful place*

CONTENTS

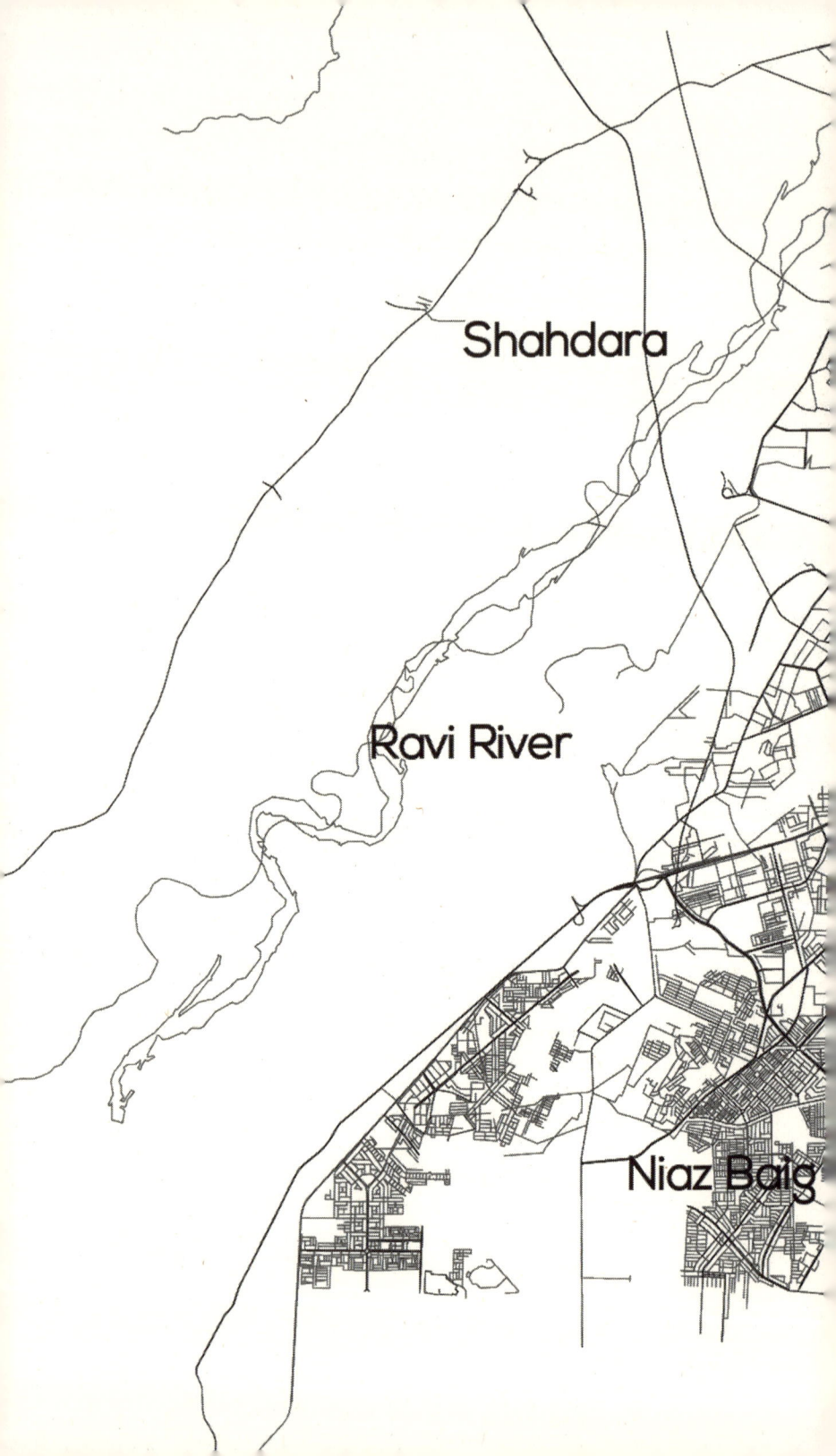

INTRODUCTION

There is a Lahore that appears to the eye—the second-largest city in Pakistan, teeming with bank-leased cars, an army of motorcyclists on its neatly laid roads, occasional heaps of garbage on the side, large multistorey buildings in the midst of hundreds of little *abadi*s, some official, others not. There is, however, another Lahore, a city as real as the one described above, yet hidden—a city that can only be imagined. Somewhere in the middle of these two worlds is my home.

Sometimes there are tangible traces of that other city: an abandoned Hindu temple standing like an anomaly in the midst of a crowded market, an old colonial structure surrounded by glass-fronted plazas. Mostly, however, that city exists in folk tales, stories and legends. These stories are scattered all over Lahore, at its junctions, around its monuments, underneath its roads and gardens, in the lives of people, in the courtyards of Sufi shrines or within abandoned Hindu temples.

Even today, as the world moves around these spaces oblivious to them, their stories continue to unfold, dancing and singing for anyone willing to listen. In these performances, Valmiki discourses with Jesus Christ, Zulfikar Ali Bhutto meets Qutb al-Din Aibak, nationalists participate in historic Mughal wars, Mughal princesses witness the heralding of a neo-liberal model of development, Bulleh Shah dances with Bhagat Singh.

Imagining Lahore is a journey through this city, in the process attempting to disentangle the story of Lahore's evolution, from its mythological origin to its contemporary status of a hegemonic capital. In the book, I have used my own travels around the city, gleaning tales in order to present a chronology of events. My travels do not necessarily follow a chronological order. They are spread over a decade, as I moved from one story to another. It was only when I began planning and writing this book in November 2014 that I started the process of bringing these diverse narratives together to map the story of Lahore. In a few instances, where some time had passed between my visit and the time of recording it in the book, I have attempted to provide the timeline of my visit. Given the rapid pace of change in the city, it is possible that the places I talk about here might have changed form since the time I visited them.

While the structure of the book takes on a reverse chronological order, there are several tangents within each chapter, exploring other stories that are associated with this historic city. In a few of these cases, the stories are apocryphal and part of folklore; they are nonetheless important to the contemporary city for they highlight how the people of Lahore imagine their home and its past. Uninterrupted, they flow through streets and alleys, making Lahore the city that it is.

1

A CONTESTED CITY

With one hand on the pressure horn, the taxi driver rolled down his window and showed me his other arm, the Punjabi version of the middle finger. Still glaring at me, he forced himself through a tiny gap in front of my car, the shiny yellow body of his car brushing against my bumper. Another wound. Another story of struggle from this arena where only the toughest survive. I honked back. Twice. 'Fuck!' 'You!'

A garbage collector on his donkey cart calmly filled the gap left by the taxi driver. A little child sat next to him, holding a cheap mobile phone on which the song 'Kitna Haseen Chehra' played loudly. It was from *Dilwale*, a popular Ajay Devgn movie from 1994. Cursed at by dozens of people who felt their space unlawfully invaded by the donkey cart, the older boy, who held the reins in his hand, sang on, oblivious to the curses and the traffic jam around him.

On the other side of the car, a motorcycle rider stood on the tips of his toes to gauge the extent of traffic ahead of him. Sweating profusely, he took off his helmet and held it in his hand, undoubtedly planning to wear it closer to the junction where there would be an army of traffic wardens, almost as helpless as the sea of humanity converging upon them from all directions.

'How long?' I asked him, as he sat back on his bike.

'A long time,' he said with the frustration that grows on you as you learn to live with the messy traffic of a developing country. Almost instinctively, both of us looked up at Shehbaz Sharif, chief minister of Punjab, who smiled down upon us from a gigantic billboard over the bridge. I wondered if this was the most appropriate picture for this spot, where thousands of commuters got stuck every day. The accompanying message suggested regret for the temporary inconvenience to the commuters for the larger good.

With no control over my situation, I honked again. Twice.

The message on the chief minister's billboard had become a part of my daily routine. Every evening, at the peak of rush hour, I would get stuck at this junction for roughly an hour. Soon after coming to power in 2008, after a decade of military rule, the chief minister of Punjab had resorted to what he knew best—construction of new flyovers and underpasses. This was one of the iconic junctions of Lahore—Kalma Chowk. A tall minaret once stood at its centre with the first Kalma, testifying to the divinity of Allah and the finality of the Prophet of Islam, engraved upon it. When the government decided to construct a new flyover at the same spot, the structure was demolished but for the part with the Kalma, which was carved out of it reverentially and preserved.

For months, day and night, seven days a week, work on the flyover continued. This is what the chief minister is known for—efficiency, his supporters claimed. It was completed in 'record time'. For a few months, life seemed to return to normal. The flyover, as expected, managed to ease the traffic flow at this congested junction. However, before one could fully recover from the trauma of its construction and appreciate its utility in a city where only a fraction of the population owns and travels by car, the chief minister was at it again.

The newly carpeted roads that had taken months to be constructed and cost billions of rupees were torn apart once again, this time for another pet project—the Metrobus. On a recent trip to Istanbul, reflective of the burgeoning relationship between the Sharifs (Nawaz and Shehbaz) and the Turkish President Recep Tayyip Erdoğan, the chief minister had become enamoured of the city. Lahore under Shehbaz Sharif was to become the new Istanbul. Automatic parking machines and garbage trucks were imported. But the most ambitious import was the Metrobus, eventually to become a bone of contention between the Opposition and the government.

Once again, for months, the junction at Kalma Chowk, along with the entire Ferozepur Road stretch, where this new facility was to be run, became a living hell. Budgets were drafted and then revised, as the cost of construction kept rising. Some accused the chief minister of distributing tenders for iron and other equipment for construction to his friends and family, while others asserted that the millions of rupees being spent on the project could be better utilized on something more useful, like the province's failing education system, or its broken health infrastructure.

Timed to perfection, the project finished just before the general elections of 2013. The Pakistan Muslim League-Nawaz (PML-N), of which Shehbaz Sharif was the Punjab president at the time (he heads it now, following the disqualification of his elder brother), had a new shiny toy to show off. The Metrobus was projected as the successful completion of Shehbaz Sharif's development agenda. It could well serve as a blueprint for development in other regions of Pakistan, if the PML-N were to be elected. Lahore, the new Istanbul, could be the future of other cities of the country. The image was readily consumed and the party swept the provincial and national elections. Soon after his

win, Nawaz Sharif inaugurated Metrobus projects in Karachi and
Rawalpindi as well.

The PML-N, in its previous incarnations, has dominated the
political landscape of Punjab since 1985, when it was propped up
by the Islamist military dictator Muhammad Zia-ul-Haq to counter
the influence of the leftist Pakistan People's Party (PPP). Nawaz
Sharif, trusted aide and protégé of Zia, became chief minister of the
province in 1985 and returned to power in 1988, even when the
PPP dominated the national Assemblies and gave Pakistan its first
woman prime minister, also its youngest, Benazir Bhutto.

In subsequent years, Nawaz Sharif emerged as a prominent
opponent to Benazir, and often resorted to undemocratic means
to weaken her government. It was a favour Benazir returned in
kind when she was in the Opposition. For example, in 1988,
Nawaz Sharif emerged as the head of a right-wing coalition called
Islami Jamhoori Ittehad, an alliance propped by the military
establishment to oppose Benazir. This tussle resulted in one of
the worst decades for Pakistan in terms of political stability. There
were four general elections in nine years, with power oscillating
between the PML-N and the PPP.

The politics of agitation throughout the 1990s dampened
the optimism of 1988, a year that marked a democratic revival
in the country after more than a decade of authoritarian military
rule. With politicians bickering and backstabbing each other,
the military's political influence only strengthened, resulting in
the coup of 1999 that saw the return of military rule for another
decade. Democracy was restored in 2008 as both Benazir Bhutto
and Nawaz Sharif joined hands against military rule. After the
political nightmare of the 1990s, this promised to be the dawn of
a new era.

While Nawaz Sharif fought bigger battles—against Benazir Bhutto and later the military establishment—in the 1990s, Shehbaz Sharif took up the post of chief minister of Punjab. After PML-N dominated the 1997 general elections, Shehbaz began his first term in a post that he would return to for a third term in 2013.

As head of the richest and most populous province of the country, Shehbaz has earned quite a reputation for himself. He is known for his hands-on approach, personally monitoring the progress of several projects, including the construction of roads. Many a time he has suspended government officials for their 'inefficiency'. Often, he is seen in the media in the midst of a flooded locality during the monsoons, earning him laurels from his supporters and even neutral observers. When compared with the bureaucratic and stuck-in-red-tape approach of other chief ministers of the country, he is lauded for his effectiveness, hard work, determination and 'no bullshit' approach. For many, he is a model chief minister.

While he is appreciated for his 'efficiency' on the one hand, his detractors censure him for his despotic approach—mistrustful of his own party members to the point that at one time, he held portfolios for eighteen provincial ministries.[1] His ad hoc dealing with state bureaucracy, suspending them on the spot without listening to their point of view, makes for flattering headlines in the media but weakens an administration already rendered inefficient by a postcolonial bureaucratic attitude. In his third stint as chief minister of Punjab, he had a dismal attendance rate at Parliament sessions. While his personal involvement in projects hastens their progress, it harms the administrative system, with only those ventures under the gaze of the chief minister being given importance and others neglected.

Shehbaz Sharif is particularly criticized for equating development with the construction of roads, and now the

Metrobus, at the expense of pressing concerns like healthcare and education. Punjab today boasts a wide web of roads and connectivity between smaller cities and villages, even as its government hospitals lack enough beds. While the elite of the country can in a mere five hours travel from Lahore to Peshawar, a journey of about 500 kilometres, many of its schools don't even have classrooms for its students. Yet, for some reason, Shehbaz's focus on bridges and roads has earned him the title of being 'development-friendly'. Many members of Provincial Assembly and members of National Assembly following suit expend a majority of their development funds on roads, completely ignoring other significant sectors. Perhaps the reason behind this skewed focus is the high visibility of road projects, which makes it easier for political parties to present themselves as 'progressive' and 'efficient'. On the other hand, development in healthcare and education would require a longer process to yield results, which cannot be marketed to the electorate. Since 2008, numerous overhead bridges and underpasses have been added to the already crowded city of Lahore.

This brings us to an apt criticism of the chief minister— that his sole focus tends to be on Lahore. Political opponents claim, and rightly so, that for the PML-N, Punjab begins and ends at Lahore. The 'development' of Punjab is equated with the 'development' of Lahore. While Lahore gets its shiny new roads, overhead bridges, underpasses, and now the Metrobus, the other, smaller cities of the province continue to function on outdated infrastructure. Lahore, it is alleged, ends up consuming a disproportionate share of the development budget. Many members of the Opposition call the government of Punjab *Takht-e-Lahore*, or the throne of Lahore, equating it to the nineteenth-century reign of Maharaja Ranjit Singh.[2] As if actively seeking to prove their detractors correct, soon after the beginning of Shehbaz Sharif's third term in 2013, the Punjab government announced perhaps its most controversial 'development project' till date—the Orange Line.

The needle of the empty syringe is still stuck to his arm. His eyes are forced shut. I can sense him struggling beneath his eyelids but the heroin proves to be stronger. He has fought this battle many times. He knows how futile it is. His head hangs to one side. Saliva dripping from his mouth sticks to his matted beard. I can almost feel the lice swimming in his hair upon my own. His brown kameez has patches of liquid—sweat, urine. A bag of rice is tied to one of his fingers. It is a small serving that he won't be able to share with his heroin-addict friends who sleep next to him in the last remaining relic of a serene Mughal garden.

There is chaos all around them—bikes, wagons, cars, donkey carts, rickshaws and buses vie for space, the one-way rule having long been abandoned. A traffic warden stands to one side, in his full-sleeved shirt, under the shade of a young tree that will soon be uprooted. He removes the straw from his glass of sugarcane juice and gulps the liquid down thirstily. He will only step in when there is a jam. Otherwise he knows there is nothing much he can do to regulate the traffic as long as work continues on the Orange Line.

The structure of Chauburji is almost like a blot of paint dropped accidentally on an intricate postmodernist painting. There is a sadistic charm to the pandemonium of Lahore. There is symmetry in its disorder. Every house is as abruptly constructed as the one next to it, all of them audaciously flouting building laws. Packed together, each new building is taller than the previous one. This is one of most densely populated areas of the city, with more than 31,000 people per square kilometre.[3]

The government too competes in its own way. Renovation of roads over the past several decades has meant the application of successive layers of tar, so that the ground floor of each house is at a different level. Even the electricity poles find themselves haphazardly aligned, bent at their own particular angle. A jungle originating from these poles heads off in different directions.

In the middle of all this is Chauburji, a structure laid according to a perfect plan, with four minarets in each corner of the square building. Perfectly shaped floral and geometrical-patterned mosaics decorate its walls. Its neatly aligned windows, arches and niches are almost an assault to the eyes of a visitor accustomed to the mayhem of Lahore. The structure belongs in a different city, in a city of gardens that no longer exists, a city that was the playground of Mughal royalty, a city of thousands, yet a city that only belonged to a handful. This, then, is our revenge, imposing on these ancient relics of oppression our authority. We introduced anarchy where once there was order. We ripped apart the symmetry of these structures and enforced upon them our own version of reality.

All that survives now is this lone gateway with its four minarets that earn it its name—*chau* (four) *burj* (minarets). The vast orderly garden, streams extracted from the nearby River Ravi, the pavilions where Mughal royalty would rendezvous, the glass palaces where the only reflection was that of royalty and the fountains that danced with the music—all these have long disappeared.

There are several contending claims to the construction of this garden and Chauburji. According to one of them, the garden was created by Zeb-un-Nissa,[4] the 'Sufi'-inclined poetess and daughter of the 'puritanical' Aurangzeb. Perhaps what gives credence to this claim is the presence of Zeb-un-Nissa's alleged mausoleum a little distance away.

The locality of Nawa Kot, or 'new fort', is only a few kilometres from here. Its name belies its condition. Thousands of houses and buildings are crowded together in this small locality, competing for space. Giant banners advertising dubious visa consulting businesses hang from every other building. Like Chauburji, there was a spacious garden here at the end of the eighteenth century, when Punjab, and particularly Lahore, was experiencing a new dawn. For almost a century after the decline of Mughal influence, Punjab and Lahore had been in a state of chaos. Squatters were gradually taking over symbols of Mughal royalty, their gardens transformed into jungles. Warlords held sway over Punjab, and the city of Lahore had been divided between three Sikh warlords. This anarchy was quelled by Ranjit Singh's conquest of Lahore in 1799.

If it hadn't been for one Mehr Muqamudin, a guard at the Lohari Darwaza, one of the twelve gateways of Lahore leading into the walled city, perhaps Ranjit Singh's march into Lahore, which symbolically marked his capture of the throne of Punjab, would have been delayed for a little while longer. Mehr Muqamudin opened the gate, allowing his armies to march into the city peacefully. As a reward for his loyalty, Ranjit Singh allotted him this garden. Razing most of the existing structures, Mehr Muqamudin established a fortified locality for the people of his ancestral village and named it accordingly.[5]

Tucked away amidst tall buildings, in the locality of Nawa Kot, is the tomb believed to be of Zeb-un-Nissa, a little building, petrified, unsure of what the future will hold for it. For now, there is hope. A government board has been placed upon its stout structure, identifying it as protected property. But danger looms at the gate. Neighbouring shops have over time extended their entrances, taking over vacant land around the tomb. Encroaching upon this protected monument is a bamboo seller's shop, with several of his freshly made ladders leaning greedily into the complex.

Built on a raised platform, the mausoleum is a single-storey structure with a wide dome on the top, typical of Mughal architecture. Two ancient trees, banyan and berry, regarded as sacred in the folk Islamic and other religious traditions of India, stand guard on either side, protecting the grave regarded as that of the Mughal princess. Abandoned by time and fate, the grave lies at the centre of the mausoleum.

At certain points, the brilliance of the sublime Mughal architecture shines through centuries of decay. Red-and-yellow floral patterns that form honeycombed shapes called *muqarna*s emerge on closer inspection. Beneath the crumbling floor, the geometrical patterns of the bricks merge into ever-growing larger ones. The red stone used widely in other Mughal buildings makes an almost niggardly appearance here, at the base of the structure, with carved floral and geometrical designs chiselled to perfection. At a time when multistorey buildings are raised in a matter of months, the meticulous attention paid to the finishing of this structure is almost embarrassing.

According to a popular story, Zeb-un-Nissa moved into a voluntary prison at the site of this tomb, where once there had been a garden, its boundaries merging into that of Chauburji Bagh. She chose to imprison herself after her father turned down her request to marry one Aqil Khan, the governor of Multan.[6] Perhaps the emperor was aghast at the princess's audacity in choosing a suitor for herself, or perhaps he was frightened by the challenge Aqil Khan or his progeny could present to him or his descendants once they were connected to the royal family by marriage. Several sisters and daughters of Mughal emperors were not allowed to marry for the same reason.

According to another popular tale, Zeb-un-Nissa was destined to ascend the Mughal throne, betrothed as she was to Suleiman Shikoh, the eldest son of Dara Shikoh.[7] The match was decided by Shah Jahan himself, who was naive enough to believe that despite his own experiences with his eldest son's ambition, his appointed heir, Dara Shikoh, would have a smooth transition to power, and thereafter his son, Suleiman Shikoh. He overestimated the political and military astuteness of Dara and underplayed the abilities of his reviled son, Aurangzeb.

Perhaps Aurangzeb could never forgive his daughter for her sympathies to his sworn enemy. Like Dara Shikoh, she too dabbled in Sufi poetry, compared to the more literalist interpretation of religion of her father. Her father might have questioned her loyalty to him and suspected her of being sympathetic to her uncle and fiancé, who too was assassinated by Aurangzeb after he captured and killed Dara.

Legend states that abandoning herself to her cursed fate, Zeb-un-Nissa found refuge in this garden, which had been constructed on her orders. Having failed to fulfil her wishes twice, she devoted her life to the needy, who were provided free food here every day. It is said that she would receive written dietary requests and would order her royal cooks to prepare meals accordingly. It was in this manner that she received a love couplet from her beloved Aqil Khan, who too had abandoned his wealth, power and prestige while pining for his unconsummated love.[8] United, finally, the lovers spent many days and nights in each other's arms, perhaps under the same watchful trees that now act as sentries to this abandoned grave. Their secret was soon betrayed and her infuriated father had her lover killed.[9] Zeb-un-Nissa, the favourite daughter of the emperor, was imprisoned in her own garden for the rest of her life, twenty years to be exact. She died a few years before the emperor and was interred in her garden.

Just behind the grave is the last remaining witness to this sad story. Hidden deep within the settlement is Chhoti Chauburji, or the lesser Chauburji, which is by no means any less in splendour than its better-known cousin. In fact, it might be the more elaborately decorated building of the two. An imposing structure, it has several windows, accompanied by small minarets on its roof. The facade of the gateway is an overdose of bright colours—green, blue, yellow—colours that closely resembled the moods, weather and nature of life in Lahore, the city of festivals, before it was whitewashed by the Victorian sensibilities of its colonizers, inherited by the postcolonial babus.

Most of the stories associated with the princess are part of folklore, devoid of historical authenticity. One must also consider the fact that during an era when royalty was perceived and treated as divinely manifested and political criticism was non-existent, rumour-mongering might have played an important role in helping common people vent their frustrations. Zeb-un-Nissa particularly must have been a ripe character for such speculation, given that she was a rare Mughal princess who was able to emerge from the shadows of the harem. Her association with Dara Shikoh and his son might also have played a part in setting her up as a target for rumours.

Lahore arose from provincial backwaters to become a metropolis thanks to Akbar, who moved the Mughal capital here in 1585. However, in 1598, when Akbar shifted his capital away from Lahore, royal funding, which saw the emergence of several building projects in the city, dried up. This was reversed when Dara Shikoh, the crown prince, was appointed governor of Lahore. The city was back on the political map, on its way to the grandeur for which it seemed destined. One can therefore imagine that in the battle between Dara Shikoh and Aurangzeb, it must have been their governor whom the people of the city must have sided with. Once Dara was captured and killed, Aurangzeb imposed his authority over Lahore as well. With no avenue available to express their sense of loss, the rumours about an alleged conflict between an emperor and his poetess daughter acquire metaphorical significance.

There is some credibility to this tale, due to Zeb-un-Nissa's alleged sympathy towards her rebel brother, Muhammad Akbar, who revolted against his father. She was publically rebuked by the emperor for this and all her property confiscated. She was imprisoned in Salimgarh Fort in Delhi where she is believed to have died in 1701 or 1702, a few years before Aurangzeb.[10] There is credible evidence to suggest that her tomb was constructed in Delhi, which was subsequently razed when the railway line was laid in 1875.[11] Therefore the so-called tomb of Zeb-un-Nissa in Nawa Kot cannot be her real mausoleum where her remains are interred.

Similarly, there are rather convincing arguments to suggest she was not responsible for the construction of Chauburji Bagh. Refuting the claims of prominent historians of the city of Lahore, there are others who assert that the garden was constructed by Jahanara,[12] the sister of Emperor Aurangzeb, another remarkable character from the Mughal harem, whose life, like Zeb-un-Nissa's, saw many ups and downs, caught as she was in the succession battle between her two brothers.

Standing as tall as the minarets of Chauburji are the pillars of another imperial symbol—Takht-e-Lahore. Only a few metres from this historic structure, the pillars run in a straight line along the road, passing in front of Zeb-un-Nissa's tomb. The accompanying road has been dug up to make way for the Orange Line, the first track of a metro train being constructed in Pakistan. Interestingly, Multan Road, upon which these pillars now stand like soldiers of doom, was completed a short while prior to being dug up once again, after years of widening and renovation, which made life hell for the residents and shopkeepers living on this long stretch.

Regarded as the new pet project of the 'talented' chief minister, the Orange Line, like the Metrobus before it, is meant to resolve the troubles of the commuters of Lahore. At the loan-signing ceremony for the project, the chief minister claimed that it would be the means of transportation for 5,00,000 people and add on average 39.38 billion rupees every year to the provincial exchequer.[13]

As soon as the plans to start the project were finalized, the government began the process of acquiring land and clearing way. This led to a series of protests by locals who were not willing to sell their properties or felt the government was purchasing them below market price. Joining hands with these protestors were proprietors who could not prove legal ownership of their properties. These included families who have been living here for several generations, some from the time of Partition and others even before them, who were now being evicted without any compensation. Traders and shop owners, who have traditionally formed the core of PML-N's support, too rose up against the project. Their businesses had still not recovered from the years of construction that took place on the Multan Road, which had turned away potential customers who would rather not get caught in traffic snarls. With a new development project under construction, the promised rewards of a revamped road seemed even more distant.

Raising their voices alongside was the civil society of Lahore, which claimed that the project threatened the city's historic heritage. A high-speed metro train passing so close to a historic monument like Chauburji would seriously damage its foundation. There are a total of eleven historic monuments along the track, threatened by this development project.[14]

Yet another criticism was of skewed priorities, a criticism which can be used to question several projects undertaken by the PML-N, including the Metrobus, laptop and yellow cab schemes. It is estimated that the 27-kilometre line would cost 200 billion rupees. Compare this to 32.80 billion rupees allocated for education development in the province for the year of 2015 and 43.83 billion rupees for healthcare in Punjab. To add to the burden, the ticket would be subsidized to the tune of 12 billion rupees, according to a report in a local English newspaper. The same report claimed that there were a hundred protests against the project between August 2015 and February 2016.[15]

Moved by the civil society, Lahore High Court in August 2016 barred the government from constructing the Metro line within 200 feet of historic structures, which the project violates in several instances. The Punjab government, adamant that the project had to be completed, decided to challenge the decision in the Supreme Court. In December 2017, the Supreme Court allowed the Punjab government to continue work on the Orange Line while taking care to not damage historic sites in its path.

The Punjab government would have liked to complete the Orange Line before national elections in 2018, which was not achieved. With the litigations against it, construction speed of the project was severely hindered. However, a major part of the project has been completed, and it is likely that the Orange Line will be up and running in the next few months, perhaps soon after a new provincial government is formed following the July 2018 elections. Despite the setbacks, this project is highlighted as a major success of the government. Lahore's Orange Line is marketed as a tangible symbol of progress and development, to be replicated in other cities if given an opportunity, reinforcing PML-N's image of being 'pro-development'. Kept in the dark about the economic realities of the project and the lopsided priorities, the voters are now being presented the Orange Line as a shiny new toy, to the envy of the rest of the country. This is a gift to the city of Lahore for its loyalty, a city which has over the years acquired the status of apex political priority.

Among the provinces, it is Punjab that acquires political priority in the country, deciding the fate of the federation. For example, in the national elections of 2013, it was only in Punjab that PML-N swept the elections, along with a few seats in other provinces. The dominant position of Punjab allowed the party to form a majority government at the Centre. In fact, Punjabis dominate the army, bureaucracy, judiciary and the media too. Punjab's political interests are the most widely represented in all forums of power. Punjab is the hegemonic power that decides the fate of the rest of the country.

Even so, it would be unfair to view Punjab as one homogeneous whole that controls the fate of Pakistan. Within Punjab, there is central Punjab, with Lahore as its centre, that wields the maximum political clout. Cities farther away from this centre, such as Multan, Bahawalpur and Mianwali, are marginalized. Funds for the entire province, which many already allege is much larger than the province's due share in the national budget, are directed towards Lahore and its immediate environment. The Orange Line is one of many such examples.

Just as Punjab symbolizes hegemonic authority within the country, within Punjab it is in Lahore where this hegemonic power converges. Lahore then is a political metaphor for not just the province but also the entire country. While Punjab's priorities are over-represented and usually dominate national priorities, it is Lahore's priorities that set the tone for Punjab and, therefore, the country. Due to its special position in the power pyramid, it yields greater power than Karachi, the largest and most diverse city in the country, and Islamabad, the capital. In this context, the Orange Line is not just another project, but rather one of the most important projects in the country that perfectly captures the essence of Lahore's colonial and hegemonic relationship with the rest of the country.

Ironically, Lahore has had to sacrifice its unique identity to ascend to its hegemonic position. A multireligious and cultural society has had to shed parts of its history and heritage to become the symbol of a monolithic religious and cultural society. As a symbol of state nationalism, understood in a narrow framework intolerant of diversity, Lahore became an epitome of this uniformity—its conformity and monolithic identity presented to other urban cities that still retain their multicultural identity as a model to aspire to. It should not come as a surprise today that Lahore is one of, if not the most, religiously and politically conservative cities, compared to other provincial capitals. Over the course of Pakistan's life, it has shown particular tolerance towards extremist religious parties and military governments. Lahore is the most politically powerful city of the country, but in the process of becoming so, has lost parts of its history and heritage, of which Chauburji could be another example.

While ascending the stairs of power, Lahore has stopped being the Lahore it used to be.

Holding an iron rod attached to the roof of the bus to steady myself, I stared sheepishly at the calligraphic graffiti on the walls as we slowly navigated a congested two-way street. Much effort had been put into its crafting—painted in black with a red border. It was almost sadistic that such a beautiful design contained such a hateful message. We emerged out of the narrow street to face the magnificent Chauburji, looking as uncomfortable in its surroundings as it always did. The fortified building was now in front of us, with barbed wire on its high walls, armed sentries standing next to the gate and a small door allowing entry to one person at a time. This is the headquarters of the Jamaat-ud-Dawa (JuD), the political and charitable wing of the Lashkar-e-Taiba, a militant organization responsible for several attacks in Indian Kashmir and the rest of the country. The graffiti on a wall next to the structure

posed a question which it also answered, 'What is our relationship
with India? That of hatred and revenge.'

In 2011, Pakistan accorded India the Most Favoured
Nation (MFN) status, an economic arrangement assuring non-
discriminatory trade between the two countries. Pakistan was
responding to India's gesture of according Pakistan MFN status
in 1996. The rhetoric easily played into the hands of anti-India
groups, spearheaded by the Hafiz Saeed-led JuD. Banners and
posters sprung up all over Lahore, asking how our arch-enemy
could be called the most favoured nation. Pictures of brutalized
Kashmiris were put up behind rickshaws, asking how this country
could be called the most favoured nation. Images of the Babri
Masjid being destroyed were also similarly used. Slogans, like
the graffiti mentioned above, appeared on the walls of Lahore,
speaking vehemently against any normalization of relations with
India. Proponents of the policy tried to explain the meaning of
this trade arrangement, but in vain. The words 'most favoured' for
India were completely unacceptable.

A few months later, passions had calmed down while the state
quietly dragged its feet. All over the city, these slogans, posters and
banners remained visible, though, like a bad hangover that lingered
on. The organization where I was working at the time was hosting
a delegation of Indian students and teachers. Having hired a bus,
we were showing them around the city. As a history enthusiast, I
had taken up the responsibility of acting as their guide. I narrated
to them stories of Lahore's multireligious and cultural past, as we
saw different monuments and spaces connected with those stories.
I wanted them to see Lahore as I do—to be able to brush past
the ugliness, congestion, extremism, and see layers and layers of
history, tradition, music, poetry, culture, religion, spirituality,
nobility and folk.

Just a little while earlier, I had spotted the graffiti I was telling
them about as we passed the Miani Sahib graveyard, the oldest

and largest graveyard of the city. Almost as old as Lahore, the entire story of the city can be narrated through it. Spread over a vast area, Miani Sahib contains thousands of graves of the city's dead, some important, others not so much. Every day newer graves occupy older ones. It is an entire city on its own, with many paths running through it.

Standing next to the driver, I had just been narrating the story of Boota Singh and Zainab. Separated from her parents during Partition, Zainab, a Muslim girl from Jalandhar district in East Punjab, remained in India. She was rescued by Boota Singh, who later married her.[16] Legends about this couple, perpetuated by movies and books, narrate how they had fallen in love and raised two daughters. However, a few years after Partition, when the governments of India and Pakistan decided to recover and return 'abducted' women at the time of Partition, Zainab too was picked up by authorities and sent to Lahore.

Following his love, Boota crossed the border illegally and reached Nurpur, a small village in the district Lahore, close to the border. Here, Zainab's family beat him up and filed a case against him. In Lahore High Court, where his case was being heard, Zainab was asked to testify, in which she refused to return with Boota.[17] Heartbroken, Boota committed suicide by walking into a running train head-on, close to Lahore's Shahdara station. He was buried in Miani Sahib. Stories of his love and betrayal were narrated in newspapers and magazines. Soon, a cult grew around Boota Singh's grave and he came to be referred to as *Shaheed-e-Mohabbat* (martyr of love).[18] Young lovers inspired by his story would visit his grave to pay homage, while those who saw his love as a blot on the nation's honour fought to remove all traces of his grave.[19] The battle over his grave and legacy went on for a long time after his death, and in many ways continues till date.

Soon after I heard about the story, I reached Nurpur, the village where Zainab settled after her arrival from India. At a barber's shop, accompanied by a few locals I had befriended, I was told that Zainab was still alive and living at the same village. But it was impossible to meet her and talk about Boota Singh. For her family, the story of Boota Singh was still a threat, so it was better not to explore it any further.

Some of the teachers of the Indian delegation had heard the story and we were still discussing it when the hateful graffiti appeared in front of me. I did not want my guests to feel uncomfortable with slogans expressing hatred for India. Hafiz Saeed and the JuD remain a bone of contention between India and Pakistan. I sought comfort in the fact that they couldn't read the script, even if they understood the language. Should I tell them what the graffiti says? Should I mention to them that we were going past the headquarters of the JuD, whose leader is the most wanted 'terrorist' in India?

I knew that they might be interested, but having spent the last two days romanticizing the city, talking about its cultural and historical depth, I didn't want to confront this reality, this ugly truth about the city of Lahore. I battled within. Was I just to present the beauty of the city, while hiding its hideousness? It's a question that still rattles me. Is my Lahore, the beautiful city I have called home all my life, the city of love and splendour, the city of allure and charm, only a figment of my imagination? Does the graffiti represent a truth I am not willing to see?

Defeated, humiliated, the turret of Jain Mandir lies at the centre of this vacant ground. In a sign of complete submission to its new political reality it kowtows to passers-by, most of whom, unaware of its existence, ignore it and move on. It only has one sympathizer who is, ironically, a *mochi*. Loyal to the temple, he sits at its entrance every day, drowning its cries with the sound of his hammer as he fixes shoes. A few decades ago, when the turret, surrounded by other sacred rooms, stood proud, piercing the sky, the sight of this mochi might have soiled its pride. Today, caged within a wall, it cannot afford to be as picky about its devotees.

For years after Partition, the temple stood on this ground, staring east, waiting for pilgrims who had long abandoned it. No one ever came back. The temple was gradually cut off from the rest of the complex. Two new roads bifurcated around it. Like Chauburji, visible from here, it too became one of the most important junctions in a new Lahore—Jain Mandir Chowk.

Just when the temple had adjusted to its new role, the fateful morning of 7 December 1992 descended. The previous day, about 1000 kilometres from Lahore, Hindu nationalists had brought down a historic mosque which had survived invasions, raids and colonization before it, but could not withstand a rising religious nationalism. The same mob, perhaps, in a different garb, gathered outside this temple. None of them knew the difference between a Jain and a Hindu temple. They did not want to know. Within hours, the proud turret was brought down, disgraced, as if the demolished Babri Masjid, 1000 kilometres from here, had somehow been avenged.

In this way, on that fateful morning, one of the last traces of Jain heritage in Lahore was decimated. According to Jain tradition there were three functional temples in the city, one close to Chauburji, one within the walled city of Lahore close to Bhatti Gate, believed to have been constructed by Emperor Akbar at the request of one of his Jain ministers, Bhanu Chandra, and one in a sixteenth-century village called Guru Mangat, named after a devotee of Guru Hargobind who used to reside there, now incorporated by the elite residential society of Gulberg.[20] The other two quickly faded away after Partition, yet somehow this particular temple had survived. Standing tall, the turret served as a junction, while its accompanying buildings, which once must have been used by pilgrims and priests, were taken over by migrants from the other side of the border, and property squatters.

The Jain heritage of Lahore was part of a rich legacy scattered all over Punjab. There are several localities in many cities of the province still referred to as 'Bhabrian', derived from Bhabra, an ancient Jain merchant community of Punjab. Lahore, Multan, Kasur, Narowal, Sialkot, Jhelum, Bhera and Rawalpindi hosted some of the oldest Jain temples in South Asia. Several prominent Jain priests have lived and preached in these areas. In fact, it is also maintained that Mahavira, the final *tirthankara*, undertook an extensive tour of Punjab, passing possibly through several cities mentioned above, where later his devotees constructed Jain temples.[21]

In recent history, Acharya Vijayanand Suri, also known as Atmaramji of Gujranwala, was a prominent Jain teacher in the first half of the nineteenth century. Directly and indirectly, he was responsible for the construction and renovation of several Jain temples in the province, including the one next to Chauburji.[22] The splendid *smadh* of Atmaramji still stands in Gujranwala, about 70 kilometres from Lahore, and now functions as a police station. One can only wonder at the irony that where once the message of non-violence was preached, now suspected criminals are incarcerated and interrogated.

The Jain temple in Lahore was constructed a few years before Partition by a rich Jain businessman from Lahore called Seth Ghazan Chand Jain, a devotee of Atmaramji. His daughter, Swaran Kantaji Maharaj became a *swaran*, a female priest, and earned a lot of respect for her services to the Jain religion.[23] The family, abandoning their ancestral property and this temple, migrated to East Punjab following the riots of Partition during which the ancient city of Lahore was burned down and this contemporary city was birthed.

It was not just Jain heritage that suffered on that fateful morning in December. Relics of Hindu temples, long abandoned by their rightful owners and being used for other purposes, as houses, schools, madrasas were also targeted, some brought down, while others continued to stand stubbornly despite repeated attacks.

The historic Sitla Mandir in Shahalami, once dominated by the influential Hindu families of the city, and the site of some of the worst riots of Partition, was another victim of religio-nationalist passion. The abandoned temple had been taken over by several refugees and its floors and rooms divided amongst numerous families. One such room was taken over by a madrasa where neighbourhood children learned the Quran. Most of the surrounding structures had already been lost, the sacred pool converted into a community garden, smadhs either destroyed or taken over by people, and community rooms converted into residences too.

On the morning of 7 December 1992, the teacher and students of the madrasa led a procession demanding the temple's demolition. A mob climbed to the top and brought down a part of the turret, in the process seriously damaging the building. Almost five decades after Partition, the locality of Shahalami once again witnessed a familiar fire that had at that time burnt through the community of Lahore. A deep crack now runs through the middle of the temple, posing a serious threat to the dozens of people who still live inside. Once the passion subsided, the students of the madrasa went back to their room within the temple to continue their education.

The story of Bheru Mandir is not much different. Located in the middle of what is believed to be the oldest inhabited locality of Lahore, Ichra, this temple was also taken over by several refugee families after Partition. Now a small town within the metropolis of Lahore, many local historians believe that it is not the walled city but Ichra where the ancient, mythological secrets of Lahore are buried. This area was once the site of some of the oldest Hindu temples of the city. Even though historical records state that Bheru Mandir was constructed in the seventeenth century, and renovated almost two centuries later on the orders of Maharaja Ranjit Singh, its actual origin might be older.[24]

Interestingly, Ichra was also home to Maulana Maududi, the founder of Jama'at-e-Islami, a right-wing religious political party. It therefore housed several passionate followers of the organization, for whom any remnant of non-Islamic heritage is a perceived threat to the historical and national purity of Pakistan. Young, passionate loyalists of the parties, along with other fanatics, surrounded Bheru Mandir on 7 December 1992, forcing its residents to flee, and began the process of its destruction. The temple proved to be stronger than expected. Despite repeated blows, it showed no sign of submission. The mob soon lost interest and the temple continues to stand till today, exhibiting only minor injuries from that battle. What it cannot hide, though, are signs of abandonment, neglect and weathering that all such religious shrines suffer once their devotees desert them.

Whereas stories of intolerance are rampant in Lahore, particularly after Partition, there are also those that present an alternative reality of the city, of a city that has resisted history. These are tales of love, resistance and harmony, which I would like to believe, despite evidence to the contrary, capture the essence of the city.

Located on the southern edge of Lahore, once marking its boundary but now another historic town incorporated into the metropolis, is the sixteenth-century Niaz Baig. The town, like several others, once had its own distinct identity, separate from Lahore. Today, however, as the city spills beyond its walls and floods the plains around it, it drowns the distinct voices of all such villages and towns, subsuming them into itself. Forced into acquiescence, these localities have a relationship with the city which has been reduced to that of a colonizer and its colony. Such hamlets also provide the city with workers, while the city rewards them with poverty.

As Lahore has prospered, its suburban localities have thrived—Model Town, Gulberg and now Defence. The wide avenues, the neatly aligned trees, fancy cars and international brands give Lahore the veneer of a leading metropolitan city, yet beyond the shiny houses is another world easily missed through the tinted windows of air-conditioned cars. Many of the new residential societies have been built on the agricultural lands of ancient hamlets, which have now been imprisoned within these communities, reduced to the status of *katchi-abadi*s.

Nowhere is this contrast more blatantly obvious than at Defence Housing Authority (DHA), the most prestigious residential society not just in Lahore but also the entire country. Like little dots sprinkled all over DHA are these tiny hamlets, some of them dating back to the fourteenth century. Walled and manned by security guards, these hamlets are closely monitored to ensure the exclusivity of the elite of DHA.

Niaz Baig, after Lahore, served as a regional capital of this area. At the time of raids and invasions, residents of neighbouring villages would retreat into the walled protection of Niaz Baig. For example, in the eighteenth century, as the wrath of Ahmad Shah Abdali descended upon the villages of Hinjarwal and Maraka, Niaz Baig, thanks to its protective wall, was spared.[25] That wall has disappeared now. What is left are the remnants of the gates and their names. Much like Lahore, the population of Niaz Baig too has spilled beyond its once-walled boundary to encroach all the way till Multan Road. The crowded community, its chaotic traffic and communal garbage disposed in vacant grounds contrasts sharply with the image of a clean city that Lahore so desperately wants to project.

Deep within Niaz Baig are the remains of another historic temple—Bhadra Kali Mandir—one of the most important Hindu temples in pre-Partition Lahore. Thousands of devotees would gather here every year in an annual pilgrimage. Like other temples around Lahore, this too was taken over by migrants coming from the other side of the border, its numerous rooms, smadhs and other buildings divided amongst different families.

One such building was a tall structure with a dome on top constructed on the orders of Maharaja Ranjit Singh, who wanted to gift the people of this community a new temple. The priests refused to shift the shrine, and so the structure remained vacant.[26] After Partition, the building was converted into a school. In 1992, when temples all around Lahore were being attacked, a mob converged here as well, adamant to bring it down. The schoolchildren, along with the elders of the community, resisted these attempts. Given its utility, they argued for its protection, and in this way, the temple was saved from destruction.[27]

Immediately after the destruction of the Babri Masjid, the religio-political parties spearheading the attacks demanded that the name of the junction be changed from Jain Mandir Chowk to Babri Masjid Chowk. A few enthusiastic shopkeepers also put up the 'new' name soon after but in official records the earlier name remained.

Almost two and a half decades after that fateful day, the rechristened junction remains a memory. Jain Mandir Chowk remained so; its name failed to die. Its memory, its legacy survived in the unconscious nostalgia of the people. Like a bittersweet thought, it continued to lurk in the recesses of Lahore's mind, a guilty conscience, a regret the city never acknowledged. Even official signs, unaware, or with a tinge of guilt, refer to this junction as Jain Mandir Chowk.

This has been the story of Lahore, its enigma. A city trying to run away from its history of a thousand years, of a Hindu past it would rather not admit. Lahore—the symbol of nationalism, the birthplace of the Pakistan movement—cannot acknowledge its Hindu heritage, for that would be tantamount to treason. Pakistan is meant to be the homeland of Muslims, a nation separate from the Hindus. For all their differences, Hindus and Muslims cannot live together and neither can their histories, it seems to say. How can Lahore then admit that before it became a Muslim city, a symbol of nationalism, a symbol of a separate civilization, it was actually Hindu? How can it admit that its ancestors, before they became monotheists, used to worship Hindu deities and sing bhajans in their praise? How can it admit that those temples which it is now keen to bring down are the same spaces it once held sacred?

Histories, like traumatic memories, cannot be easily cast away. They come back to haunt us. Surviving as tiny repositories of traditions are some of these names, preserving within them histories and stories not otherwise officially acknowledged. Despite the imposition of other narratives and propaganda, these names endure, highlighting how, at the level of lived experience, Lahore carries along its past, which the state would rather have it forget.

Some kilometres from Niaz Baig is another historic hamlet, Qila Gujjar Singh, 'fort of Gujjar Singh', named after an eighteenth-century Sikh warlord, Gujjar Singh Banghi, who, along with two others, Lehna Singh and Sobha Singh, had carved up Lahore amongst themselves. Their tumultuous rule was ended by Maharaja Ranjit Singh. Pakistani nationalist history projects the Sikh period, also incorporating the time period of Ranjit Singh, as a devastating time for the Muslims of the city. Mosques, it says, were converted into stables, the sound of the azan was banned, the religious freedom of Muslims was curbed. In the nationalist historiography, history is divided according to religious sub-groups, while in school textbooks non-Muslim history is hardly mentioned. Thus, an average educated Pakistani grows up completely unaware of the non-Muslim history and heritage of Pakistan.

Even so, the country's non-Islamic history keeps popping up through localities like Qila Gujjar Singh. Sometimes the state consciously attempts to remove any last traces, as it tried to do in the case of Krishan Nagar. Established in the 1930s, this residential society, with its geometrical layout, parks, sewage system, clean drinking water and bungalows, was meant to fulfil the needs of the growing Hindu middle-class of the city.[28] After Partition, with an influx of hundreds and thousands of migrants, it soon transformed into another locality Lahore was trying hard not to be. In contemporary Lahore, it is a crowded, congested part of the older city.

With the change of political reality, the name, however, inspired by Lord Krishna, continued to survive, a threat to a nascent, insecure state. In 1992, it was finally changed to Islampura, but the new name was never accepted by the residents of the city. Krishan Nagar remained Krishan Nagar. Now in a homogeneous Lahore eager to hide and pretend that it does not have a non-Muslim past, localities like Qila Gujjar Singh and Krishan Nagar raise some rather uncomfortable questions.

For years, as the turret of Jain Mandir rested on the ground, it found solace in the fact that its sister buildings, rooms which were once linked with the entire temple complex, still stood tall, providing residence to thousands of people. Surrounded by a fast-changing Lahore, they were a few remaining specimens of pre-Partition architecture, a unique blend of British, Hindu and Mughal influences.

What two conflagrations of nationalism could not accomplish in 1947 and 1992 was achieved by the demons of development. Skirting the fragile structure of Chauburji, the track for the Orange Line headed straight in the direction of Jain Mandir. These historic buildings, the last surviving evidence of Jain heritage in the city, fell in the way, and so were demolished. The turret would now have to find happiness in the fact that its city, its Lahore, is rapidly 'modernizing' and 'developing'.

It was called the largest political *jalsa* in the history of the city. Generous estimates suggested there were over 2,00,000 people. Others put the number at around 1,00,000.[29] Many took offence at the statement. Benazir's jalsa in 1986 was the biggest political gathering, they said. Others suggested Bhutto's historic jalsa in Lahore was even bigger. But those were different times, making simplistic comparisons difficult. This was 2011. Imran Khan's Pakistan Tehreek-e-Insaf (PTI) had mastered the tool of social media. Party trolls had learned the art of drowning the voices of anyone criticizing their *kaptaan*. If elections could be won by popularity on social media, Imran Khan would have been the undisputable leader of Pakistan.

There was no other news on 30 October 2011. News vans had cast their anchors outside Iqbal Park, while camerapersons had set up their equipment in front of the stage since early morning. It was an iconic background—Minar-e-Pakistan, the symbol of Pakistani nationalism—with a backdrop that placed an overblown image of Imran Khan alongside Muhammad Ali Jinnah. Next to Jinnah was a portrait of Allama Iqbal, the national poet, who is buried at walking distance from here, in the embrace of the seventeenth-century Badshahi Masjid, shadows of whose tall minarets fall on this iconic ground.

The story of this ground is as old as Lahore. Several historians suggest that in the Mughal era there was a fruit garden here, between the fort and the river. In fact, just behind the garden is Badami Bagh, the last remaining oral testimony to the almond garden that once existed here.[30] It was also used as a ceremonial military parade ground by the Mughals, a tradition that was continued by Maharaja Ranjit Singh.[31] During the colonial era it was christened Minto Park, in honour of Lord Minto Gilbert Elliot (1751–1814), the ninth governor general of India from 1807 to 1813.[32]

It was here that the All-India Muslim League held its three-day general session from 22–24 March 1940. Referred to as the Lahore Resolution at that time, it demanded that Muslim-majority provinces within India be given autonomy. As the movement for Pakistan gained momentum, the resolution was relabelled as the 'Pakistan Resolution', a title it continues to hold.

There is some disagreement regarding the interpretation of the resolution. A majority within Pakistan believes this was a clear-cut demand for a separate state, while others feel it was a demand for provincial autonomy within one country.[33] For Pakistanis it is a symbolic day, which marks the first time that an unequivocal demand for a separate homeland was formally raised, and which was achieved seven years after the resolution was adopted. Even though the resolution was adopted on 24 March, the country, every year, celebrates 23 March as Pakistan Day, marked by a national holiday. It is in the spirit of the resolution that after the creation of Pakistan, Minto Park was renamed Iqbal Park, and the junction close by came to be referred to as Azadi Chowk. Sometime in the 1960s, Minar-e-Pakistan was installed at the centre of the garden to further solidify its importance in national memory.

For Imran Khan, on 30 October 2011, the choice of the city and the garden were of paramount importance, a fact he mentioned in his speech that evening. He said that Lahore had been in the vanguard of all significant political movements in the history of Pakistan, as the images of Iqbal and Jinnah looked on benignly from the background.

More than its historical significance, perhaps it was the city's contemporary political symbolism that was on Imran Khan's mind.

Lahore, since 1985, when Nawaz Sharif first became the chief minister of the province, has been the hub of PML-N's political strength. Besides a decade of military rule, from 1999 to 2008, when the province was ruled by his cronies, most of whom were former allies of the PML-N, the party for the most part has been in power in the province. Many of the party's bigwigs, including Nawaz Sharif, Shehbaz Sharif, Ayaz Sadiq, Saad Rafique and now Hamza Shehbaz (Shehbaz's son), contest elections from Lahore. For decades they have swept Lahore, symbolic of their control over the political landscape of the province. While Punjab retains its hegemonic grip over the country, it is Lahore that becomes a symbol of that power, the ultimate crown, representing the pinnacle of political strength.

In 2008 the PML-N won eleven out of thirteen seats in Lahore, reflective of its dominance over Punjab. In 2013, its grip tightened even further, with twelve out of thirteen seats, a result replicated in other regions of Punjab as well, where it secured many more seats than in the previous elections, completely rooting out any other political party.

Perhaps not anticipating such a clean sweep of Lahore by the PML-N, Imran Khan felt that his party had more than a fighting chance in Lahore. His political rally in 2011 had taken the nation, and perhaps even his own party, by storm. Prior to the jalsa, no serious politician or political commentator had taken him seriously. He was still regarded as a political pariah who at best would win a couple of seats. But the Lahore jalsa forced political commentators to sit up and take notice. He had made an impression on Lahore and those who are successful in seducing this city always gain politically.

The tsunami, a word that Imran Khan, quite inappropriately, used for his political movement, started gaining momentum. His next jalsa in Karachi was claimed to be a bigger success. The PTI had emerged as a third wheel in the almost dual political party system of Pakistan, and the social and electronic media was loving it.

Right until the elections, Imran Khan was everywhere. Many felt he had a fair chance of becoming the next prime minister. He was contesting elections from four national Assembly seats, one of which was in Lahore, his home town. He was standing against his old college mate from Aitchison College, Ayaz Sadiq. Both the PTI and the PML-N knew that in terms of numbers, a victory for the PTI in Lahore would be the same as any other, but symbolically it could have far-reaching political repercussions. The incumbent PML-N government had to make sure that it retained Lahore.

It is perhaps because of this that following the elections, and the complete dominance of the PML-N, not just in Lahore but also in the entire province, allegations of rigging by Imran Khan and the PTI outshouted any other political narrative. In August 2014, when Imran Khan, along with a large contingent, sat in Islamabad in protest, the entire federal government came to a gruelling halt. Several other political parties and candidates raised concerns of rigging, but it was Imran Khan's voice that was getting the most ears. The allegations of rigging were concentrated in four constituencies, all of them in Punjab. Two of these seats were in Lahore. It is hard to believe that a similar hue and cry would have been raised had these constituencies not been in Lahore.

In one of the by-elections in these contested constituencies, the PML-N once again emerged victorious, giving the incumbent government enough political armament against the PTI, but what both the parties eyed carefully was the decreasing margin of victory. In fact, this is a pattern that can be noticed in all the twelve seats the PML-N won in Lahore in 2013, in most of which the PTI gave it a run for its money.

Cracks are appearing in the Takht-e-Lahore. The PML-N knows that if Lahore is lost, all is lost. Standing on the stage on 30 October 2011, Imran Khan perhaps saw these cracks appearing.

2

A CITY OF DISSENT

It is a perfect metaphor for the city of Lahore, a city in transition, between two worlds, a city unsure of itself. Sabzazar Housing Scheme skirts the imaginary boundary of the city, fenced by Motorway, Multan Road and Bund Road on three sides, all marking the breached limits of Lahore. This was before the river, the lifeline of the city, the reason for its existence, was turned into sewage, with industrial pollutants being dumped into it and no source of fresh water.

The housing scheme promises a suburban lifestyle to its residents, which continues to evade them. Its geometrical avenues and aligned trees give the illusion of an upper-middle-class neighbourhood, yet, engulfed by three major highways, it can never rise above its geographical surroundings. Its broken roads, vast empty plots converted into dumping grounds and the congestion right at its doorstep render its suburban dream a farcical joke. As I drive through the locality, I notice Avicenna School, named after an eleventh-century Persian intellectual, one of the great minds who ushered the Muslim civilization into its

Golden Period. His original name was Ibn-e-Sina, Avicenna being its Latin corruption. Yet today, in a country that claims to take immense pride in its Islamic heritage, he is referred to by the Latin corruption of his name.

As if consciously trying to shatter the illusion of suburban utopia, the Khadak nala flows on one side of the housing scheme, containing within it the filth of hundreds of small-scale industries operating within the locality of Khadak that lends its name to the nala. The nala forms the division between two contrasting localities—one acting out a fantasy, the other true to its element. Here houses, buildings, schools, factories, showrooms crawl upon each other. There aren't any straight roads. There is no apartheid either. Pedestrians, rickshaws, trucks, cars, bicycles, vendors, schoolchildren, beggars all share these roads equally. There is dynamism on the streets. Sometimes it is expressed through festivals.

A few years ago, I visited the locality on the occasion of Eid Milad-un-Nabi, an annual celebration of the birthday of the Prophet of Islam. The locality of hundreds of thousands appeared as one big family. Houses turned inside out, flowing into the streets. Families had decorated the corners of their homes with symbols of Islam—Kaaba, Mount Hira, the shoe of the Prophet. There was no one indoors. There was a sense of friendly competition, with each corner trying to outdo the other with its decorations.

Sometimes this kind of raucous dynamism can explode, burning the people caught in its radius. In the year 2012, a fire in a factory operating in the locality took the lives of fourteen people.[1] For a few months after, there was much government scrutiny as hundreds of factory owners and workers looked on with bated breath. Public memory soon faded away, and nothing changed in Khadak.

Facing Khadak is the popular housing scheme Allama Iqbal Town, one of the largest such schemes in the country. Now infested with numerous housing societies, this area was once a vast jungle, interspersed with a few settlements, one of which is Khadak, formed in the eighteenth century, during the time of the three Sikh warlords.[2] Due to its vulnerable location, Khadak was subjected to raids by bandits. Eventually, the people of the community decided to take up arms and protect their village. 'Khadak' in Punjabi means an exhibition of strength, the name an oral historical testimony of the violent times the community faced.

Sabzazar, Allama Iqbal and several other housing schemes were constructed on the agricultural lands of Khadak and other surrounding villages. Now caged in from all sides by housing schemes eager to protect themselves from the defiling touch of Khadak, the village has become a collective dump for all of these communities. In the avenues, communities and markets of suburban localities, much of the city's folk history is lost. Their desperation to disassociate from their 'mother' villages is reflective of a schizophrenic postcolonial mentality. The transition from 'village' to 'city', from 'old Lahore' to 'new Lahore', becomes a class symbol and a lifestyle choice. Progress and modernity are understood as breaking away from traditional communities, architecture and precolonial urban planning. The colonial blueprint of a perfect 'planned community' finds crass replicas all over the city.

However, there is sometimes a whiff among suburban communities that is reminiscent of a Lahore unaware of colonial sensibilities. At times it is the graveyards that continue to accumulate tales of these localities and their origins. For instance, the graveyard in the middle of Sabzazar. Surrounded by a complex network of roads, dominated by vehicles of all sorts, honking loudly, negotiating for space, is a small island of serenity. At its entrance is a seventeenth-century Sufi shrine that lends its name to the graveyard—Shah Fareed. It's a new building, freshly renovated, with a green dome on top. There is an old keekar tree at the entrance where a handful of *malang*, devotees of the shrine, sit together smoking cigarettes and sharing tales of political intrigues. Their thick bangles, several rings and beads set them apart from others who enter and exit the shrine to pay homage to the saint. A small plaque records nothing other than the dates of the birth and death of the saint interred here.

There are several such shrines across the city, raised in hundreds of graveyards dotting its landscape. Much like the uncodified Hinduism of the precolonial era, these too represent local cults, which might not necessarily be connected with any meta-theological narrative. Even though there has occurred an unprecedented formalization and uniformity of religious practices after the advent of mass media, several of these shrines continue to attract devotional followers looking for a localized, immediate intermediary.

At the other end of the graveyard of Shah Fareed, protected by a small enclosure and accompanied by the graves of his wife and daughter, under the cool shade of a giant peepul tree, is the final resting place of the 'poet of the people'—Habib Jalib. His verses are inscribed on plaques on the wall of this enclosure. I stood facing his grave, unsure of what to do next. A committed communist, Habib Jalib was an atheist, hence sceptical of religious ritual and dogma.

While Lahore is undoubtedly a symbol of hegemonic authority, it is also the city of Habib Jalib, the rebel poet, who challenged this hegemony his entire life. His was one of the loudest voices against the first military dictator of the country, Ayub Khan. At a time when all intellectuals, poets, writers and artists were silenced by the military regime, Jalib defied convention. Instead of focusing on romanticism and beauty, he talked about the streets of the country under military rule. Defying all guidelines, on a live mushaira being aired by Radio Pakistan, a state-run enterprise, Jalib went on to recite:

The stench of teargas lingers
The hail of bullets persists . . .[3]

His rendezvous with incarceration began after this episode and continued till the end of his life.

'Mein ne us se yeh kaha' (I said this to him), a satirical poem, is one of his most memorable verses from that era. The poem reminds the dictator how only he can salvage Pakistan, how only he can take it from night to day. It reminds him how a hundred million people of Pakistan are the 'epitome of ignorance', 'completely mindless', and how the dictator is the 'Light of God' and 'Wisdom and Knowledge personified'. Jalib does acknowledge in the poem that there are a handful of people who oppose his rule and he, Ayub Khan, should 'tear out their tongues' and 'throttle their throats'.[4]

Jalib was a member of the Progressive Writers' Movement, a left-leaning literary organization that aimed to use writing to inspire people to create a just and equal society for all. After Partition, Lahore became the centre of this organization in Pakistan, earning the city yet another title, that of the cultural capital of the country. It is through the Progressive Writers' Movement that writers like Faiz Ahmad Faiz, Saadat Hassan Manto, Ahmad Faraz and Hameed Akhtar challenged a state that was cosying up to the United States of America and increasingly defining itself in religious terms. Even in the poem quoted above, Jalib mentions China and its 'system'. He mentions the friendly relationship between China and Pakistan and yet the paranoia against leftist politics in his country. 'Stay clear of that [system]', he suggests, these masses 'could never become rulers'. At the end he expresses the desire, 'You [Ayub] remain our President forever.'[5]

Even today, as Pakistan flirts yet again with democracy, the nostalgia for one-man authoritarian rule continues to surface sporadically. The narrative of a messiah who would save the country continues to dominate political discussions.

Imran Khan's entire political career is based on these romantic notions of a true Pakistani hero, who would finish off corruption and restore Pakistan to the glorious stature it is meant to achieve. Even Shehbaz Sharif's success in Punjab can be attributed to a 'messiah' image he has successfully crafted for himself over the years—one man, with an iron determination to get things done.

In the past, however, such romanticization has been associated with the men in khaki, who have ruled the country three times directly and continue to exert immense pressure on the civilian government indirectly. Despite their failed attempts at governing and providing stability, parts of the populace continue to be enamoured of them.

Particularly in the past few years, the cult of Raheel Shareef, the former army chief, exemplifies what Jalib was talking about in the 1960s. As the ratings of politicians fell, Shareef's popularity continued to soar. All good things in the country became associated with him, while all the failures were blamed on the politicians. On various occasions, posters exhorting him to overthrow a 'corrupt' democratic system to establish a dictatorship were raised in various cities of the country.

Ayub's dictatorship marked a fundamental shift in Pakistan's foreign policy, the effects of which can be experienced till today. Breaking away from non-alignment, the state under him openly sided with the US in the Cold War that was being fought in every continent of the world through the respective proxies of the US and USSR. In compensation for US military aid, Pakistan's airbases were leased out to the CIA to spy on the Russians. The balance of domestic politics in the country also shifted forever, in favour of the military establishment. American support for military dictators, beginning with Ayub, then Zia and finally Musharraf, has been fundamental in not only the dictators' international legitimization but also in suppressing domestic democratic resistance to them.

For all his atrocities, Ayub Khan today is remembered fondly in Pakistan. His image plastered to the rear of trucks is a ubiquitous sight. While dictators after him were worshipped during their time in power and vilified after they exited the scene, Ayub continues to be held in esteem. School textbooks recall his time as the 'Golden Period' of Pakistan, a narrative that continues to dominate popular political discourse. 'Ideologically' aligned with the Americans, Pakistan under Ayub saw a rapid introduction of liberal economic reforms. While poverty remained rampant, the elite benefited from these policies and hence the narrative of 'economic growth' became dominant. Many today acknowledge that wealth at that time remained confined to twenty-two of the richest families in the country. Talking about this uneven distribution of income, Jalib observed:

Twenty households prosper
As a million people suffer
President Ayub live forever[6]

In 1962 when Ayub Khan introduced his Constitution, Jalib was one of the few to criticize it openly. One of his best remembered poems, 'Dastoor', rejected the dictator's Constitution.

This constitution
This dawn without light
I refuse to acknowledge
I refuse to accept[7]

Even today Jalib's 'Dastoor' is recited both by rebels and members of the political establishment. One of the most memorable moments in recent years was Shehbaz Sharif reciting it at one of his political rallies.[8]

Jalib, during his long career, particularly aligned himself with women on political issues. His first foray into feminist politics was in 1965, when he wrote a poem in honour of an actress, Neelo, who refused to be pressurized to perform for a state guest, the Shah of Iran. During the Pakistani presidential elections of 1965, when Ayub Khan was pitted against Fatima Jinnah in a battle rigged before it even began, Jalib supported the latter, calling her the mother of the nation.[9]

In 1971, as Pakistan headed towards the darkest chapter since its creation, Jalib's was one of the only voices from West Pakistan, dominated as it was by Punjabi hegemony, to speak out against atrocities committed by the army in East Pakistan under the guise of Operation Searchlight. Flooded with state propaganda interspersed with legends of the gallant and chivalrous Pakistani soldier, West Pakistan supported the operation that was meant to silence Bengali nationalist sentiment.

With the arrival of Zulfikar Ali Bhutto and his slogan of Islamist socialism, there was hope in the country's leftist circles. Jalib maintained an ambivalent relationship with the new prime minister. There were moments of warmth, but also of persecution. He was put behind bars for his opposition to the dismissal of the provincial government of the North-West Frontier Province (NWFP), now called Khyber Pakhtunkhwa, and high-handedness in dealing with the separatist movement in Baluchistan by Bhutto.

Despite a bittersweet relationship with Bhutto, on the occasion of his death at the hands of Zia, Jalib wrote:

His magic has not been broken
His blood has become a slogan[10]

The years to follow were to shape the nature of Pakistani society for generations to come. Today, as religious extremism raises its head not just in Lahore but every other city of the country, its roots can be traced to the hateful years of Zia, who actively mixed religion with politics, leading to an unprecedented Islamization of state institutions. Infused with righteous piety, Zia was on a self-appointed crusade to 'rectify' the country's moral issues. His Islamization of the state and its institutions was meant to further 'purify' the land of the pure. Petty criminals, but mostly political opponents belonging to Bhutto's PPP, were flogged in public. Under the pretence of a religious system, Pakistan was ushered into one of its darkest periods. For Zia and his cronies, Pakistan was finally on the right path, heading towards enlightenment. Zia, the messiah, through Islamization of state institutions, thought he had rectified all of Pakistan's problems. It is in this context that Jalib made a few objections in his poem, 'Zulmat ko Zia'. He said he could not call this cruelty kindness, this dark night dawn, this desert a rose garden, nor a human being God.[11]

In another poem that mocked Zia's referendum of 1984, an attempt by the dictator to legitimize his position, Jalib wrote the following:

The city was desolated
Was it a jinn or was it a referendum?[12]

Jalib's role during the Woman Action Forum's (WAF) protest on 12 February 1983 against the recently passed Law of Evidence, which reduced the weight of the testimony of a woman to half of a man's, resulted in one of his most iconic photographs of the times. Surrounded by a sea of women, Jalib was the only man invited to join the protest and recite his poetry of rebellion. The police descended upon the protestors to drag them to jail. In one photograph, young policemen are pulling an aged Jalib from both sides. In another, Jalib receives a blow to his head.

Even today, when the old guard of the WAF gathers every year on 12 February to commemorate that event, Jalib's poem is recited like an anthem. Set up in Karachi in 1981, the WAF had a strong presence in Lahore, led by some of the most prominent feminists of its time. The organization was originally initiated to oppose the Hudood Ordinance, which was part of Zia's programme of Islamization. The ordinance prescribed punishments for adultery and fornication, suggested public whipping, deprived women of their property rights, prohibited alcohol and reduced the value of women's testimony. While some of these laws were later revised, others continue to be a part of Pakistan's penal code.

The WAF's struggles against Zia are shining examples of brave opposition to a ruthless dictator. At a time when political activists were being tortured, whipped in public and even killed, a few hundred women walked the streets of Lahore, raising their voices for their rights. While most of them came from liberal education and upper-middle-class backgrounds, their class privilege did not stand in the way of their street protests. Harassed and 'manhandled' by the police of the state, they continued to march and created an example of a heroic feminist political movement.

The movement has a special significance in the history of Lahore and Punjab. It publicly protested against a dictator at a time when the rest of the city and the province had passively accepted its fate. While anti-Zia movements, under the banner of the Movement for the Restoration of Democracy (MRD) raged in other parts of the country, particularly in Sindh, the Punjabi middle class, traders and businessmen reaped the benefits of Zia's liberal economic policies. After Bhutto's haphazard nationalization, which had a serious economic impact on Punjabi businessmen, most of them were relieved by the dictator's economic policies.

While Sindh burned, Punjab basked in the glow of economic prosperity. Its position as the hegemonic centre was further solidified. Soon, the MRD emerged as a Sindhi nationalist struggle. In this docile and passive environment, the voices of the WAF and Habib Jalib rang even louder. Jalib could not help but resent Punjab's apathy. He felt it was Punjab's support of the establishment that had led to the country's dismemberment in 1971. He could see history repeating itself in Sindh, where the MRD had turned into a full-blown civil war between Sindhi nationalists and the Punjabi establishment. Jalib knew Punjab had to realize the situation before further damage could be wrought to the country. His poem 'Jaag Mere Punjab' is a plea for such an awakening.

Awake O Punjab, Pakistan is in danger[13]

On 12 March 1993, this rebel poet of Lahore, who had been at the forefront of protests against two military dictators, breathed his last at Lahore's iconic Ganga Ram Hospital. He was buried at Sabzazar graveyard, where he had spent the last few years of his life. While during his lifetime his activism and poetry were seen as a threat by the political establishment, after his death he was appropriated by everyone. His poetry is now recited by politicians of all ideologies. Once incarcerated by the state for his opinions, in 2009 Jalib was awarded the highest civil award in the country,[14] which was received from the President of Pakistan by Jalib's daughter, who is now buried next to her rebel father.

Scattered in the courtyard of Data Darbar are the sins of the city of Lahore. For a thousand years, people of all religions, castes, sects and creeds have found refuge here. The shrine has provided food and shelter to anyone seeking them. At the centre of a mammoth courtyard is the actual shrine, containing the grave of the eleventh-century Sufi scholar Ali Hujwiri, also known as Data Ganj Bakhsh. Covered by a small building with latticed windows looking into the shrine, not everyone is allowed into this sacred space. To these windows, devotees tie their supplications in the form of a thread, beseeching the saint to intercede on their behalf. The threads are removed when there is no room for any more, only to be replaced once again with new ones.

Tradition dictates that one enters the abode of a Sufi saint with an offering. There are dozens of shops outside this highly guarded complex to ensure this tradition is not discontinued. *Chadar*s with Quranic verses hang from the roofs of these shops, mostly in green—a colour associated the most with Islam. The dome of the shrine is green. The bigger dome of an imposing mosque behind the shrine is also green. Offerings at the shrine include overpriced flower petals and incense sticks. After passing through the police picket and its metal detector, a devotee is stopped once again at the entrance, where a group of boys asks for his or her shoes. Irrespective of the weather, a devotee needs to walk barefoot on the shrine's white marble, whether it is burning in the heat or freezing in the cold. A coupon is handed to a devotee for his or her shoes and an amount charged on return.

Inside, the administrators watchfully monitor the arrival of devotees. Not everyone's chadar is important enough to adorn the saint's grave. Not everyone's incense stick can spread its fragrance in this holy space.

Perhaps there was a time when devotees would bow before the grave, as they still do in some of the other Sufi shrines. This is a major bone of contention between different sects of Islam. Puritans believe 'shrine-worshipping' is an act of *shirk*, a serious sin of worshipping someone other than Allah. They assert one should only bow before God. I remember my grandmother reiterating the fact to me many years ago, when I first visited the shrine with her. With the rising influence of the puritanical school of thought and the increasing significance of the shrine in the political and social landscape of the city, such 'heretical' traditions have been abandoned. There are signs at the shrine warning pilgrims against such practices. Guardians rebuke 'ill-informed' devotees who attempt to bow before the saint.

Even within the puritanical streams of thought, there are variations. There are those who believe all forms of 'grave-devotion' are un-Islamic. The Sufi saints were highly learned men, they assert, who need to be respected, but no form of devotion can be shown towards them. Everyone is equal in the eyes of Allah. Others believe that while it is 'un-Islamic' to bow in front of a grave, one can pray to the Sufi saint to intercede on a devotee's behalf because of their closer association with God. According to them, praying to the saint for intercession is not equivalent to worshipping the grave.

For centuries these debates have existed in Muslim societies. Sometimes, patronized by the state, certain traditions have overshadowed others; however, never before in the history of the religion have they faced the kind of existential threat that they do today. There has been an unprecedented increase in the number of attacks on Sufi shrines all across the country, with 'un-Islamic' practices being cited as justification. In March 2009, the popular shrine of Rahman Baba was attacked in Peshawar.[15] In the same year, the iconic shrine of Abdullah Shah Ghazi located on top of a cliff facing the sea in Karachi was attacked.[16] In 2017, the shrine of Lal Shahbaz Qalandar in Sehwan Sharif, a symbol of religious syncretism in the country, was bombed.

Data Darbar's fate has been no better. On 1 July 2010, it was attacked by two suicide bombers. One blew himself up in the courtyard, the other in the basement. The attack took place on a Thursday evening, the busiest day of the week, when hundreds of devotees gather to listen to qawwali. A musical rendition of the spiritual experience, qawwali is also regarded as 'un-Islamic' by puritans. The blasts at Data Darbar resulted in the deaths of at least forty-five people, injuring many more.[17]

Lahore was in a state of shock. Never before in its millennium-long history had this sanctuary ever been desecrated. It was respected when the Mughals established authority over Punjab. It was treated with care during the bloody raids of Nadir Shah and Ahmad Shah Abdali. Even during the period of the Sikh warlords, when the entire city was in chaos, the shrine stood as it is, providing comfort to all its devotees. Under Ranjit Singh, even as the neighbouring Badshahi Mosque was converted into a stable, the shrine of Data Darbar continued to be regarded as sacred and treated accordingly. The British too always upheld its sanctity. For the first time in the history of this ancient city, it seemed that the shrine was up against an enemy unlike any in the past.

The attack on the shrine was an attack on the soul of Lahore. For contemporary Lahore, Data Darbar is not just a shrine but also a vibrant symbol of the city—of its prosperity, wealth, power, beauty, austerity and religiosity. It has been appropriated and manipulated by all the major political leaders of the country at different times.

Born at the end of the tenth century in Ghazni, Afghanistan, Ali Hujwiri moved to Lahore after the conquest of Punjab by Mahmud of Ghazni. Instead of settling inside the walled city, he found a place for himself a little distance away, in the wilderness. From here, he is popularly believed to have preached the new religion, converting many. Unlike some of the other Sufi saints, like Mansur al-Hallaj, Lal Shahbaz Qalandar and Bulleh Shah, Ali Hujwiri upheld the supremacy of the Shariah and the religious rituals associated with it.[18] It is perhaps the orthodox Islam preached by the saint that allowed for easy appropriation of him and the shrine by contemporary politicians looking for religious validation.

Contrary to its present state—a vast complex divided into male and female sections, with a gigantic mosque in the background, an open courtyard, a large hall in the basement for qawwali, a madrasa and a library—Ali Hujwiri's shrine has been a modest structure for the longer part of its life. Situated opposite the Bhatti Gate of the walled city, the shrine was first constructed in the eleventh century as a single building with a grave at its centre, a form it retained for centuries. The simple building at the centre of the courtyard is reminiscent of the original shrine. Even during the Mughal reign, the shrine failed to attract imperial funding.

Defying popular historical narratives in Pakistan, it was rather during the reign of Maharaja Ranjit Singh that the shrine rose in significance and began to rival other popular Sufi shrines like Mian Mir and Shah Hussain. A library containing the imperial collections of handwritten copies of the Quran donated by Maharani Jind Kaur, the youngest wife of the Maharaja, was constructed on her orders.[19] This was the first such public collection of copies of the Quran in the city and raised the status of the shrine. Its social and political significance only increased thereafter. Under the colonial regime, as a new sort of urban religious identity developed, the shrine acquired centre stage. Particularly after the creation of Pakistan, all governments have viewed the patronage of the shrine as an important act in terms of acquiring political legitimacy.

During his years in power, Bhutto donated the shrine's fabled silver gate with gold decorations.[20] Bhutto's successor, Zia, too donated generously, and was responsible for the construction of the giant mosque that overshadows the modest structure containing the grave.[21] Patronage of Data Darbar was an important political move in his quest for legitimization of his illegal rule and his Islamization programme.

It was at the shrine's doorstep, outside the Bhatti Gate, that the scene of PPP loyalists, *jayalas*, protesting against the military regime and immolating themselves to save their leader's life had unfolded in 1978.[22] With Karachi and Sindh erupting, Pakistan seemed on the brink of another civil war. The dictator understood the political significance of Punjab and Lahore. He knew he could not afford to lose Lahore as he was losing Karachi.

Religious patronage became his primary propaganda tool and it
worked. Islamization in conjunction with economic liberalization
earned the dictator support among the trading class of the city, its
economic backbone. Patronage to the shrine of Data Darbar, the
benefactor of Lahore, patron saint of the city, thus served a crucial
political purpose.

It was a moment replete with symbolism when Benazir turned
towards the shrine before heading down to Iqbal Park to address
her mammoth jalsa, still believed by many to be the largest
political gathering in the city, counter to what Imran Khan claims.
Zulfikar Ali Bhutto had done the same when he reached Lahore
to challenge the authority of Ayub Khan. Now Benazir was up
against another dictator, a more brutal version of the former, and
she was at the shrine of Data Darbar to seek his blessings in her
political mission.

This act acquired even greater significance in the background
of almost a decade of malicious propaganda against the Bhutto
family. Ever since snatching power, Zia had unleashed the
state propaganda machinery against Bhutto, his family and the
PPP. They were called a threat to Islam and Pakistan, atheists,
libertines and Westernized elites. There was a strong religious and
moralistic undertone in his political opposition to Bhutto and
Benazir.

The education system and the media (completely owned by
the state) had undergone years of Islamization by now. There
was a new generation of Pakistanis who knew no other reality.
With public executions, caning and other religious laws, Pakistan
under Zia had increasingly aligned itself with the Saudi state, as
opposed to the liberal Islamic democratic country that Bhutto had
promised in the 1970s.

In conjunction with the US, Zia had funded several Wahabi madrasas all over the country to support the Afghan Jihad. The nature of religion in the country underwent a fundamental change during his decade-long rule, the ripples of which can still be felt in the country. A literal and puritanical interpretation of Islam, espoused by the Wahabi ideology, slowly seeped into the social fabric of the country, which had earlier been dominated by an inclusive Sufi interpretation. Religious clerics amassed immense power under Zia. Supported by the state and with a cadre of young, passionate followers, religious leaders acquired unprecedented street power. Along with looking after the law and order situation, the police force was given the added responsibility of moral policing, such as asking young couples sitting together in public for marriage certificates and punishing them if they failed to produce one.

Moral policing, sanctioned by the newly introduced religious laws of the country and strengthened by street vigilantes, radically decreased the space for women in public. Whereas in the 1960s and 1970s, at least in cities like Karachi, Lahore and Rawalpindi, young women wearing skirts and jeans would cycle to work or colleges, in the 1980s, hounded by a zealot state and its proxies, women began to disappear from public spaces. Those who braved the onslaught had to conform to a certain display of 'modesty'. Western clothes were shunned. A dupatta over the head became a regular feature. Cycling to work became unimaginable if you were a woman.

The Afghan Jihad led by Zia brought in a vast and unaccounted supply of weapons, funnelled into Afghanistan via Pakistan by the US, fighting a proxy battle against its arch-enemy, the USSR. Large tranches of those weapons routinely found their way into illegal arms markets in the bigger cities of the country. Perhaps using the same weapons, the government armed its allied parties to counter its political opponents. The Muttahida

Qaumi Movement in Karachi, headed by Altaf Hussain, which began as a student political group a year after Zia overthrew the civilian government, was pampered by the military government to counter the stronghold of PPP in its home city. In Lahore, it was the Islami Jamiat-e-Talaba (IJT), the student wing of the Jama'at-e-Islami, that received government support. Their student leaders were given weapons so that they could gain an upper hand in the universities and colleges where the left-leaning National Students Federation, sympathetic to the PPP, held sway.[23] Violence gripped the campuses of Lahore and Karachi. Politics became bloodier under the shadow of the gun. Alongside entered heroin. Under Zia, Pakistan became the chief exporter of heroin in the world, which arrived into the country from Afghanistan. Millions of Pakistanis took to this new addiction.

All this was accompanied by the worst form of political repression. For eight years the country remained under martial law, with all expressions of political dissent severely penalized. PPP supporters were jailed, tortured and even killed. Prominent political leaders critical of the government were thrown behind bars without any charges. There was an arid sense of fear in the country. Paranoia swept through the major cities. Government informants, it was feared, roamed among the public, eavesdropping on conversations in restaurants, bus stations and other public spaces. Uttering the name 'Bhutto' in a public space could lead to severe repercussions. In this environment, perhaps the military dictator convinced himself that he had erased Bhutto's memory. He had started believing his own propaganda. Little did he realize that, like molten lava, the memory of Bhutto lay just beneath the surface, waiting to erupt through the first crack.

Even before dawn on 4 April 1979, defying all protocol, the first democratically elected prime minister of the country, Zulfikar Ali Bhutto, was hanged in Rawalpindi. It had been only eight years since the breakaway of East Pakistan, and the country had finally begun to move on from the traumatic experience. This execution sent shockwaves around the country. There hadn't been a more popular leader in Pakistan until then. Bhutto had a cult following. People dressed like him, wanted to be like him. Like Mao's *Little Red Book*, books of Bhutto's quotations were sold throughout the country. In power, he had shown the dispirited country a dream of a great future, of becoming an Islamic superpower, strong enough to not only fight its giant 'Hindu' neighbour but also take on the superpowers of the world. With his death, that dream died too.

There could be no public mourning. Martial law was at its peak. No political gatherings were allowed. His followers cried in the confines of their homes. His body was flown to Larkana in the dead of night and buried in the family graveyard, with no members of his family present. Benazir and her mother were jailed, while her two brothers were in exile.

As a new repressive regime spread its tentacles, the trauma of the loss only grew bigger in the public subconscious. Whatever flaws Bhutto had during his lifetime, his death rendered him a 'saint'. Compared to the 'monster' that followed him, Bhutto appeared better, brighter. As the military dictator tried suppressing his memory, his legend only grew stronger.

For seven years after the overthrow of her father's government on 5 July 1977, Benazir was incarcerated by the military dictator, sometimes with her family members and sometimes alone. PPP's distraught supporters had no leader. Her brothers, Murtaza and Shahnawaz, shocked by the death of their father, decided to adopt a more radical approach and militarily challenge the dictatorship. Benazir, on the other hand, advocated a non-violent democratic approach. Her peaceful opposition to Zia even from behind bars was to earn for her a reputation not only within the country, but also internationally, similar to Aung San Suu Kyi's during her opposition to Myanmar's military junta.

It was a potent image. A beautiful young woman carrying forward her father's democratic struggle, in a deeply patriarchal and religious society. Also, a 'complete' woman, who understood family values along with political compulsions—a 'daughter of the East', as her autobiography was called. While her father's rise to political popularity had been on the shoulders of a military dictator, Ayub Khan, Benazir's political star rose opposing a brutal military dictatorship. She was finally able to exit the country in 1984 on the pretext of medical treatment. She remained in exile for two years, trying to harness global support against the military dictator who had by now become a champion of 'freedom' in the West due to his leading role in aiding the fight against communism in Afghanistan. It was also during her exile that her younger brother was secretly poisoned and killed in France, a murder she believed was orchestrated by the establishment. This was the second 'sacrifice' the Bhuttos had made for 'democracy'. 'Democracy is the best revenge,' became her slogan.

In 1986, when Zia lifted martial law, Benazir decided to head back to Pakistan to continue her opposition to him. Instead of Karachi, her home town, she chose to land in Lahore. A young Benazir understood how politically significant the city was and how any political movement that began here found resonance across the country. It was in Lahore that her father had started his independent political career by opposing Ayub Khan. It was in Lahore that he had talked to the largest gatherings. Lahore, under Bhutto, had been a bastion of the PPP. Punjab and Sindh had swept him to power. It was also in Lahore that Bhutto had hosted his Islamic Summit in 1974, believed to be his greatest foreign policy achievement, that cemented an Islamic bloc to counter the cultural threat from the West. Thus it was in Lahore that Benazir wanted to mount her challenge to the mighty Zia.

However, Lahore presented another problem. A majority of the cadres within the Pakistani army came from Punjab.

Thus, Punjab was also the heart of the establishment. Aside from a few protests, Lahore and Punjab had remained passive throughout the long decade after Bhutto, even as Sindh and Karachi burned. After the economic slump of the Bhutto years, liberalization and American aid had brought much-needed respite for the industrialists and traders of Punjab, who quietly stood behind the dictator. The return of a Bhutto to power brought back unpleasant memories of nationalization, when thriving businesses were taken over by the government and turned into economic liabilities. Lahore—and Punjab—were divided. While Bhutto's land and labour reforms had earned him everlasting love and support from the working classes, the upper classes looked at the new Bhutto with suspicion. Interestingly, this is an image the PPP continues to conjure in urban Punjab, a narrative that Nawaz Sharif was successfully able to hijack and manipulate, presenting himself to be the more economy-friendly alternative. Benazir's return to Lahore, therefore, was also meant to be a symbolic challenge to the establishment and its supporters at its very core.

Lahore remained conflicted. It continued to pose the greatest political challenge to Benazir, opposed as she was by Nawaz Sharif, who was, at least in the early half of the 1990s, the face of the establishment. The loss of Lahore to her arch-rival would be, till the end of her life in 2007, one of her biggest political defeats. It's a loss from which the PPP has still not recovered; a loss that represents the loss of Punjab. It is a bastion the party needs to conquer if it ever wants to form a federal government again.

The situation was different on 10 April 1986. Lahore was still not lost. A city that had been muted for almost a decade roared in support of Benazir. The slogan *'Jiye Bhutto'* (Long Live Bhutto) resonated in the air. The tripartite colours of the party's flag, black, red and green, adorned the streets. For a people yearning to publicly mourn the loss of their fallen leader, the joyous return of Benazir became a celebration of Bhutto's death. In Sufi tradition, it is not birthdays but rather the death anniversaries of the saint that are commemorated. For it is believed that death represents the ultimate union of the Sufi, the lover, with God, the Beloved, which is the final goal. At this point, for the city of Lahore, Bhutto had ceased to be a Machiavellian politician. He had become a saint. At a time of extreme censorship, 3 million people, according to PPP sources, gathered to welcome his daughter back.[24] Police authorities assigned to maintain 'law and order' quickly disappeared.

Standing atop an open truck, Benazir waved back and clapped along with her supporters. A journey that usually takes fifteen minutes stretched over ten hours.[25] It was not just a political gathering, it was a celebration, a public mourning, a 'tamasha' as her political opponents later suggested. It is this tamasha, politics intermingled with music and dance, which was eventually appropriated by all political parties. A young Benazir was the ultimate symbol of protest. Habib Jalib's famous poem 'The Gunmen Are Afraid of Unarmed Girl' was written for her.[26]

Before she headed to Iqbal Park to formally challenge the dictator, she needed the blessings of the patron saint of Lahore—Data Darbar. Data Darbar was the symbol of Islamization under Zia. Benazir was not the atheist, socialist, libertine monster that Zia had portrayed her as. She was rooted in the culture of the land. What better way to show that than by offering a chadar at the grave of the saint?

Benazir was now ready to take on the military dictator. In the shadow of the shrine, at the historic Iqbal Park, she addressed the largest political gathering in the city. Two years later, she was sworn in as the youngest and the first woman prime minister of Pakistan, the first woman head of state of any Muslim country in the modern era. This, though, was only the beginning of her woes.

On his drive to Kot Lakhpat Jail in Lahore, along with his cousin Mumtaz Bhutto, once the powerful governor of Sindh, Zulfikar Ali Bhutto must have realized he had underestimated the threat the military regime posed to him. According to several reports, Bhutto, immediately after the coup, even when he was kept in 'protected custody' in Murree, had been in high spirits and was convinced he would be able to intimidate his captor by using his famed power of rhetoric.[27]

Perhaps till this point, Bhutto could not imagine that his handpicked army chief, promoted out of turn over six other senior generals, a meek-looking army man, could present a serious threat to him, the most popular and powerful man in the country, loved by the entire Muslim world, and destined to lead it, along with the rest of the Third World. For someone with as much knowledge and appreciation of history, it is rather strange that Bhutto did not realize that a similar out-of-turn promotion of Ayub Khan had led to the first military coup in the country. Incidentally, twenty-two years after the coup against Bhutto, another out-of-turn promoted general, Pervez Musharraf, led a coup against his premier.

It is a simple roundabout with a colourful fountain, which connects Ichra, Shahjamal with Shadman. The fountain is usually dry. It was here, on a cold November evening in 1974, that Ahmad Raza Khan Kasuri, a former colleague turned vehement critic of Bhutto, was intercepted as he was returning from a wedding with his father, mother and aunt. A similar attack had been made on the young rebel politician in Islamabad earlier, which he had managed to escape. He survived but his father was not as lucky. Rushed to the nearby United Christian Hospital, he was pronounced dead soon after. When asked by police officials to name suspects, Kasuri blamed Bhutto, the prime minister of Pakistan.

Soon after his release from 'protected custody', Bhutto was granted bail by Lahore High Court despite pressure from the military regime. Perhaps till this point, Bhutto felt he could garner public support and fight his way out of this alleged conspiracy to murder. The case against him was three years old and lacked evidence. Zia, however, knew well enough it was either his own life or Bhutto's.[28]

It was a well-known fact that Bhutto did not take well to criticism. Often, he resorted to personal attacks, mocking the body language or manner of speaking of his opponents.[29] His inability to tolerate criticism had turned many of his former allies into enemies. Several of his loyal supporters, who had helped him reach the pinnacle of power, had been sidelined following his years in office. One such example was J.A. Rahim, one of the original founders of the PPP, the intellectual theoretician behind the party, who was manhandled by members of the Federal Security Force (FSF) loyal to Bhutto, for his criticism of their chief.[30] Late to a dinner, Rahim had called Bhutto 'King of Larkana' and marched off. Had Bhutto's intolerance for criticism reached a new level with Ahmad Raza Khan Kasuri? The murder of Nawab Mohammad Kasuri was pinned on the prime minister's loyal paramilitary force, FSF, created by Bhutto in 1972. Bullets used for the murder allegedly belonged to the guns used by the force.

Having shed off military martial law, Bhutto, as the head of a newly established democratic regime, understood the precariousness of his political position. The powerful army establishment had only recently been humbled in the debacle of 1971. Two wings of Pakistan were now left with only the western wing.

Even though it was Yahya Khan, the martial law administrator who launched the military operation titled Operation Searchlight to curb Bengali nationalist sentiment, Bhutto was equally responsible. In the first general elections of Pakistan in 1970, Mujib-ur-Rehman's Awami League had swept the elections in East Pakistan, while Bhutto's PPP had dominated Sindh and Punjab. Mujib-ur-Rehman should have been invited to form the government and would have been elected prime minister. It is argued that Yahya Khan had even begun calling Mujib-ur-Rehman prime minister, but Bhutto was not ready to allow his Bengali compatriot to govern both the wings.[31] He argued that his party should be allowed to rule the western wing, which was unacceptable to Mujib-ur-Rehman. A stalemate ensued, with the army eventually stepping in to control the 'law and order' situation in East Pakistan. It was not Yahya Khan but Bhutto who was the most hated person in East Pakistan which became Bangladesh, at least in the days preceding the operation.

Ironically, it was Bhutto who benefited the most from the fiasco, first becoming the civilian martial law administrator, and then prime minister. By then, Pakistan had had enough of military rule. It wanted to take its fate into its own hands and Bhutto was the man elected to be at the helm of affairs. Despite his powerful position and the weakened state of the army, Bhutto knew the balance could tilt in the latter's favour. Seeking inspiration from Hitler's SS, he raised the FSF, a force that would be loyal to him and shield him from the army. Little did Bhutto realize that the FSF would lead to his downfall. His fate in the case of conspiracy to murder was sealed on the testimony of Masood Mahmood, his handpicked director of the FSF, who admitted to Bhutto's involvement in the plot. The FSF was disbanded by Zia on his seizing power.

The earlier war, in 1965, had set in motion a chain of events that would bring Bhutto closer to power, another debacle for which Bhutto shoulders as much responsibility as the military establishment. A member of the dictator Ayub Khan's cabinet, Bhutto was the young and talented foreign minister who had impressed his boss at home and others abroad with his elegant and passionate speeches. A young firebrand, he was a supporter of the

Kashmir cause. It was because of Bhutto's persistence and planning that Ayub Khan launched Operation Gibraltar, a secret operation in which clandestine fighters from Pakistan would cross the Line of Control and instigate the local population to rise up against the Indian forces.[32] Once there was a general uprising, Operation Grand Slam, a full-scale military operation, could have been launched.

Bhutto, with a keen eye on the international situation, had seen India cosying up to the Americans, while maintaining a warm relationship with the Soviet Union. It was in the process of upgrading its military hardware. Bhutto realized that soon the Indian Army would be too powerful for Pakistan to compete with in conventional war. It was therefore imperative for Pakistan to wage a war with India while there was still some kind of a balance between the two armies.[33] An act of aggression was brilliantly presented as a defensive approach.

What the regime and Bhutto had not taken into account was a counter-attack by the Indian forces on the western front. Bhutto believed, and had managed to convince his President, that India would rather attack Pakistan on the eastern front, in East Pakistan, as opposed to the western front where there was a strong army presence. He also believed that China would come to their rescue in East Pakistan, which did not happen. In case of that attack, the Pakistani army would easily be able to cut off Kashmir from India. The lives of millions of Bengali Pakistanis were put in jeopardy and perhaps regarded as collateral damage in this operation, which became a strong cause of resentment in East Pakistan.

Contrary to expectations, the Indian forces, instead of marching into East Pakistan, moved into Punjab and headed towards Lahore. Bhutto, Pakistan's political establishment and intelligence agencies were all caught off guard. There was a real threat that the Indian forces could march into the provincial capital. The Pakistani establishment could have sacrificed Dhaka for a chance at Kashmir, but Lahore was never an option.

On the outskirts of the city, close to the Indian border, relics of the war survive till today. Three layers of mounds were constructed to halt the progression of Indian tanks, in the middle of which were camouflaged posts, still numbered and well maintained. Several villages along the border were occupied by advancing Indian forces, but Lahore was saved. Despite being caught off guard and outnumbered, the Pakistani army managed to keep the Indian forces away from the city.

Ayub Khan, who had by now become disillusioned by his ambitious foreign minister, took it upon himself to seek peace. He met with Indian Prime Minister Lal Bahadur Shastri in Tashkent where, snubbing Bhutto, he signed the Tashkent Declaration, a ceasefire deal, on 10 January 1966. Humiliated, Bhutto returned to Pakistan perhaps having made up his mind to overthrow the powerful field marshal. He called Ayub a coward and accused him of having agreed to ceasefire so close to victory. A battle he had lost on the ground, he managed to win through clever rhetoric. Ironically, using the rhetoric that Bhutto had crafted then, the Pakistani establishment continues to project the war of 1965 as a victory even today.

Situated within the locality of Ichra, not far from Shadman Chowk, where Nawab Mohammad Kasuri was shot, is the house of Maulana Maududi, the cleric who founded the Jama'at-e-Islami. Once opposed to the creation of Pakistan, the Jamaat led by Maududi started demanding that Islamic law be introduced in the country after its creation. Maududi regarded Bhutto's leftist rhetoric as a threat to his Islamic agenda. Bhutto too returned the compliment, with his criticism often directed against Maududi in his speeches.

After almost six years in power, Bhutto's popularity was not what it had been in the 1970 election. However, the Opposition was divided and the PPP would have easily swept the elections.

Bhutto's strongest rival, Wali Khan, was jailed and barred from campaigning. Bhutto did not just want to win the elections, though. He wanted to win by a landslide, with a two-thirds majority, so he could bring about the constitutional changes he wanted.[34] This included jettisoning the parliamentary system, with all its checks and balances, in favour of a presidential system that would give him even more power.

To his surprise, several Opposition parties came together to form a united front against the PPP, under the banner of the Pakistan National Alliance (PNA). It was an unlikely coalition, with leftists joining hands with rightists to overthrow the 'tyranny' of Bhutto. Despite a strong opposition, the PPP was still able to win the elections by a landslide, a verdict the PNA refused to accept. Allegations of rigging spread like wildfire, with street protests bringing life to a halt in Lahore and Karachi.

From March 1977, when the elections were held, till July 1977, chaos reigned on the streets of Pakistan's cities. In Lahore, the Jama'at-e-Islami led the charge. Its highly organized cadres of young and passionate boys clashed regularly with state authorities. Both the Opposition and the government refused to budge and conditions continued to worsen. Eventually, Bhutto decided to concede to certain demands of the PNA. At the end of April 1977, he arrived at Ichra to meet Maududi in his home. Two days after the meeting, alcohol, gambling, nightclubs, cinemas and other 'anti-Muslim' activities were banned. Lahore was directing the country towards 'Islamization', which would be taken up full throttle by Zia.

There is reason to believe that the Opposition and the government were heading towards a settlement at the start of July.[35] Rioting, protests and state brutality, which turned Lahore and other major cities of the country into battlegrounds, had taken their toll on the resolve of both sides and they were now looking for a way out. General Zia, the army chief, was aware of this. On 4 July, the prime minister conducted a meeting with his trusted cabinet members which included Zia and declared that the 'deadlock' would break the next day.[36] The same night, Bhutto and his family were taken into 'protected custody' by General Zia and martial law was declared.

Similar to the fate of Mujib-ur-Rehman, who, along with members of his family, was assassinated during a coup d'état, Zia too would have liked his soldiers to kill Bhutto on the morning of 5 July. However, Bhutto astutely cooperated and urged his family members to do the same. The soldiers were provided with no reason to assassinate the prime minister. The tedious task of finding a reason to assassinate his former boss came to Zia. Former allies of Bhutto were interrogated. Old files revisited and all orders from the prime minister's office carefully studied. A pretext was required and it was eventually found in this almost forgotten police report, in which Bhutto had been accused of conspiring to murder Ahmad Raza Khan Kasuri on the night of 9 November 1974.

Disappointed when Lahore High Court granted bail to Bhutto, Zia took it upon himself to handle the case. Bhutto was arrested once again, to be tried by a military court. However, soon after, Zia allowed the case to be heard in Lahore High Court, where he had handpicked a judge who had a personal grudge against the former prime minister. By referring the case directly to the high court instead of the civil court, the cunning military dictator had deprived Bhutto of one step of appeal. The case was heard and Bhutto was found guilty. In Lahore, a city that had once embraced Bhutto, his death warrant had now been issued.

The judgment was split 4–3, with all Punjabi judges upholding the penalty and non-Punjabi judges disagreeing with it. Punjab was standing behind the military establishment. Bhutto spent the last days of his life in Rawalpindi Jail, where he was eventually executed. The judgment was appealed in the Supreme Court which rejected it and upheld Lahore High Court's decision.

Bhutto, sitting in his cell awaiting the Supreme Court's decision, must have realized that the judgment would be against him. It was in jail that he made his last political move which was to make him immortal in a way. He took his cue from other famous political prisoners, particularly Jawaharlal Nehru, someone he had deeply admired since his youth.[37]

Fashioning his writing on a pattern similar to Nehru's letters to his daughter from jail, later published as *Glimpses of World History*, Bhutto wrote to his political successor, Benazir, encouraging her to continue his incomplete political journey. This powerful letter written to a future prime minister from death row has today become part of history. Bhutto reiterated that he would prefer dying at the hands of the military; he would rather live in history. His writings from jail, including this letter, were to serve this particular purpose. His last bout of rhetoric made him immortal—a giant of a politician, whom every politician today wants to emulate. Bhutto, as he had wished, managed to stay alive in history.

In the company of tall plazas that house shopping malls and offices, this spacious single-storey house stands out like an anomaly. A vast garden with old trees spreads out across its front yard; the house itself with its chipping paint shows signs of neglect. The boundary wall is low and the gate see-through, reminiscent of a time when the city was much safer. Mubashir Hassan, the occupant of the house, it seems, still wants to live in that city of yore.

This historic house is located on one of the most important roads of the city, Main Boulevard, a long, signal-free stretch running through Gulberg. A modern suburb constructed in the 1960s, Gulberg, with its large bungalows, became home to the gentry. Its distance from the city centre made it a calm island in the chaos of Lahore. Today, however, it serves as the city centre, while still retaining its prestigious status. Even as new plazas emerge from the earth all across Gulberg, old bungalows with tall pillars, high walls and spacious gardens, constructed in a colonial architectural tradition, continue to exist.

In the middle of this locality, an anomaly exists almost like an unpleasant truth, in the form of a town known as Guru Mangat. This fourteenth-century town gets its name from a devotee of Guru Hargobind who constructed a gurdwara here to commemorate the Guru's presence at the spot as he passed through the city.[38] There are at least two other gurdwaras in Lahore that commemorate the same trip, all marking the different halting spots of the Guru.

Just off Mall Road, the ultimate symbol of colonial Lahore, is Temple Road which passes through the locality of Mozang, another small town that dates back to the sixteenth century, incorporated into the metropolis of Lahore.[39] Temple Road derives its name from another Gurdwara of Hargobind, constructed to commemorate his visit to the locality.

About 12 kilometres from here, in the middle of the village of Amar Sidhu, now part of Lahore's prestigious DHA, there is another gurdwara that commemorates the Guru's stop at the locality. Guru Mangat lies in the middle of these two towns. Slowly, as the city of Lahore spilled beyond its old borders and looked hungrily outwards at the agricultural land surrounding it, Guru Mangat too made way for sprawling postcolonial bungalows. Today, the area undergoes another transition as the bungalows cede ground to the shining plazas.

On 30 November 1967, after Bhutto had acquired nationwide popularity by defying Ayub Khan, a public convention was organized on the sprawling lawns of Mubashir Hassan's home in the heart of Gulberg. The PPP, one of the largest and most important political parties in the country, was formed here.

With Islamic socialism as its manifesto, the party was a unique amalgamation of political opinions, with its members ranging from committed communists to feudal lords and spiritual leaders. In the years to come, these contradictions were laid bare as Bhutto rushed through half-hearted land reforms and nationalization, while at the same time unleashing the state machinery on protesting labourers.

Right from the beginning, the city of Lahore was at the centre of Bhutto's political movement. In June 1966, Bhutto resigned from the cabinet and travelled to Lahore, where, at the historic railway station, he was greeted by a sea of supporters, the largest show of support Bhutto had ever had till that point.[40] Lahore was also home to several colleges and universities, with their political students groups, many of which had leftist leanings and were charmed by the socialist rhetoric of Bhutto. They became his most passionate supporters. With Lahore safely behind him, Bhutto knew he could challenge the military establishment. He would go on to speak in front of gigantic crowds in the city, vying in numbers with gatherings in the largest city of Pakistan, Bhutto's adopted home town, Karachi.

Bhutto's show of strength in Lahore and Karachi leading to the elections of 1970 were to translate into a landslide victory in Punjab and Sindh, making the PPP the strongest party in the western wing. Even in the 1977 elections, the PPP remained dominant in these two provinces, which easily allowed it to dominate the federation.

There are several accomplishments attributed to Bhutto's years in power—the Constitution, the country's nuclear programme, democratization of politics and foreign policy successes being a few of them. However, one of the least talked about was the forging of a uniquely Pakistani identity. Despite his demonization by the subsequent military establishment and his political opponents, his vision of a Pakistani identity, inspired by an Islamic ethos, remains a central feature of the military establishment's perception of Pakistani identity as well.

Fresh from a civil war after the country's dismemberment, Bhutto felt it was imperative to carve a national identity, especially with Indira Gandhi proclaiming the death of the 'Two-Nation Theory'—the raison d'être of Pakistan. Despite his secular views, religious identity acquired a stronger presence in Bhutto's conception of national identity. His rhetoric and sloganeering against India contained elements of this, where he presented Pakistan as a distinct Islamic civilization in perpetual conflict with its Hindu neighbour.

It was during his tenure that history as a subject was replaced with Pakistan studies in schools to inculcate a sense of national identity. The country's Hindu past was removed from the curriculum and history was reinterpreted to project Islamic rulers as heroes and Hindus as demons in order to justify the creation of Pakistan. A civilizational framework, similar to Huntington's *Clash of Civilizations*, was used to study the historical relationship between Hindus and Muslims, presented as full of antagonism, as two distinct groups forced to live together despite irreconcilable differences. This extremely biased subject which has experienced several revisions over the years is one of the most important legacies of Bhutto.

Perhaps taking a cue from Nehru's India, Bhutto worked actively to promote the country's culture, through film, theatre, books and music. He established government institutes to promote art and culture rooted in an Islamic spirit. The boundaries between culture, religion and national identity became blurred. Even today, several of these institutes survive, actively seeking to promote a Pakistani identity, an identity they are trained to see through a monolithic lens, which since Bhutto's time has become even narrower.

Bhutto's mortal enemy, Zia, did not deviate much from the nationalist agenda the former had set for the state. His Islamization policies and an attempt, particularly during the Afghan War, to project himself as the leader of the Islamic world, were adopted from his predecessor. All the major politicians of the country, including Nawaz Sharif and Imran Khan, in more ways than one, share this nationalistic vision. Almost three decades after the creation of Pakistan, Bhutto moulded Jinnah's vision of Pakistan in a way that the country continues to internalize till today.

However, today it is Zia more than Bhutto who is held responsible for this narrow interpretation of the Pakistani identity. The blame for the intolerance and violence that emerge from a monolithic view of national identity is laid at his doorstep as opposed to that of Bhutto, the original architect of this vision. Bhutto, when compared to Zia, is almost seen as a saint, his 'martyrdom' making him immortal, beyond any criticism. Zia becomes a demon, to be blamed for every ill the country faces today. The nuance of history is lost in this polarization of political characters. The continuity of vision and policy from Bhutto to Zia is overlooked.

You could well say that in the popular imagination of Pakistan, Bhutto is Ram, while Zia is Ravana.

3

TO THE LEFT, NO RIGHT

I stopped my car in front of a tall metal gate and honked. The walls were several feet high. There was no chance of anyone getting in unnoticed. A small window in the gate opened and a pair of eyes peeped out. A young man with a long beard looked at me with inquisitive eyes. 'I want to go to Brigadier Saeed's house,' I told him. He asked for my identity card, and the gate of Dar-us-Salam opened.

The irony of the name of this community was not lost on me. Dar-us-Salam means an abode of peace but, in Islamic terminology, it also refers to a place where Muslims are free to practise their religion. Located in the heart of urban, middle-class Lahore, flanked by Muslim Town and Garden Town, is a small community of a few dozen houses, all belonging to members of the persecuted Ahmadiyya community.

Till a few years ago, before members of the community were hunted down in the streets of Pakistan, before their houses and residential communities were ransacked at the slightest 'provocation', security at Dar-us-Salam was lax. It was like any other housing society without the barbed wire, surveillance cameras, metal gates and vigilant security guards.

Lahore, however, is a changed city. This is a city that has tasted blood and would not settle for less. This is a city pushed beyond the precipice of sanity, consumed by its own paranoia. Graffiti inciting acts of hatred against members of the community does not even raise eyebrows any more. The report of an Ahmadi killed in the city is one more addition to a pile of several such stories. Often, these stories appear unexplained. There is no need to explain why an Ahmadi was shot. There is no public condemnation, no word of consolation from the political elite. No one dare humanize them any more.

On 28 May 2010, the city of Lahore saw one of its worst massacres. Two Ahmadiyya 'places of worship' were attacked by the Punjab Wing of the Tehrik-i-Taliban. According to the laws of the country it would be illegal to call them mosques. More than eighty people were killed and several more injured.[1] A few days later, the victims were attacked once again at Jinnah Hospital where they had been taken after the incident.

Salman Taseer, then serving as the governor of Punjab, was the only prominent government official to visit the leaders of the community after the attack. He was accused of being an Ahmadi agent and a threat to religion.[2] Less than a year later, he was assassinated by his bodyguard for his support to a Christian woman accused of blasphemy. Nawaz Sharif would not dare to meet members of the community, but condemned the incident, calling it an attack on Ahmadi brothers. He too was severely criticized. 'How can Ahmadis be our brothers?' he was asked. He eventually had to retract his statement.[3] Whereas a majority of the citizens of the city would have condemned the brutal assassination of members of the community, opposition to Taseer and Sharif made it clear that they shared with the Tehrik-i-Taliban a pathological hatred towards Ahmadis.

The Ahmadiyya movement was founded by Mirza Ghulam Ahmad, born on 13 February 1835 at Qadian, a village in the district of Gurdaspur. His forefathers had been given a large *jagir* in the village by Babur, founder of the Mughal Empire. They temporarily lost favour during the Sikh era, when their properties were taken away and they were forced to move out of Qadian. However, towards the end of his rule, Ranjit Singh re-established Mirza Ghulam Ahmad's family in Qadian and his father was given a high post in the army. During the colonial regime, they lost part of their jagir but continued receiving a pension from the British state.[4] Mirza Ghulam Ahmad was a religious scholar and author who wrote numerous books and articles.

In many ways, the Ahmadiyya movement was a product of its time. The colonial state had spread its tentacles all across Punjab. Christian missionaries had a strong presence in the cities and towns through their schools, colleges and hospitals, and were free to proselytize in remote villages. Several marginalized members of the community, particularly those who belonged to the lowest rungs of the Hindu caste hierarchy, found an attractive escape in a new, 'egalitarian' religion.

Both Hindus and Muslims reacted to this in their own way. The Arya Samaj, founded in Lahore in 1877, reacting to the Christian missionaries, criticized some elements of 'Hindu religion' and offered a rationalist interpretation of the Vedas. They found much support in the province. Mirza Ghulam Ahmad saw the Arya Samaj movement and the activities of Christian missionaries in Punjab as a threat to Islam, which led him to begin his own movement for Islamic revivalism. His was meant to be an intellectual response to the ideological threat posed by the other two proselytizing movements.[5] It was similar to several Islamic revivalist movements launched in colonial India that saw the dying influence of Muslims in the political arena as a lack of Islamic religiosity.

In March 1882, Mirza Ghulam Ahmad made a controversial claim that earned him the ire of religious traditionalists. He claimed that he had received a revelation from God, entrusting him with a special mission.[6] This became controversial because of the traditional Islamic belief that God only speaks to prophets, who ceased to appear after the last Prophet, Hazrat Muhammad (Peace Be upon Him). Mirza Ghulam Ahmad made another controversial claim in 1891, challenging Christian theology and traditional Islamic belief when he said that he had received a revelation that Jesus Christ had neither died on the cross nor had he been lifted to heaven, but rather survived his crucifixion and escaped to Kashmir, where he died a natural death and was buried.[7] Challenging the belief that Jesus Christ would reappear in his original body close to the Day of Resurrection, he said that another man with similar attributes would appear from the community of the Prophet of Islam. He claimed that he himself was that Promised Messiah—the second coming of Christ.[8]

There is a similar concept in Islamic eschatology, of 'Mahdi', the prophesized redeemer of Islam, whose appearance will coincide with the second coming of Christ. Together Christ and Mahdi will battle Al-Masih ad-Dajjal, the Antichrist, the false Messiah. It was claimed that Mirza Ghulam Ahmad was the promised Mahdi.[9] Many Islamic theologians turned against him. They argued that by claiming to be the promised messiah, a prophet, he was defying the basic tenets of Islam. His movement was termed un-Islamic, with personal attacks against him becoming widespread. Despite the opposition, Mirza Ghulam Ahmad continued to present his movement as Islamic.

The Jama'at-i-Ahmadiyya, or the assembly of Ahmadiyya, was first founded in 1889 when Mirza Ghulam Ahmad took a pledge of allegiance from his initial supporters.[10] However, it was not until 1901 that it was formally recognized as a separate sect of Islam. In 1901, the British colonial government conducted its fourth census of British India when, with the permission of Mirza

Ghulam Ahmad, the Ahmadiyya community was for the first time registered as a separate entity.[11]

There has been much criticism of the census conducted by the British, for it is seen as a tool implemented by the colonial administration to control the population instead of learning about them. Many historians have identified it as a mechanism of social engineering.[12] Instead of understanding the population better, the census imposed British biases and categories on Indian society.

One such example is that of religious communities. For example, the census only allowed one to be either a Muslim or a Hindu and not identify as a member of both religious communities. Such exclusivity was perhaps a feature of a homogenous British society, but for a multireligious and cultural society like India, at times divisions between Hindus and Muslims were not always so distinct. There were, and still are, both in India and Pakistan, religious communities that adhere to two or more religious traditions.[13]

Critics of surveys have also identified that caste was another such category that was understood by the indigenous population differently from what was imposed by the colonial administration in its surveys. It has been identified that in precolonial India, castes were not rigid and frozen as they were understood by the British. There was fluidity in caste structures, and communities and individuals sometimes flowed between different castes, which the census reports solidified.

This became problematic because the colonial government then brought about constitutional changes that granted political representation to certain groups identified in the census reports. Identifying with a particular group was no longer just a matter of identity but now had political consequences. Over the years people started identifying with the categories that were imposed on them by the British and traditional classifications slowly faded away. This can explain why, after living together for hundreds of years, borrowing and lending from each other's cultures, traces of which can be seen even today, Muslim nationalists could claim that Hindus and Muslims were two different 'civilizations' that could not live together, a claim that Hindu nationalists also endorsed. The riots during Partition can be seen as a consequence of the social engineering that was institutionalized by the British through their census.

Like other social groups, perhaps Mirza Ghulam Ahmad also felt that it was important to form an identity separate from the larger religious group, which eventually led to the creation of a new category in the census. It might have been a way to ensure that his followers or group did not eventually merge with the larger community. The census further solidified distinctions, giving them formal recognition, sanctioned by the state. There already were indications of such a separation, due to criticism from members of the traditional Islamic community.

The creation of Pakistan provided a fresh impetus to anti-Ahmadi sentiments. Soon after Partition, the Majlis-i-Ahrar, a Lahore-based religious organization, initiated a violent movement against the community demanding that it be declared constitutionally non-Islamic. Fierce riots broke out in Lahore in 1953, which eventually spread to other parts of the country.

The Majlis-i-Ahrar was a radical, conservative, nationalist organization founded in December 1929. Politically aligned with the Congress, it took part in the failed Khilafat Movement. It was opposed to the Muslim League and rejected the proposal of Partition. One of its leaders, Maulana Mazhar Ali Azhar, called Jinnah 'Kafir-e-Azam' in a couplet he composed.[14] Pakistan was repeatedly called Palidistan, Kafiristan and Khakistan by members of the organization prior to the country's formation.[15] However they did an about-turn post Partition. In January 1949, the Majlis-i-Ahrar announced that it would cease to function as a political group and would only operate as a religious organization, aligning itself politically with the Muslim League.

In its struggle against the Ahmadiyya, the Majlis-i-Ahrar was joined by the Jama'at-e-Islami under the leadership of Maulana Abul Al Maududi. Much like the leaders of the Majlis-i-Ahrar, Maududi too had been opposed to the creation of Pakistan.[16] Ironically both these organizations found themselves at the forefront of shaping the Islamic national identity of the new country. Part of their newfound patriotism was a plan to exclude the Ahmadiyya community from the nationalist project, despite the fact that the community had given its full support to the struggle for Pakistan.[17] The focus of this anti-Ahmadiyya movement became one person, perhaps the most prominent member of the community—Mohammad Zafarullah Khan, the first foreign minister of the country.

Chaudhary Zafarullah Khan was an old stalwart of the Muslim League and was responsible for drafting the Lahore Resolution in 1940.[18] He had also represented the party at the round table conferences and the Radcliffe Boundary Commission that determined the border between India and Pakistan.

During the anti-Ahmadiyya movement, the Majlis-i-Ahrar claimed that because of his religion, Zafarullah Khan would work against the interests of the country. A man who had worked tirelessly for the country's creation was being called anti-Pakistan by those who had vehemently opposed it. The government was given an ultimatum to remove members of the community from important government positions. A new definition of what it meant to be a Pakistani was being implemented.

On 5 March 1953, thousands of Majlis-i-Ahrar members along with the Jama'at-e-Islami marched in Lahore, raising slogans against Mirza Ghulam Ahmad, Zafarullah Khan and the Ahmadiyya community. They were joined by college students, traders, shopkeepers, workers and others. Members of the Ahmadiyya community were attacked, their houses and shops ransacked. Government property, including police vans, was also vandalized.[19]

According to the Munir Report, an inquiry into the riots published by the government in 1954, the government was complicit in allowing the situation to worsen. Prior to the riots in Lahore, anti-Ahmadiyya rallies had been organized in several other cities, while members of the community had also been attacked. The government was aware of the activities of the Majlis-i-Ahrar, but remained passive, arguing that taking any action against its leaders would make martyrs of them and add fuel to their movement. The government's lack of foresight led to one of the worst riots that the city of Lahore has ever seen.

Other cities in Punjab, including Sialkot, Gujranwala, Rawalpindi, Lyallpur (Faisalabad) and Montgomery (Sahiwal), followed Lahore's lead. According to unofficial numbers, 200 Ahmadis lost their lives all over the country.[20] There are others who claim the number was as high as 2000.[21] The situation in Lahore was so bad that the governor general, Ghulam Muhammad, implemented the first martial law of the country, dismissing the federal cabinet, effectively also removing Zafarullah Khan from his post.

Thus, out of expediency, the government accepted one of the demands of the protesters. A new standard had been set that would see the appeasement of the mob become a norm. The religious right had been conceded a space that only increased in subsequent years. The Majlis-i-Ahrar became a predecessor to all the Sunni extremist organizations that were to follow in its wake—the Sipah-e-Sahaba, the Lashkar-i-Jhangvi, the JuD and so forth—which would take it upon themselves to determine who was a true Pakistani and which community or individual was not. Only five years after the creation of the country, its narrative had been hijacked. Adherence to the Sunni faith became a criterion for patriotism.

The riots represent another historic turning point. On 6 March 1953, martial law was implemented in Lahore. Law and order was established soon after, but only after the army had been invited into the political arena. Five years later, Ayub Khan overthrew the civilian government and established military rule, the first of many to come. The image of the army as the saviour of Pakistan, as civilian state institutions failed, was first crafted during these riots.

The 1953 anti-Ahmadiyya riots in many ways laid out the path for the future course of the country. I wanted to talk to someone from the Ahmadiyya community who had witnessed the events, which led me to Dar-us-Salam to interview Brig. Saeed and some other members of the community.

Next to the entrance was a 'place of worship'. It had no dome or minaret so 'Muslims' may not be offended by the similarity of its architecture to a 'mosque'. According to the laws of the country, it is also a crime for members of the community to 'pretend' to be Muslims by using 'Islamic' symbols, which would include domes and minarets. I parked the car outside and walked into the house.

Brig. Saeed belonged to a sect within the Ahmadiyya community known as the Lahore Party, a minority within a minority, so to speak. The other group is referred to as the Qadiani Party. The split occurred in 1914 after the succession of Mirza Ghulam Ahmad's son, Mirza Bashir-ud-Din Mahmud Ahmad, as the second Khalifa of the Ahmadiyya community. The reason was the status of the founder of the movement: While the Qadiani Party believes Mirza Ghulam Ahmad to be a prophet, a cause of concern for the larger Muslim population, the Lahore Party, led by Maulvi Muhammad Ali, asserted he was a *mujaddad* who denied any claim to prophethood.[22] Mujaddad is an Islamic term used to refer to someone who enables a religious 'revival'.[23] There is a long tradition of mujaddad in Islamic history and it is not a particularly controversial issue as such. However, this is a fine point that is lost upon the state and vigilantes, for whom there is no distinction between the two Ahmadiyya factions. The Lahore group moved to the city after the split and set up an organization called Ahmadiyya Anjuman-i-Isha'at-e-Islam.[24]

Eighty-one-year-old Nasir Ahmad, who was called in from a neighbouring house on my arrival, had been a young college student when the 1953 riots broke out in Lahore. He was living at the Ahmadiyya Buildings, located on Brandreth Road—a prominent Ahmadiyya locality which constituted the Jama'at's 'place of worship' and several residential blocks. It was often visited by Mirza Ghulam Ahmad and it was where he breathed his last on 26 May 1908.[25] The central office of the Ahmadiyya Anjuman-i-Isha'at-e-Islam was moved there after its secession from the Qadiani Party. Several Ahmadiyya families were living there around the time of the riots. In later years, the residential blocks were converted into commercial markets known as Ahmadiyya Markets, but as the religious sentiment of the city and the country changed, these were rechristened Muhammadiyya Markets by the tenants.

I remember a visit to the market. It was rush hour at Brandreth Road. Cars, pickups and bullock carts were jammed in a narrow street with shops on both sides. Right across from us was the walled city of Lahore, with the Mochi Gate and Akbari Gate, a few steps away. I walked down the road, not sure if there would be any way to identify the market. I had no reason to worry. 'Muhammadiyya Electric Market', announced a green board at the entrance of an old building. A couple of window air conditioners jutted out. Another board atop this one proclaimed the same. As if there was a need to reinforce the name.

I walked past the building casually, afraid of how the shopkeepers would respond if I were to begin photographing it. The systematic persecution of the Ahmadiyya community is one of the most controversial issues in the country. Any sympathy for its members is immediately perceived as a sign of disaffection for Islam and one's country. Standing here, in the midst of a sea of shopkeepers, I felt perhaps a fraction of the anxiety that thousands of members of the community experience every day.

On the side of the building, in fading white paint, I could make out letters that spelt 'Ahmadiyya Buildings'. The sign was once large enough for everyone to see. But these weren't those times. Facing the building is the Government Islamia College. On its lawns, leaders of the Muslim community had gathered to protest Mirza Ghulam Ahmad's presence in the building. They had celebrated when he died.[26]

'There were processions everywhere,' recalled Nasir Ahmad, when I asked him about the anti-Ahmadiyya riots of 1953. 'They would make it a point to abuse Mirza Ghulam Ahmad when they passed our building during the riots of 1953. There were a few police officials posted outside our building to keep the rioters away. We were stuck inside for days. It was scary.'

Sabiha Saeed was then a child living with her parents at Aitchison College. 'My father was a teacher there. We were aware of the rioting outside. We were instructed by the administration to remain within the protection of the school.'

Established in 1886, Aitchison College was originally called Punjab Chiefs' College, an institute meant to train local chiefs to become prototypes of Englishmen and assist the colonial administration in administering the 'indigenous population'. It was renamed Aitchison College in honour of Sir Charles Umpherston Aitchison, lieutenant governor of Punjab from 1882 to 1886. Two of his greatest contributions to the city were the establishment of this school and of the University of the Punjab, the largest university in the province.

Aitchison College is still the most prominent all-boys boarding school in the country, which continues to churn out 'brown sahibs' who, since the creation of Pakistan and even earlier, have formed the country's political elite. Prominent alumni include Aitzaz Ahsan, Syed Babar Ali, Talal Akbar Bugti, Zafarullah Khan Jamali, Imran Khan, Farooq Leghari, Shah Mehmood Qureshi and Sardar Ayaz Sadiq.

Spread over 200 acres, the college is a beautiful specimen of fusion architecture, combining Mughal techniques with British ones. It is a gated community and therefore was safe from the protesters and the rioters in 1953.

'In fact, our relatives from other parts of the city too came and stayed with us for a few days because they knew it was safe to be with us,' recalled Sabiha Saeed.

Our conversation jumped from one topic to another, from the Munir Report to Salman Taseer, to the Majlis-i-Ahrar and the role of the Muslim League leaders during the riots.

'The 1974 riots began with a small conflict at Rabwah,' said Ahmad.

Rabwah is about 170 kilometres from Lahore and became the headquarters of the Qadiani faction of the Ahmadiyya movement, after the shift in 1948 from Qadian in East Punjab when a large proportion of the community migrated to Pakistan. The word 'Rabwah' is mentioned in the Quran and means an elevated place. In 1998, the Punjab Assembly, offended by the 'appropriation' of the Quran by 'non-Muslims', passed a resolution changing the name of the city first to Nawan Qadian and later to Chenab Nagar. However, it is still popularly referred to as Rabwah.

'There was a group of young student-members of the IJT travelling to Peshawar from Multan in 1974,' recalled Ahmad. 'When the train stopped at the Rabwah station, these boys got out and began cursing Mirza Ghulam Ahmad and the Ahmadiyya community. The train then left the station and so did these boys. However, when young boys from Rabwah heard about the incident, they decided to confront these boys on the way back. This led to an altercation and the Jamiat boys were given a thrashing. News of the conflict spread like wildfire throughout the country.'

The student wing of the Jama'at-e-Islami, the IJT, is the largest students' organization in the country, with its headquarters in Lahore. While it has always been a prominent pressure group, operating through street protests, since the 1980s it received the patronage of Zia-ul-Haq and thus established control over several public universities in the city, closely monitoring their environment and sometimes even the curriculum. Punjab University, Government MAO College, Dayal Singh College, Islamia College, are all places where the IJT still has a strong hold.

Control over government colleges and universities has played a pivotal role in the Islamization of society. Every year thousands of students graduate from these universities having spent years being fed the propaganda of the IJT. Through their college years they are indoctrinated with a certain ideological viewpoint influenced by political Islam. It is no wonder then, that these students become tolerant of Sunni extremist organizations like the JuD and the Sipah-e-Sahaba. Given that Lahore is the education centre of the country, with its hundreds of colleges and universities, it is not surprising that the city has over the years, particularly after the 1980s, also emerged as the hub of the religious right in the country. It is now a deeply conservative city, reflective of the Islamization that has spread to other parts of Pakistan as well.

In 1974, the news of the IJT students being attacked at Rabwah spread like wildfire. Despite the arrest of seventy-one members of the Ahmadiyya community from Rabwah, protests against the community continued unabated throughout the country.[27] Several other religious parties and bar associations joined the Jama'at-e-Islami and Majlis-i-Ahrar. The protests soon turned violent as mobs started attacking Ahmadis and their property in different cities in Punjab. Several members of the community lost their lives during these riots. The protesters demanded that Ahmadis be removed from their posts in government departments and also be excommunicated from Islam.

In the National Assembly, the Opposition, which was a confluence of several religious parties, insisted that a bill be introduced in Parliament declaring Ahmadis as non-Muslims. A bill to this effect was consequently passed in Parliament on 7 September 1974.

'In 1974, I was stationed in Multan,' said Brig. Saeed. 'My parents and some family members lived in our ancestral house in Abbottabad. It was a big house built on a hilly slope with various portions at different levels. As the riots spread through the city, all our relatives and other members of the community came to our house for protection. There were a few police officials posted outside, but when the rioters came, they did nothing. In fact, they aided the mob in entering the premises.

'Someone from my family saw the approaching mob and warned the people inside. When the heavily armed mob started firing, everybody moved to the lower portion of the house to face this trial together. The upper portion (the main house), my father's car and his nearby clinic were burned down. They made repeated attempts to break into the lower portion with the intention to kill. My brother-in-law was shot in the thigh and was in a critical condition as he had lost a lot of blood by the time they eventually evacuated. Some others suffered pellet wounds.

'It was a miracle that the lives of about seventy-five innocent, unarmed people were saved that day, which included a large number of women and children. My elder brother, who was also in the army, was posted as the commandant of the Pakistan Military Academy in Kakul, Abbottabad, at that time. He called his superiors and the local administration, informing them of what was unfolding, but there was no help. By sunset, the mob dispersed with the resolve to attack again at night. However, before any more harm could befall our family and friends, they were evacuated to safety in an army bus. They narrowly escaped death that day. My father had constructed a mosque next to our house which was used by the community for prayers. The Kalma was inscribed on the wall of the building. Some years later, that was also removed and the mosque was locked up. It still remains locked.'

From the corner of my eye, I saw Brig. Saeed's ten-year-old granddaughter listening to the accounts of oppression. She had heard them before, internalized them. What is her concept of home? I wondered. What is her concept of safety? What does Lahore mean to her? What does Pakistan mean to her?

'You know, I have been told Bhutto refused to attend the Parliament session the day they passed the anti-Ahmadi bill. He was with his friends, one of whom was an Ahmadi. That day he told his Ahmadi friend, "Don't worry, my friend, with this bill I have signed the death warrant for myself and my children." You know what happened after that,' said Sabiha Saeed.

It is impossible to imagine that such a beautiful place could be the site of such pain. The vast garden outside the Diwan-i-Aam provides a vista of the walled city of Lahore. It is one of the highest points of the fort and the city.

The river once used to flow at the base of this mound, caressing its thick boundary walls. Many saints and ascetics have sat on the edge of these walls to preach. Most of them transcended religious boundaries. For example, next to the boundary wall of the fort is the smadh of Bava Jhengardh Shah. A Hindu by birth, he became a disciple of Guru Har Rai, the seventh Sikh Guru.[28] A square structure topped by a dome, his smadh too is an example of syncretism, a combination of Muslim and Hindu architectural traditions. A few steps away is the smadh of Wasti Ram, another Hindu, whose father was a disciple of Guru Gobind Singh.[29]

These boundary walls narrate the story of Lahore Fort. Facing the majestic elephant wall, with intricate and colourful motifs depicting elephants and other imaginary scenes from the royal court, is an austere but stout wall constructed by the British after they took over the fort. Next to this wall are several rooms that were constructed at the same time and are now used as offices by government officials. The distinct architectural traditions of Lahore Fort could not be more obvious here.

Rising from behind the thick walls are the minarets of Badshahi Masjid, the most iconic mosque in Lahore. The golden dome of Guru Arjan's smadh shines next to it, behind which is the splendid smadh of Maharaja Ranjit Singh. Between the fort and the mosque is Hazuri Bagh, with a *baradari* brought from Emperor Jahangir's mausoleum and placed in a garden constructed by Maharaja Ranjit Singh to celebrate the acquisition of the famed Koh-i-Noor.[30] The city of Lahore, capital of the Sikh Empire, was beyond Roshani Gate (the gate of lights) next to this bagh.

Located inside the fort, the Diwan-i-Aam was to the Mughal kings what Hazuri Bagh was to Maharaja Ranjit Singh. Here, the Mughal emperor, surrounded by his courtiers and advisers, would appear before his audience of common petitioners. Cases were heard and decided in this space. It was also here that Lahore and Punjab were handed over to the British by a young ten-year-old Maharaja Duleep Singh, the youngest son of Maharaja Ranjit Singh.[31]

Despite its dilapidated condition, it is easy to get lost in the fort's magnificence with its Sheesh Mahal, the chamber of Emperor Jahangir, and Moti Masjid, among so many others. Visited by hundreds of people every day, it is an easy way to partake in the lives of Mughal royalty. Even though the fountains run dry and the sound of music no longer pervades the atmosphere, it is easy to conceptualize that world while standing at the hub of Mughal power in Punjab.

Below this world of beauty and art lurks a dark reality, the dungeons where the Mughal authorities threw prisoners and then forgot about them. Their screams drowned before they could escape the earth and rise above the rhythm of the dancers' *ghungroo*s. Visitors are not allowed into this dark world upon which the foundation of the Mughal Empire was built. Entry has been barred to all because it is structurally unstable, according to the local guides. But they lie, repeating a story they have been told to convey. The dungeons hide an ugly reality. Hundreds of political prisoners were brought and tortured here during the regimes of military dictators.[32] Blinded by a deep darkness, most of the prisoners were kept in solitary confinement and tortured systematically for their political beliefs. Their screams and cries never reached the ears of the hundreds of tourists walking above them, marvelling at the Mughal heritage of the country.

Several prisoners—journalists, politicians, activists—returned to tell stories of horror and inexplicable torture. Many others were not as lucky. Salman Taseer, the slain governor of Punjab, was one such prisoner kept here during the darkest days of Zia's military regime.[33]

On 12 December 1960, Zohra Alambardar Hussain reached the Miani Sahib graveyard in Lahore to do what no mother should be asked to do. She had come from Hyderabad in India on 4 December after hearing about her son Hasan Nasir's death in police custody.[34] Nasir, a devoted communist and member of the leftist National Awami Party (NAP), had been picked up by state authorities from a shanty town in Karachi, where he was hiding, and brought in chains to Lahore Fort for 'interrogation'.[35] Aligned with the Americans, the military regime of Ayub Khan was hunting down communists across the country. Nasir, the former secretary general of the banned Communist Party of Pakistan (CPP) and later the office secretary of the NAP, was one of the most prominent communist leaders in the country.

Memories of the Rawalpindi Conspiracy Case of 1951 were still fresh, turning public perception against the communists, thus allowing the state a free hand in dealing with them. Journalists, editors, activists and others sympathetic to the cause had been silenced, afraid of being labelled anti-state, as the communists were being called in the aftermath of the failed conspiracy. Emboldened by the meek opposition a few years ago, Ayub Khan's military regime felt confident that it could pick up leftists and communist activists without being held publicly accountable.

The Rawalpindi Conspiracy was allegedly planned by the Lahore-based leadership of the CPP headed by Sajjad Zaheer, along with certain members of the army disgruntled with the government of Liaquat Ali Khan, to overthrow the government and instead instal a communist regime. Within the army, General Akbar Khan, an Ahmadi, was leading the plot, supported by Brig. M.A. Latif, a brigade commander at Quetta. Akbar Khan was officer-in-command during the first Indo-Pakistan war of 1948 over Kashmir. He felt that his prime minister, Liaquat Ali Khan, had let him down by failing to send him reinforcements at a time when his forces had made considerable progress in Kashmir.[36]

The CPP was keen to overthrow a government that was increasingly aligning itself with the Americans. Ever since its creation in 1948, an offshoot of the Communist Party of India (CPI), the party had failed to garner much public support.[37] There are several reasons for this but one of the foremost ones was that much of its leadership did not have roots in this part of the country.[38] The general secretary of the party, Sajjad Zaheer, belonged to an aristocratic family from Oudh, United Provinces. Other prominent members of the party, Sibte Hasan and Ashfaq Baig, too belonged to north India and had moved here after the creation of Pakistan, with no prior inroads in the city or Punjab. With its headquarters at McLeod Road in Lahore, the party managed to gain some support in the city, such as among the railway workers at Mughalpura, but largely failed to achieve grass-roots popularity.

Another reason was its distance from other regional nationalist struggles.[39] In what was a multilingual society, most of the leadership of the CPP came from an aristocratic Urdu-speaking background. For Bengali and Sindhi nationalists, fighting for the rights of their languages that were being overpowered by a minority language, Urdu, the leadership of the CPP represented the same literary establishment that they were up against.

Similarly, in a deeply religious country that had been created on the basis of religion, leaders of the party refused to conceptualize their theories in an Islamic framework and continued to root them in orthodox atheistic Marxist principles.[40] Thus they spoke in a language alien to the local populace in more ways than one. The state had begun using a religious language to further its agenda. This 'anti-religious' stance of the CPP made it easy for its opponents to call it an enemy of religion and hence of Pakistan.

The party was also seen as operating under the shadow of the CPI, its mother party, which in turn was perceived as being under the influence of Kremlin. Whereas the CPI initially opposed the demand for Pakistan, calling it regressive, it eventually accepted it in a convention in Calcutta in 1948 and decided to form a separate Communist Party for Pakistan headed by Zaheer, a member of the Central Committee of the CPI.[41] Members of the party knew that with no industrial class and no local representatives, they needed to build the party from the ground up in the new country. Its initial opposition to the partitioning of India and support to the Indian National Congress remained a liability in the newly established country.[42]

Despite these political shortcomings, the party played a seminal role in fomenting a literary and intellectual movement in a Pakistan that was still trying to find its political and cultural bearings. Soon after coming to Lahore, Sajjad Zaheer, a prominent Urdu writer, set up the Pakistan Progressive Writers' Association, an offshoot of the Progressive Writers' Movement of the 1930s, of which Zaheer was one of the founders. The association attracted several prominent leftist writers and intellectuals into its fold, such as Faiz and Manto. With regular meetings and gatherings, Lahore became a hub of literary activity. Several of these prominent writers sat in Lahore's famous tea houses and coffee shops surrounded by college students, engaging in discussions about what should be the direction of literature in Pakistan.

The wall fan creaked as it rotated slowly overhead. There was an air conditioner above the fan but it was switched off. The walls of the tea house were decorated with pictures of intellectuals, leftists mostly, who had spent a large portion of their youth sipping tea and smoking cigarettes in this hall. There was Manto in front of us, Faiz on an adjacent wall, Ustad Daman facing him. Next to him was Ahmad Faraz and many more. There was a menu listed on a pillar next to our table. I could see the dimly lit kitchen behind it, with waiters, sweaty on a humid summer afternoon, walking in and out of it, their heads covered by a net cap. I decided to order only a cup of tea.

Next to the entrance was a plaque noting that Nawaz Sharif had inaugurated the tea house in 2013. The government purchased the building and leased out the cafe to keep it alive. History had come full circle.

In the early days of Pakistan, Pak Tea House located on Mall Road, within Anarkali Bazaar, emerged as a hub of the Pakistan Progressive Writers' Association. Every day stalwarts of this movement would gather here and sit for hours, engaged in serious political and literary discussions with other writers and intellectuals. Students from the neighbouring Punjab University, National College of Arts and Government College would flock to them, crowding on chairs around them, listening intently to their debates.

Every week the Pakistan Progressive Writers' Association would organize a formal meeting on the top floor of this cafe, where writers ideologically aligned with the movement would read out specimens of their writing, which would then be critically analysed by connoisseurs. It is here that some of the greatest pieces of Urdu literature, including Manto's short stories and Faiz's poems, were first read and appreciated.

As the state began aligning with the Islamists and Americans, the leftist intellectuals became increasingly critical of its policies. These opinions were vocally expressed here, in the hall of this cafe, with members of intelligence agencies discreetly lurking behind the haze of cigarette smoke.

The history of Pak Tea House is closely linked with that of the leftist movement in Lahore. As long as there was a thriving leftist literary culture, Pak Tea House remained at the forefront of the movement. Hounded by the state, which was becoming increasingly powerful, the movement slowly faded away, particularly after the Islamization by Zia in the 1980s.

Pak Tea House, which had become a symbol of revolutionary talk, also took up a new identity. Under an unabashed spree of privatization and economic liberalization, a tyre market started up at Anarkali. With the writers gone, Pak Tea House was taken over by a tyre vendor who used it as his godown. The dictates of free market had taken hold of the last bastion of the leftist cultural movement in the city.

There was much hue and cry about the fate of Pak Tea House amongst a new breed of intellectuals who romanticized the Lahore of the 1950s and 1960s as being an intellectual peak. Blogs and newspaper articles were written and petitions moved for the government to do something about the tea house. The government finally decided to act in 2012, when the cafe was purchased and renovated. From being at the centre of anti-state rhetoric, Pak Tea House in 2013 was resuscitated on the back of government support.

Looking around the cafe, I tried to take stock of the other customers there. A family of travellers sat in front of me, the women at one table with the children and the men at another. There were several students, in groups of two and more. A man in his mid-sixties sat behind me, his chair touching mine, sipping a cup of tea.

There are still some weekly literary meetings organized at the tea house, but there is no doubt that Pak Tea House is a shadow of its former self. The intellectual activity that had awarded a distinct status to it has receded. The intellectuals who once made Lahore the cultural capital of the country live today only in the frames hanging on these walls. From a thriving space that was at the centre of crucial literary debates, Pak Tea House today serves more as a museum useful only to display the achievements of the past.

Soon after the constitution of the Pakistan Progressive Writers' Association, there was serious debate about its place in a country created on religious rhetoric. There were several contesting opinions, ranging from those who argued that literature should help bring about political and social change to those who opined that literature reflects an inherent beauty and that itself is reason enough to pursue it. Perhaps no other writer from the movement has been able to reconcile these two opposing points of view better than Faiz, the poet of protest, who, despite using classical Persian poetic imagery managed to include in it political references.[43] A committed communist, he was one of the accused in the Rawalpindi Conspiracy Case and spent four years in jail. He died in 1984 in Lahore and is buried in a Model Town graveyard, close to where he spent the last few years of his life.

Even today Faiz continues to be a symbol for leftist activists and writers. His poems, particularly those with overt political symbolism, are recited from leftist political podiums. The genius of his poetry and intellectual depth can be gauged from the fact that even those who might have disagreed with his political opinions have embraced his poetry. On many instances, Qazi Hussain Ahmad, chief of the Jama'at-e-Islami from 1987 to 2009, recited Faiz's poetry at political rallies.[44] Faiz continues to be one of the most widely read Urdu poets in Pakistan among all segments of society, irrespective of their political opinions.

Whereas Faiz represented the literary establishment, rooted as he was in the classical Urdu and Persian poetic traditions, another writer from the movement became a literary pariah. While Faiz was celebrated by everyone, Manto, at least during his lifetime, was rejected by all. The progressives called him regressive, the traditionalists called him progressive.[45] Rejected by both, Manto, who had moved to Lahore from Bombay in 1948, found himself in a literary wilderness, which eventually took a toll on him and resulted in his untimely death in 1955. Shunned and banned during his lifetime, his writings today are widely acknowledged for their literary merit. In 2012, the Pakistani state awarded him the Nishan-i-Imtiaz, the highest honour given to a civilian. It was the same state that had haunted him during his lifetime, accusing him of promoting vulgarity by writing about the sexual violence committed during Partition.

Ahmad Nadeem Qasmi, another member of the organization, disagreed quite publicly with Zaheer on the role of religion in the state of Pakistan. Unlike Zaheer, Qasmi argued for a reconciliation of Islamic history with the egalitarian principles of the CPP.[46] Perhaps he was attuned to the cultural sensibilities of the people of the land much more than Zaheer.

While the Pakistan Progressive Writers' Association remained the foremost literary organization in the country, there were many writers and intellectuals who either refused to associate themselves with it or were turned down for their political opinions. Another literary organization that became a rallying point for writers who did not necessarily agree with the constraints of the Pakistan Progressive Writers' Association was the Halqa Arbab-e-Zauq, established in 1936 in Lahore. With these two organizations, which were often at odds with each other, Lahore emerged as a literary and cultural capital of the newly formed Pakistan, a title that it still, jealously though arguably unfairly, holds on to.

Perhaps one reason why the CPP was able to leave a greater literary imprint on the country was because most of its leaders were better writers and intellectuals than political organizers.[47] People like Sajjad Zaheer and Sibte Hassan were more at home when theorizing about Marxism than implementing those principles.

Due to its lack of political impact, the leaders of the party were perhaps in a hurry to bring about a revolution.[48] A top-down approach, supported by sections of the army, seemed like a quicker way to social justice. A meeting did take place, in which some leaders of the army were quite keen to overthrow the government and allow the CPP to seize power, but, it is believed, members of the party, including Zaheer and Faiz, turned down the offer.[49] The government found out about the meeting and used it as a pretext to arrest the leading proponents of the 'conspiracy'.

A media trial followed which asked for the summary executions of all those involved. The communists were called anti-state and anti-religion, with their initial rejection of Partition used as evidence of their treachery. Along with Chaudhary Zafarullah Khan, General Akbar Khan too became a symbol of the 'treachery' of the Ahmadiyya community during the riots that followed a couple of years later. The CPP was banned. Upon the intervention of Nehru, with whom Zaheer had ties, the latter was allowed to leave for India. The nascent movement was clipped in the bud. It was a turning point in the history of the left in Pakistan.

With prominent leaders either arrested or underground, workers of the party were rudderless. They were eventually brought together in 1957 with the formation of the NAP.[50] However, one year after its creation, the party was banned under the martial law of Ayub Khan, along with all other political parties in the country. A severe crackdown followed, resulting in the arrest of several workers of the party, including Hasan Nasir.

In November 1960, an army veteran and a prominent Marxist, Major Ishaq Mohammad, and Mahmud Ali Kasuri, a lawyer and one of the founders of the NAP, filed a habeas corpus appeal in Lahore High Court[51] to locate Hasan Nasir. Maj. Ishaq Mohammad, who was also imprisoned and tortured at Lahore Fort, had reason to believe that Nasir too was being kept there.

A court inquiry disclosed that Nasir had indeed been kept and 'interrogated' at Lahore Fort, but as of 29 October 1960, the inquiry had ended and he was to be sent to Karachi. However, on 13 November, according to police officials, Nasir was found hanging in his cell at Lahore Fort.[52] They claimed that he hanged himself after finding out he was to be transferred to Karachi because he had become anxious after disclosing the names of his comrades during his 'interrogation'.[53] Another reason stated was that he had become depressed after receiving a letter from his mother and hearing about the declining health of his father. He had hanged himself using his pyjama cord. Government officials buried the deceased at Miani Sahib in Lahore.

Nasir's comrades suspected foul play. They wanted his body to be exhumed and a postmortem conducted to determine the reason for his death. On 12 December 1960, following court orders, in the presence of Nasir's mother, his body was exhumed. However, due to the advanced stage of decomposition, the body was unrecognizable.[54] Zohra Alambardar Hussain refused to accept that the body belonged to her son and did not take its possession. The body was reburied, while Nasir's mother returned to India.

4

A CITY FORGOTTEN

A small stream flows meekly through a parched riverbed. Nomads who have camped on the dry bed, with the arrival of summer and the subsequent monsoon, will evacuate it and move to a higher area, as the Ravi will pretend to be a river for a couple of months. The silhouette of the city of Lahore is before us—the Minar-e-Pakistan is trying to catch up with the towering minarets of Badshahi Masjid. The rest of the city is lost in a haze.

This is the busiest part of the city, one of the main entries into Lahore. It was once the gateway of the kings—Shahdara— now a small town on the western bank of the river, an industrial hub, emptying its waste into the river. On a clear morning, when the particles in the polluted air have settled, one can still see the minarets of the mosque at Data Darbar, the white dome of the smadh of Maharaja Ranjit Singh, the tall buildings of the walled city behind Badshahi Masjid.

The river was once whimsical, wild, impervious to the sufferings of those living close to it. In its generosity, it would sometimes assume the incarnation of Vishnu, the preserver of life. Lahore would not exist without the blessings of the Ravi. But sometimes, it would become Shiva, the deity of destruction. In an ecstatic dance of death, it would break out of its banks, destroying everything that stood in its way. No force could tame its violent energy. Life would eventually sprout from the seeds of destruction the river would leave in its wake, and hence the cycle of life—of death and birth, hand in hand—would move forward.

Aware of the untapped energy of the river, many rishis, yogis, dervishes and tantrics have sat on its banks, praying to the mighty goddess to share with them its unlimited boon. For seventeen years, every day, Guru Nanak would take a dip in the river as he worked in his fields north of Lahore. Asked for his last wish before his impending capital punishment, Guru Arjan wished for one last bath in the waters of the river that flowed next to Lahore Fort at the time. He never emerged from it, choosing to pass on to the next world on his own terms. According to folk tradition, Valmiki composed the Ramayana on the banks of the Ravi.[1] It also talks of the riverbank as the site of the Battle of Ten Kings—an epic confrontation mentioned in the Rig Veda in which the tribal kingdom of Bharata emerged victorious, eventually lending its name to India.[2]

Standing on the edge of the river, it is hard to imagine the mighty Ravi of the past, one of the six sacred rivers to flow through Punjab. This river system is the cradle of the Indian civilization, giving birth to the Indus Valley Civilization, before the Gangetic river valley civilization emerged in northern India following the demise of cities like Mohenjo-Daro and Harappa. The little stream flowing at the edge of Lahore today is a sad reminder of the changing political landscape as well. In 1960, Prime Minister Nehru and President Ayub Khan met in Karachi to determine the control of rivers flowing in Punjab emerging from Indian territory. Control of the eastern rivers, Beas, Ravi and Sutlej, was handed to India, while that of the western rivers, Chenab, Jhelum and Indus, was given to Pakistan. Over the years, as India built dams and barrages on 'its' rivers, these once mighty ancient rivers began to dry up. Where the Sutlej has almost disappeared, the Ravi too seems headed towards imminent extinction in Pakistani territory. Once the source of life for Lahore and its surroundings, the river today begs for survival.

On 31 December 1929, as a cloud of mist hung over the river, one by one, the leaders of the Indian National Congress, the largest political organization in pre-Partition India, stepped into the cold waters of the Ravi to take a pledge of complete freedom, Purna Swaraj.[3] The cold water in the midst of a bitter Lahori winter symbolized the ultimate sacrifice the pledge would demand—self-control. The Gandhian doctrine of turning the other cheek was to be the road to freedom. Freedom in this context did not just mean political autonomy, a government of Indians, but also spiritual autonomy, which could only be achieved through self-mastery, the ultimate expression of Swaraj. Internal Swaraj was to be a prerequisite for political Swaraj.

Mahatma Gandhi's entire life was an exemplification of this kind of self-control expected of his followers. This self-control was not just a process but an ultimate goal—moksha, salvation. Political Swaraj, for Gandhi, was to be the sum total of Swaraj for individuals, every individual in control over his or her impulses.[4] This would lead to the ultimate social order, with complete harmony, no exploitation—Ram *rajya*. Nationalism, for Gandhi, was not an expression of citizens being assured their civic rights but rather it was them fulfilling their duties towards society, which they could only accomplish after achieving complete self-mastery.[5] Political autonomy would have no significance if self-control was not achieved.

It is this internal Swaraj that provided members of the Congress the strength to face the brutal persecution of the colonial state without violent retaliation. During a severe lathi charge in

Lucknow, just a little before the event in Lahore, members of the party held their ground and only raised their hands to protect their faces, when with their numerical strength they could have fought back, dismounting the police officers from their horses.[6] The vicious, violent state was helpless in front of unarmed protesters exhibiting the pinnacle of self-control. Similar self-mastery was exhibited by members of the Khudai Khidmatgar, led by Abdul Ghaffar Khan, an ally and close friend of Gandhi, on 23 April 1930, at the Qissa Khwani Bazaar in Peshawar, when the colonial police fired at peaceful protesters, resulting in the death of over 200 people.[7]

Gandhi and Congress supporters at the end of 1929 were a step closer to this internal Swaraj after the debacle at Chauri Chaura. In 1922, in a small town called Chauri Chaura in the United Provinces, a mob burnt down a police station after being fired at, at the height of Gandhi's satyagraha during the nationwide Non-Cooperation Movement, resulting in the death of about twenty-two policemen.[8] So disappointed was Gandhi at the lack of discipline shown by protesters, who had taken to the streets following his call of strike against the colonial state, that he halted the movement. Political autonomy for Gandhi, and the Congress under his shadow, was not acceptable without the prior disciplining of the self through non-violence. Freedom meant nothing without this internal freedom.

While on the one hand stepping into the cold waters of the Ravi on New Year's Eve symbolized self-control amidst adversity, on the other, it illustrated another concept of nationalism, deeply intertwined with religious expression. Taking a dip in a holy river signified spiritual purification through *snan*. Religious rituals and symbols were a regular feature of Gandhi's political gatherings. Often, he would organize public readings of the Gita and the Quran. Self-autonomy leading to political autonomy, for Gandhi, would be a product of earnestly following one's religion, dharma.

For several other nationalists too, the downfall of Indian civilization, culminating in its colonization by the British, was a result of people moving away from the true teachings of their religion.[9] Several Muslim allies of the Congress party were a product of such Islamic revivalist movements. Representatives of the urban educated classes, many of them felt that a staunch adherence to Islamic doctrine would result in a political revival of Islam in South Asia. It, therefore, was hardly a surprise that the Indian National Congress, under the leadership of Gandhi, threw its weight behind the Khilafat Movement of 1919, which was a politico-religious movement to preserve the Caliphate under threat after the defeat of the Ottoman Empire at the hands of the Allied Powers, which included Britain.

It is interesting to note here that Jinnah, the founder of Pakistan, did not support the Khilafat Movement. An Anglicized Indian, Jinnah's concept of nationalism, inspired from the British, was premised upon a secular state that had particular responsibilities towards its citizens. For him, it was adherence to constitutional law that ensured the well-being of citizens, rather than religious revivalism. He remained sceptical of religious revivalist movements and they, in turn, had their reservations about him and his call for Pakistan. Jinnah's speech to the Constituent Assembly of Pakistan on 11 August 1947 sums up his notion of nationalism, in which religion was to have no role in the functioning of the state. It was this ideological difference that had earlier led to Jinnah's exit from the Congress in 1920.[10] While the Congress under its old guard shared Jinnah's vision of nationalism, it took on a more religious outlook after the arrival of Gandhi, affiliating with other religious revivalist movements.

Particularly in Punjab, Hindu nationalism played a pivotal role in promoting the cause of Indian nationalism, where cadres of the Arya Samaj joined the Indian National Congress.[11] Founded in Lahore in 1877 by Swami Dayanand Saraswati, the Arya Samaj was a Hindu revivalist movement that looked to 'modernize' Hinduism by removing some of its 'corrupted' influences to seek the essence of a pure Vedic culture, which for them represented the true form of religion.

While several of its members actively engaged in political activities, the organization itself never expressed political aspirations. Some of its doctrines did invoke a Hinduized version of patriotism. The Arya Samaj believed in the greatness of India's past, a past that was solely associated with Hinduism, and wanted to revive its lost glory. In its ideological framework, the downfall of the 'Indian' civilization began with the arrival of Islam in the subcontinent. The Muslims, similar to the British, were seen as a foreign colonizing force. The organization set up several educational centres with the sole focus of nationalizing education in India.

The 'Hinduization' of Indian nationalism also led to communal polarization in Punjab. Some members of the organization were responsible for the publication of inflammatory material, offensive to Muslims, sometimes leading to communal violence.[12]

This rather motley collection of diverse ideologies and at times antagonistic political opinions within the Congress shows the organization's unique position in Punjab. Unlike the United Provinces or Gujarat, it never found a stable footing in Punjab.[13] Several members of the party from Punjab were not necessarily those who believed in its anti-imperialist stance, but became affiliated with it, as they did with other political organizations, to address more local concerns. For example, particularly for the urban Hindus and Muslims, separate electorates and extra weightage given to minorities in assemblies were a bone of contention, which they wanted to take up through the platform of the Congress.[14]

There are several reasons why the Congress was not able to find the same kind of stronghold in Punjab as it did in other parts of the country. First, Punjab was firmly entrenched within the colonial apparatus. It was the bread basket of British India, with most of its agriculture converted into cash crops and exported to Britain. The rural economy was the backbone of the province. Local zamindars, who had benefited from the colonial state, were staunch supporters of the British. The rising nationalism in Punjab, therefore, remained limited to urban centres like Lahore and Rawalpindi. The most prominent political party in pre-Partition Punjab, the Unionist Party, was a staunchly pro-Empire organization.[15]

Punjab was also the main recruiting ground for the British imperial army. Soldiers from Punjab had played a crucial role in not only the First World War but also in 1857 when, through Punjab's loyalty, the British were able to quell the 'Mutiny' in other parts of north India. It was therefore essential for the British to maintain control over Punjab to ensure the perpetuity of the Empire.

Under its broader programme of anti-imperialism, the Congress had managed to find several local partners all over India to spread its agenda. For example, in Gujarat it was Vallabhbhai Patel, and in the NWFP (Khyber Pakhtunkhwa) it was Abdul Ghaffar Khan. In Punjab, it lacked a political ally who could further the cause. For a little while though, towards the end of the 1920s, it seemed as if the Congress had found the perfect ally.

Located within a congested residential community of small houses in Lahore is the spacious Bradlaugh Hall. With its windows and doors shut, the building is now abandoned. While the 'indigenous' population remained confined within the boundary of the walled city, this area, off Mall Road, was reserved for the British elite. Spacious bungalows with sprawling gardens used to dominate the landscape of this area that is now largely taken up by small houses.

Before it became a congested locality, the tall bell tower of the Government College, a gorgeous specimen of Gothic architecture with its tall pointed buildings piercing the sky, must have been visible from here. At walking distance from the Hall is the office of the superintendent of police. Behind the recently renovated facade of the building, one can still see remnants of colonial architecture, which amalgamated Victorian design with existing Indian traditions. Facing the office is the Government Islamia College, founded by another politico-religious organization called the Anjuman-i-Himayat-i-Islam, formed in Lahore in 1884, which, like the Arya Samaj, conjoined nationalism with religious revivalism.[16] Interestingly, the building of the college originally belonged to the Dayanand Anglo Vedic (DAV) College, set up by members of the Arya Samaj as part of their 'nationalization' of education.

Since the creation of Pakistan, Bradlaugh Hall has assumed various incarnations. Abandoned at the time of Partition, it was re-appropriated as a food warehouse. Sometime in the 1980s, it was converted into the Milli Technical Education Institute. Soon a conflict broke out between the directors of the institute, with one of them occupying the Hall and renting it out to private academies.[17] Finally the Evacuee Trust Property Board (ETPB) took over the Hall in 2009. The ETPB is a government institution established in 1960 to administer properties left behind by non-Muslim refugees during Partition. It argued that the occupants of Bradlaugh Hall had taken over the property illegally after Partition. Since 2009 there has been a giant lock placed by the ETPB at the gate of the Hall.

A nineteenth-century political activist, Charles Bradlaugh was one of the few Englishmen of his time who were sympathetic to the plight of the Indians under colonial rule. He, along with a handful of other well-wishers, asked for greater representation of Indians in the Indian government. Bradlaugh was roped into politics by Allan Octavian Hume, a member of the Imperial Civil Service later known as Indian Civil Service (ICS), who is regarded as the 'Father of the Congress'.[18]

Set up in 1885, the Indian National Congress at its inception was a pro-Empire organization that believed in the benevolent nature of British colonialism for providing 'political liberty', which had never been available to Indians prior to the arrival of the 'White Man'.[19] It is for this reason that the Congress was initially seen as a friendly organization by government officials who regularly attended its sessions. Some of its earliest resolutions dealt with the spread of education, cutting back of military budgets, abolition of excise tax and, most importantly, availability of government employment for Indians.

Towards the end of the nineteenth century, with the spread of British education, several Indians believed they were qualified enough to participate in the ICS. While on paper the service was open to them, in practice there was widespread discrimination in their being inducted into it, resulting in much resentment.[20] A need was felt for a political organization that would channel the grievances of Indians to the colonial state. This became one of the most important reasons for the establishment of the Congress.

Till the First World War, Englishmen sympathetic to the plight of Indians played an important role in the functioning of the Indian National Congress. For example, till 1917, Hume served as the head of the Congress Secretariat. Sir William Wedderburn, another bureaucrat of the ICS and one of the founders of the Congress, was elected twice to serve as its president, in 1889 and 1910. Sir Henry Cotton, another ICS officer, served as president of the Congress in 1904.[21]

The situation began to change drastically after the arrival of Bal Gangadhar Tilak, a Marathi lawyer who was among the first to raise the voice of Indian nationalist sentiment.[22] Tilak joined the Congress in 1890 and resented its passive attitude towards the Empire. He wanted it to demand greater autonomy for Indians, eventually resulting in a division within the party, between the Moderates and the Extremists.

Accepting the providential character of the British in India, the Moderates argued that Indians must first reform their own society by removing its social and religious evils. Only then would they be ready for political reform. The Extremists, on the other hand, led by Tilak, argued that political reforms would result in the implementation of the required social and religious reforms.

Joining hands with Tilak was Lala Lajpat Rai from Punjab. A graduate of the prestigious Government College in Lahore, Rai became acquainted with Tilak during the first session of the Congress held in the city in 1893.[23] A prominent member of the Arya Samaj, Rai believed in the 'golden era' of Hinduism and argued that adherence to the Hindu faith would result in the revival of the country. He, along with Tilak and Bipin Chandra Pal, a Bengali politician, formed what came to be known as the 'Lal Bal Pal' trinity and laid the foundation of the assertive Indian nationalism that would eventually sideline the Moderates.[24]

Lala Lajpat Rai became the face of the Congress in Punjab. The party's popularity soared when another session was organized in Lahore in 1900. It was held in the newly constructed Bradlaugh Hall, raised particularly for the occasion with funds collected from sympathizers of the party in the city and beyond. Even today, at the main entrance of the Hall is a plaque that records its inauguration on 30 October 1900 by Surendranath Banerjee, a Bengali politician, two months before the session of the Congress. Thereafter, Bradlaugh Hall in Lahore became home to all Congress sessions in the city. In fact, it was at Bradlaugh Hall that members of the Indian National Congress met on 19 December 1929, which culminated in the declaration of Purna Swaraj on 31 December on the banks of the Ravi.[25]

The Partition of Bengal in 1905 became a turning point for the nationalist struggle in India,[26] with the Extremists eventually elbowing out the Moderates. The colonial administration claimed that Bengal had been divided into two for administrative purposes, the west becoming Hindu-dominated and the east becoming Muslim-dominated. The Partition also trigged communal tensions, with Muslims in the province happy about the situation.[27] For the Hindus of Bengal this was an example of the divide and rule policy of the colonial state.

The Indian National Congress under the leadership of the 'Lal Bal Pal' trio launched the Swadeshi Movement, boycotting British products and services in favour of Indian products, a precursor to Gandhi's Non-Cooperation Movement in 1920. In many ways, the Swadeshi Movement was aligned with the Arya Samaj's philosophy of the regeneration of India's greatness.

From 1905 onwards, there was no stopping the growing consciousness of Indian nationalism. In 1909, the Indian Councils Act was introduced, also known as the Morley-Minto Reforms, which, along with giving greater representation to the Indians in legislative councils, also introduced separate electorates for Hindus and Muslims. This move fanned communal tensions, with the Muslims supporting separate electorates and Hindu leaders rejecting it.

The next big nationalist tide came with the Rowlatt Act of 1919.[28] Under this new legislation, war-time restrictions imposed during the First World War were made permanent. The act provided the government with the authority to search or arrest any Indian without warrant or confine suspects without trial for up to a year. It also took away an offender's right to appeal. Compounded with economic woes brought on by the prolonged war in Europe, large-scale protests sprung up in several cities of India. On 9 March 1919, a huge public meeting was organized at Bradlaugh Hall.[29] A spontaneous protest turned violent in Amritsar, with protesters throwing stones at police, who retaliated by firing back. The violence spiralled out of control and several government buildings and other properties were ransacked by protesters.

The British could not afford to lose control over Punjab, its bread basket and primary supplier of recruits to the colonial army. They were also afraid of a repeat of 1857, when Indians, including their forces, had united against the British. The colonial administration wanted to stem this budding tide even if it meant resorting to vicious violence. It is in this context that the Jallianwala Bagh massacre took place in Amritsar on 13 April 1919, when the colonial force opened fire on unarmed protesters and others gathered at Jallianwala Bagh, resulting in the deaths of over a thousand people, according to nationalist sources. Government records limited the casualties to 379.[30]

Jallianwala Bagh inspired a wave of outrage throughout the country. It became the ultimate symbol of colonial repression. The British strategy of attempting to stifle nationalism with brute force had backfired.

This was also the time when a new leader had entered the political arena and provided a fresh impetus to the Indian National Congress and the nationalist movement. In 1915, after returning from South Africa where he had earned quite a reputation fighting for the rights of Indians settled there, M.K. Gandhi joined the Indian National Congress. Immediately after the Jallianwala Bagh massacre, Gandhi was selected as the Congress representative to compile a report on the massacre, contesting the official version.[31] After the death of Tilak in 1920, Gandhi was to emerge as the chief architect of the ideology of the Indian National Congress.

At the end of 1921, after being elected president, Gandhi redefined the party's goal to Swaraj—self-government—and, building upon the swadeshi policy of former Congress leaders, launched his Non-Cooperation Movement. Politically, at least, Swaraj at this point meant complete autonomy for Indians, but not necessarily a breakaway from the Empire. While Lala Lajpat Rai, the 'Lion of Punjab' as he had come to be known, decided to throw his weight behind Gandhi's non-cooperation, he also predicted its failure.[32] He argued that the repressive environment in the country after Jallianwala Bagh was not conducive to 'passive resistance', his interpretation of Gandhi's satyagraha. The Non-Cooperation Movement did come to an unceremonious halt after the Chauri Chaura incident on 4 February 1922.

An alliance between Gandhi and Rai that could have made the Congress more popular in Punjab was weakened after the incident. The Congress or Gandhi could not find any formidable ally from the province thereafter.

A miniature train, profusely lit, balanced on the roof of the railway station took circles on its tracks. The railway station was decorated with green bulbs. The Kalma, placed on the building after the creation of the country, sparkled in glowing lights. It was as if the entire city of Lahore had come to the station to see this spectacle. Thousands of visitors gaped at the fort-like station. On 14 August every year, the Lahore railway station becomes one of the most visited sites in the country by enthused citizens celebrating the birth of their country.

Even without the decorations, the railway station is a sight to behold. Unlike several other colonial monuments which depict an amalgamation of colonial architectural traditions and indigenous designs, the railway station seems more British. The thick boundary wall with its dual clock towers is interspersed with a couple of bastions on each side. The bastions almost come across as an anomaly, a forced inclusion into the structure. But they were special times requiring special measures. Constructed just a couple of years after the war of 1857 that had shaken the foundation of the Empire, the British wanted the station to fulfil the dual purpose of acting as a fort in case of a siege.[33]

A few kilometres from the station is the walled city of Lahore, home to a majority of the population of the city. The British had already torn down its walls after the nightmare in Delhi. The intermingling of the colonial masters and their subjects, which happened frequently during the earlier phase of colonial rule, came to a complete halt after 1857. A new colonial state emerged in its aftermath, a much more vicious state, convinced of its superiority over the 'natives'. It was this new state that expressed itself during the Jallianwala Bagh massacre.

Two cities were emerging in Lahore after 1857 too—one for the locals and the other for the British. The city was expanding westwards where new avenues and bungalows for the colonial masters were being constructed. The railway station was placed right in the middle of these two worlds. It was to become the most important tool in the hands of the colonial state to extend its bureaucratic hold over the rest of the province. It was also a symbol of the 'progress' that came with the 'modernizing' colonial state.

Whereas the railways benefited the colonial state economically, it also played a crucial role in forging a sense of common national identity.[34] For the first time, Punjab was connected with other parts of the country. With the intermingling of people, there arose a sense of not only a common culture and heritage but also a realization of common problems and cases of discrimination at the hands of the colonial state. The nationalist leaders took full advantage of this growing interconnectivity, travelling to cities and towns far away from their home towns, forming political alliances that culminated in a unified nationalist struggle.

On 30 October 1928, the Lahore railway station was in a way able to unite the whole of India. The Simon Commission was visiting Lahore and there was a massive protest against it at the station, headed by Lala Lajpat Rai, among others.[35] The commission was composed of British parliamentarians visiting India to study the situation and propose constitutional reforms to address demands for self-government and the controversial issue of separate communal electorates.

This was a crucial period in the history of the Indian National Congress. Inspired by the Bolshevik Revolution in Russia in 1917, several young Indians were sceptical of the traditionalist attitude of the old guard of the Congress. Two prominent critics of the old leadership of the Congress were Jawaharlal Nehru and Subhas Chandra Bose.[36] Both felt that the leadership, including Gandhi and Motilal Nehru, were not revolutionary enough. They wanted the Congress to demand complete independence from the British Empire, as opposed to dominion status, which assured self-autonomy to the Indians albeit within the Empire, similar to Canada and Australia.

While leaders of the Congress and other political organizations sat together to determine their united front against the British-imposed Simon Commission, a young Jawaharlal became increasingly critical of them, including his own father and his mentor, Gandhi.[37] He felt any reference to dominion status would be a betrayal of the revolutionary spirit of the country.

The arrival of Jawaharlal Nehru on the scene heralded yet another phase of nationalism. Moving away from the religious revivalist concept, his understanding of religion and history was inspired by the historical materialism of Marxism. Communal tension was for him a result of economic conflict. Swaraj meant a socialist revolution that would fundamentally alter economic structures and redistribute wealth. He openly talked about the nationalization of large-scale industries, causing anxiety amongst the industrialist backers of the Congress.[38] Self-autonomy with dominion status were politics of appeasement and too mild for his revolutionary nature. The old guard of the Congress was sympathetic to some of his revolutionary ideas, but felt he was moving too fast. Many were sceptical too. They would have preferred the moderate temperament of his father, Motilal.

Quite unexpectedly, Jawaharlal Nehru was elected president of the Congress on 28 September 1929.[39] For several days prior to the meeting, Motilal, who was tipped to be the new president of the Congress, was trying to convince Gandhi to choose his son instead. Motilal had been in poor health for some time and believed his time was limited. Several members of the Congress felt that Gandhi should be president. As expected, Gandhi's name was recommended by the Provincial Committees; however, he, at the last minute, turned it down and recommended Jawaharlal's name instead. With Motilal's and Gandhi's support, Jawaharlal became the president of the Congress during this defining period in its history.

The Nehru Report, composed by Motilal Nehru, was the Congress's response to the Simon Commission. Disappointing Jawaharlal, the report still sought dominion status within the British Empire. Jawaharlal was made to accept the demand by Gandhi's intercession. Gandhi said that if the British Parliament did not accept the recommendations of the report in a year, he would wholeheartedly throw his weight behind Jawaharlal's demand for complete independence and lead a non-violent, non-cooperation struggle for it.[40]

Unresponsive to nationalist demands, the Simon Commission visited several cities of the country in an attempt to glean its political picture. On 30 October 1928, as the Simon Commission stepped on to the Lahore railway station platform, a huge contingent of Congress members shouted slogans of 'Simon Go Back'. A police lathi charge followed, seriously injuring an ageing Lala Lajpat Rai.

Even though Rai had distanced himself from the Indian National Congress after Gandhi's suspension of the Non-Cooperation Movement in 1922, he still held great political clout, particularly in Lahore, where his social welfare projects had earned him quite a reputation. He had set up a National College at Bradlaugh Hall, which became a hub of revolutionary activities in pre-Partition Lahore. It is here that Bhagat Singh met his comrades Sukhdev Thapar and Yashpal. Rai had also established a library close by, the Dwarka Das Library, which housed thousands of books with a particular focus on Marxist literature. He founded a weekly magazine as well. In 1927, he had formed a trust to run a TB hospital for women in the city, in honour of his mother, Gulab Devi, who had died of TB. The Gulab Devi Chest Hospital continues to function till today.

Lala Lajpat Rai succumbed to his injuries on 17 November 1928. His death shook the entire nation.[41] A confrontation between the nationalists and the colonial state seemed imminent. Those who had argued for dominion status were now pushed to the other side. Jawaharlal Nehru, in subsequent protests, emerged as a central leader, and his ideology for complete independence was soon to become the official ideology of the Indian National Congress. By the time the Congress gathered in Lahore on 19 December 1929 under the leadership of Jawaharlal Nehru, a year had lapsed since the Nehru Report. Gandhi now stood firmly behind the new leader.

Standing on the banks of the river on the night of 31 December 1929, the flag of an independent India was unfurled. Jawaharlal Nehru addressed the delegation, beginning his tryst with destiny. Gandhi asked all his supporters to celebrate 26 January 1930 as National Day. Rallies were organized on the assigned day with millions of people taking a pledge of freedom.[42] The Congress, from 1930 to 1947, celebrated 26 January as Independence Day.

Lahore had been Jawaharlal Nehru's coronation. He was to become a legend, almost a modern-day version of the Buddha, who abandoned the luxuries of the world for the salvation of his people.

The titles bestowed upon him included 'Bharat Bhushan' (Jewel of India) and 'Tyagamurti' (Embodiment of Sacrifice).[43] His vision of nationalism and of India that he articulated in Lahore that night would become central to the agenda of the Indian National Congress. For the next several decades, till his death in 1964, it would power the vision of the Indian state. India became Nehru and Nehru became India. However, when the goal of Purna Swaraj was finally achieved, the city where he had first taken the pledge was no longer part of Nehru's India.

There was an unexpected knock on the door. It was still a couple of hours before morning prayers. Perhaps it was his younger brother in need of something for *sehri*. The entire cycle of life had been turned upside down because of Ramzan. Shops and eateries remained open till sehri, then were closed the entire day to reopen around the time of *aftari*. Iqbal Qaiser opened the door to find a posse of police officials at his door, some in civilian clothes. Without an explanation he was asked to sit in the police van and driven to the Township Police Station.

'A couple of our friends had been arrested for the murder of this other friend of ours, who belonged to the Ahle-Hadith group. Of those arrested, one was a Shia while the other was an Ahmadi. It was being framed as a sectarian murder,' Iqbal Qaiser told me at his house in Township on a quiet Sunday morning. Only a few restaurants serving breakfast were open, as the market was still in deep slumber. A cyclist rode down the street ringing his bell before the impending turn.

'But I was not being questioned about the murder. Instead they were asking me about my poem. Why did you write this poem, what does it mean, who asked you to write it? I had recently returned from a trip to India, so they were asking me questions about the trip. Why did I go, who did I meet there? What was my agenda? For thirty-four days, I was detained at the station without any official report against me. For thirty-four days they only asked about the poem.'

About fifteen-odd days prior to his arrest, Iqbal Qaiser, a young upcoming Punjabi poet, had been invited to recite his poetry at a conference arranged at the historic Faletti's Hotel. Just off Mall Road, adjacent to the provincial Parliament, this hotel, constructed in 1880, is regarded as one of the finest in the city.[44] Organized when martial law was at its peak in 1983, by several nationalist Punjabi organizations along with splinters of socialist and communist political parties, this widely attended conference was the first of its kind.

Called the Bhagat Singh Conference, it was held a few days after Singh's death anniversary on 23 March. Lahore was the hub of his political activities. He had been schooled here, exposed to revolutionary Marxist literature here, had formed his first political party here and had been hanged here too. After his death, his supporters had managed to wrest his and his comrades' remains from the colonial administration and cremated them on the banks of the Ravi.[45] Several of his former comrades wanted to construct a memorial for him in Lahore, but that was not to be. Instead, a memorial was constructed on the other side of the border, in 1968, in a village called Hussainiwalla.

Even though Lahore, Punjab and, in fact, the whole of India showered their love on Bhagat Singh both during his lifetime and after, his legacy in Pakistan became a victim of history's communalization. Only leaders of the Muslim League or those historical Muslim 'heroes' that fit the narrative of the most dominant party of the country were to be celebrated in Pakistan. Roads, buildings and institutions were renamed to honour our new heroes. Muhammad Ali Jinnah, Allama Iqbal and Fatima Ali Jinnah continue to be the most popular names of roads and institutions. Slowly and gradually, all traces of the non-Muslim League political leaders were erased.

At the end of the lower Mall, at a place called Gol Bagh, there was a statue of the 'Lion of Punjab' Lala Lajpat Rai, with his index finger raised towards his audience. Following the riots of Partition, when statues around the city were being vandalized, this statue was removed from its location and placed in the parking lot of Mayo School of Arts. It eventually found its way to Mall Road in Shimla, India.[46]

Bhagat Singh fared no better. The annual festival on the occasion of his death anniversary, attended by thousands of people in Lahore and Banga, his home town in district Faisalabad, ended abruptly in 1947.

Similar to what would happen in Zulfikar Ali Bhutto's case almost five decades later, Bhagat Singh, along with Rajguru and Sukhdev, was hanged at 7 pm on 23 March in Lahore Central Jail as opposed to the scheduled time in the morning of 24 March.[47] Anticipating massive protests, the administration pre-empted any interference by executing them before the appointed hour. The bodies of the three men were then hacked, placed in sacks and, through the rear gate of the jail, driven to the banks of the Sutlej, to a jungle near Ganda Singhwalla village, about 70 kilometres from Lahore.[48] Here, while the remains were being burned, the officials were intercepted by protesters from Ferozepur and Lahore, leading them to abandon the half-completed project. The protesters then took the remains back to Lahore, Bhagat Singh's political home.

Bhagat Singh's incarceration from 1929 to 1931 had captured the political imagination of the people of India. He became the only other political leader of the pre-Partition anti-colonial struggle who at one point rivalled Gandhi's popularity.[49] He provided an alternative to the Mahatma's non-violent political struggle. They became symbols of competing political ideologies, representing two distinct means to achieve the same goal—independence. Independence itself meant two different things to them. For Gandhi, Purna Swaraj was a spiritual journey, a self-discovery, leading to self-control and self-mastery. This internal spiritual autonomy was to align with the external political reality. For Bhagat Singh, whose struggle too required immense self-discipline, the Gandhian confluence of spirituality and politics held no significance. Purna Swaraj for him was a socialist revolution, the abolition of class and the disappearance of religion. While in Gandhi's India, the capitalist would look after the needs of the proletariat in a paternalistic manner,[50] in Bhagat Singh's India, there was to be no capitalist, only a dictatorship of the proletariat.

Even while the younger leadership of the Congress, including Jawaharlal Nehru, was sympathetic to Bhagat Singh—Nehru even visited him in Lahore Central Jail—Gandhi remained vehemently opposed to the young revolutionary.[51] His critics argue that Gandhi at that point could have used his good offices with the British to procure clemency for Bhagat Singh and his comrades, but he was too adamant to acknowledge anyone else's concept of revolution if it did not consort with his.

Eight years after the abrupt end of the Non-Cooperation Movement, the country braced itself for another movement— the Civil Disobedience Movement of 1930. Revolutionaries like Bhagat Singh and Chandra Shekhar Azad were a fallout of the previous abandoned movement.[52] Having thrown themselves into the movement, they had been disappointed by its sudden abandonment. They had argued that in a country where an incident like Jallianwala Bagh could happen, incidents like Chauri Chaura were also bound to happen. Deeply disillusioned by Gandhi's call to end the movement, both Bhagat Singh and Azad had decided to confront the colonial state through the very violence it espoused.

Bhagat Singh, in particular, became a vocal critic of the Indian National Congress and Gandhi. He had no patience for their oscillation between appeasing the government and opposing it. A committed Marxist, for him, violence was an essential feature of a revolution, thus making him sceptical of Gandhi's non-violence mantra.

This time as well, despite a nationwide response, the non-cooperation movement did fizzle out, as Gandhi began his talks with Viceroy Irwin. The talks led to the Gandhi–Irwin Pact resulting in the discontinuation of the movement, as the British government agreed to release political activists, except those who had committed acts of violence.[53] This it seemed was particularly angled to keep Bhagat Singh and his comrades in jail.

On 8 April 1929, Bhagat Singh and B.K. Dutt threw two bombs in the Central Legislative Assembly in New Delhi from the visitor's gallery. They were deliberately thrown in a vacant part of the gallery to avoid harming attendees. Leaflets thrown with the bomb read, 'It takes a loud voice to make the deaf hear.'[54]

Bhagat Singh was an incredibly well-read revolutionary. At a young age, he had established a deep bond with books and emerged as an exceptional writer. He spent numerous hours studying Marxist literature at the Dwarka Das Library in Lahore, the home of revolutionary literature in the city. His jail notebook contains passages from writers such as Plato, Descartes, Hobbes, Locke, Rousseau, Trotsky, Marx, Engels, Lenin, as well as Rabindranath Tagore and Lala Lajpat Rai. Even on the day of his hanging, he was engaged in reading till a few minutes before his death.[55] He understood the important role literature played in political revolutions.

He had extraordinary knowledge of global affairs, particularly revolutionary history. In his writings one finds references to global events, analysed in the local Indian context. Even in the act of throwing bombs in the Assembly, he had taken a leaf from a similar revolutionary act in the French Parliament with the aim of directing the Parliament's attention towards the poverty of the people. That act too had been accompanied by the one-liner, 'It needs an explosion to make the deaf hear.'[56]

Both the bombers courted arrest after the explosion. This was part of the strategy devised by Bhagat Singh. He knew that he could not expect a fair trial from the British, but wanted to use the platform provided by it to raise awareness about their revolutionary agenda. Applying the Marxist interpretation of history, they felt that India was still not ripe for revolution, hence it needed a dramatic act, such as the one committed by them, to raise political consciousness. Their sham of a trial was to offer them the perfect opportunity to do so.

Bhagat Singh was one of the main theoreticians behind the revolutionary Hindustan Socialist Republican Association (HSRA). It was under his influence that the party added 'Socialist' to its name and socialism to its political agenda. His comprehensive understanding of global revolutionary movements and his deep knowledge of statecraft outshone even that of Chandra Shekhar Azad, his mentor and the founder of the party.[57] It was therefore deemed that he would be the perfect candidate to represent the party's agenda during the trials.

The bombings drew sharp criticism from the nationalist movement. Several leaders of the Congress, including Gandhi and Motilal Nehru, severely condemned the act.[58] Bhagat Singh had yet not become the revolutionary folk hero he was to become. Things changed dramatically during their imprisonment.[59] In jail, Bhagat Singh along with his comrades began a 116-day hunger strike in what was to become the longest hunger strike of its time. The protesters were force-fed on several occasions, severely damaging their fragile health. On the sixty-third day of the protest, one of their comrades, Jatin Das, passed away.

Forcible feeding of milk had damaged his lungs, but he refused to give up his fast even on his deathbed, choosing instead to give up his life in protest.[60]

In a letter written by Bhagat Singh to the superintendent of Mianwali Jail where he was kept for a little while, he argued that they were political prisoners and should not be treated like common criminals. In addition, he demanded a better diet, no forced labour, books, newspapers, better clothing and toiletries. He also argued that political prisoners be treated as European 'special class' prisoners.[61] Upon receiving no response, he and his comrades decided to go on a hunger strike.

The colonial state was particularly reluctant to accept them as political prisoners. So far it had cast them as 'terrorists', stripping them of political motive. Allowing them to be termed political prisoners would also require the colonial administration to acknowledge their political grievances, thus making it difficult to present them as terrorist demons.

The hunger strike quickly changed public perception in favour of Bhagat Singh and his comrades.[62] His parent party, Naujawan Bharat Sabha, which he had formed in 1926 in Lahore, worked tirelessly to garner support in his favour. They organized several meetings and even celebrated an All-India Bhagat Singh-Dutt Day. Jatin Das's death added fuel to the fire.

Bhagat Singh was also successfully using the trial for propaganda. His political speeches were being reported and consumed by the entire country. Nationalistic fervour in the 1920s was already at fever pitch, with the Rowlatt Act agitation, the Jallianwala Bagh incident, the Non-Cooperation and Civil Disobedience movements, and now Bhagat Singh. He became a national icon. His slogan 'Inquilab Zindabad' became a rallying cry across the nation.[63] Prominent leaders including Nehru and Jinnah spoke in his favour, yet the British government remained unmoved.

At this time, Gandhi met Lord Irwin, the viceroy of India. There was an expectation that he would intercede on behalf of the prisoners. Jatin Das's death had pricked the conscience of the nation, yet Gandhi remained quiet, adamant that 'violent' tactics were not the correct path to freedom. He completely ignored the fact that through their non-violent hunger strike, these prisoners had adopted an approach Gandhi had often used himself. In this, they were not unlike Gandhi's satyagrahi.[64] Yet Gandhi could not look past their 'violent' act. His reluctance to engage with Bhagat Singh and others played into the hands of the British, who could hang them for they had quite unexpectedly found the link to another unresolved case—the Second Lahore Conspiracy Case.

During the Khalistan militancy phase in the 1980s in India's state of Punjab, Bhagat Singh quite strangely emerged as an icon of the movement. His posters became widely available in Punjab, perhaps to emphasize the point that one man's revolutionary can be another's terrorist. One such iconic poster depicted Bhagat Singh holding a pistol, standing behind a tree facing the superintendent's office, waiting for J.A. Scott to emerge.[65]

The lathi charge during the Simon Commission protests, in which Lala Lajpat Rai had sustained life-threatening injuries, had been ordered by Scott, superintendent of police.[66] Rai held a special place in Bhagat Singh's life. He had studied at the college Rai had founded. His library had played a crucial role in fomenting his revolutionary ideas. Rai had also been a comrade of Bhagat Singh's revolutionary uncle, Ajit Singh, and the two had founded the Bharat Mata Society.[67] He also represented a breed of Congress leaders whom Bhagat Singh could trust. They were seen as revolutionaries, and not 'appeasers' as Bhagat Singh labelled other Congress leaders.

Despite holding Lala Lajpat Rai in high respect, Bhagat Singh and his party also had major political differences with him and criticized him on several occasions. They were particularly critical of Rai's communalization of the national struggle. Even so, they saw Rai's death as a blow to the pride of Indians. A sense of despair had descended on the political landscape of the country. Not even one of the senior-most national leaders had been spared.[68]

Bhagat Singh and his comrades in the HSRA wanted to avenge Lala Lajpat Rai's death. On 17 December 1928, all of them took their positions, waiting for Scott to leave his office. Bhagat Singh and Rajguru had been given the responsibility of shooting Scott. They both stood behind a neem tree facing the office, waiting for their target.

That neem tree still stands tall, just behind the gate of Islamia College. Graffiti of the IJT is painted in a calligraphic style on the wall. Almost nine decades after Bhagat Singh, this college, that was once the DAV College, is still home to vibrant student politics. One of the agendas of the Naujawan Bharat Sabha was to politicize students and form associations with other student bodies. They were particularly successful in Lahore. So perturbed was the colonial government at the revolutionary politics at DAV College that the governor of Punjab threatened this college and others with grave consequences if things did not change.[69]

When I visited the site of the incident, I noticed how, under the shade of the tree, on the footpath facing the superintendent's office, clerks were filling up forms for petitioners heading into these offices. With their years of experience, they knew well enough which documents needed to be forged and how to answer particular questions. The road in front of the office was blocked with barbed wire and cement. Armed police officials manned the tall walls and entrances into the office, as a sea of people rushed in and out with different petitions. Traffic was limited to only one road, where everyone was honking incessantly.

It was not Scott but his assistant superintendent of Police, J.P. Saunders, who exited the building. A signal was given to Rajguru and Bhagat Singh, but before Bhagat Singh realized this was not their man, Rajguru had already fired. Bhagat Singh followed suit, pumping three or four bullets into his body. They tried escaping but were chased by the head inspector, Chanan Singh, who was shot dead by Chandra Shekhar Azad.[70]

Bhagat Singh and his comrades disappeared into DAV College, where the student body was sympathetic to their ideology. The colonial state was aware of this and clamped down heavily on students' groups. Several students were detained for questioning, but in vain. While the Indian National Congress officially distanced itself from the shooting, it spoke out in support of these students being harassed by the state.[71]

There was countrywide condemnation of the act. Even *People*, a weekly magazine started by Lala Lajpat Rai in Lahore, criticized it.[72] Gandhi compared the attack to the murder of the Hindu publisher Rajpal in Lahore at the hands of Ilm-uddin.[73] Bhagat Singh and his comrades had 'avenged' their country, but had failed to win its support. Something was required to stir its political consciousness, which came in the form of the plan to throw the bombs at the Central Legislative Assembly in New Delhi on 8 April 1929.

During the course of investigating the bombing, police found evidence of Saunders's murder. A special tribunal heard the case and, on 7 October 1930, Bhagat Singh, Sukhdev and Rajguru were sentenced to death. Bhagat Singh had already earned nationwide fame by now. His death would turn him into a folk legend. Songs were written about him, legends were crafted about his valour in a vein similar to other Punjabi folk legends, like Dullah Bhatti, Heer-Ranjha and Bulleh Shah.[74] His death anniversary became an annual festival, just as the death anniversary of a Sufi saint is celebrated, for that is the day he is supposed to become one with his maker, his beloved. Bhagat Singh came to be revered not just in Punjab but also the whole country.

In the 1960s, some barracks and gallows of Lahore Central Jail were demolished. These included the room where Bhagat Singh and his comrades had spent the last few days of their lives. Later, a roundabout was constructed at the spot where the gallows of the jail used to be. This roundabout, connecting Shah Jamal, Shadman and Ichra, came to be known as Shadman Chowk. Bhagat Singh, Sukhdev and Rajguru were hanged at this spot on 23 March 1931.

Every year, since the beginning of the new millennium, a handful of activists have been gathering here demanding that the name be changed to Bhagat Singh Chowk. For years the authorities turned a deaf ear to them. Over the years, the movement has gained momentum. Leftist organizations in search of an icon also joined in. Street theatre was organized on the day. A few Indian activists also participated, including Mahesh Bhatt and Kuldip Nayar.

One year, I was one of the first to get to the protest. I noticed Syeda Diep spray-painting 'Bhagat Singh Chowk' on a board next to the roundabout. I walked up to her and whispered, 'You know this is illegal.'

'This won't be the only illegal thing done in this country,' she replied. For years Diep, a political activist who runs the Institute for Peace and Secular Studies, has been organizing a small protest at Shadman Chowk every 23 March. While the rest of the country celebrates Pakistan Day, these protesters demand the renaming of the roundabout to Bhagat Singh Chowk.

In 2011, the head of the ETPB, Asif Hashmi, promised to rename the chowk. A notice eventually came through in

2012, when the City District Government of Lahore passed a notification rechristening the chowk in Bhagat Singh's name. This was in conjunction with other similar notifications that saw the naming of roads in honour of other 'heroes' of the land, such as Faiz Ahmed Faiz, Waris Shah and Mir Chakar.

It felt as if the state was in the process of redefining itself. Years of Islamization had taken a severe toll. Religious extremism and sectarian violence had resulted in the loss of thousands of lives. As religiously motivated militants exported jihad, Pakistan's global reputation suffered immensely. The Pakistani state, under a democratic regime, seemed to be actively seeking to portray a softer image. These developments were also happening in tandem with changes in the educational curriculum to rectify the promotion of religious extremism.

The situation had changed drastically since 1983, when a poem read by Iqbal Qaiser at the Bhagat Singh Conference landed him in police custody on a false pretext. The poem did not have any overt references to Bhagat Singh. It didn't need to. At the peak of Islamization and state oppression, Bhagat Singh was a symbol of secularism and protest against a brutal state. Just the symbol itself was intolerable to the authorities.

This symbol had been reincarnated at the time of another dictator. With leftist politics in a shambles and religious intolerance at its peak, this symbol represented an alternative society, a classless society, with no religious violence. The state, this time at the receiving end of this religious violence, was not averse to embracing this symbol, hence the renaming of the chowk.

However, soon after the notice, opposition came from the JuD. 'We will not allow the renaming of places after Hindus, Sikhs or Christians,' said the spokesperson of the organization at a hastily arranged press conference.[75] The state quickly returned to its default position as Lahore High Court restrained the government from renaming the roundabout.

Instead of pushing back, the leftist activists, the Opposition, rather fuelled their movement. The gatherings on the roundabout on 23 March grew larger. Another group of activists from Faisalabad started travelling to Bhagat Singh's ancestral village, Banga, and began to organize a Bhagat Singh festival there. His ancestral home and the primary school where he studied in the village were renovated. Just as in 1931, when he had become a symbol of protest against a repressive state, today in Pakistan he is emerging as a symbol of protest against religious extremism.

His prediction did come true. 'After I am hanged the fragrance of my revolutionary ideas will permeate the atmosphere of this beautiful land of ours. It will intoxicate the youth and (prepare them) for freedom and revolution . . .'[76]

The younger brother brought in a framed photograph and sat on a charpoy facing us. The person in the picture, Rehmat Ali, was a middle-aged man with short hair and a trimmed beard. He was wearing a black suit with a red tie. The man holding the frame couldn't be more different. His hair was untrimmed, with patches of white. His unshaved beard hid parts of burned skin that clung to his bones. He was wearing a worn-out white shalwar kameez. I looked at both these faces closely to see if I could detect any sort of similarity. I couldn't look past their contrasting states of hygiene.

The elder brother was in a better state, wearing a clean grey shalwar kameez with a brown skullcap. He had a long white beard. He was a schoolteacher, and the younger brother a farmer. 'My father, Fateh Shah, brought this picture from India when he was invited to visit our ancestral village of Wajidke, in 1978, by the Indian government. This picture was given to him with an award for the services our grandfather rendered to the country,' said the elder brother. There was a sense of embarrassment in his tone.

On a Sunday evening, while we were on our way back from a trip down Multan Road exploring its monuments, my mentor and friend Iqbal Qaiser asked me to take a short detour. We drove into a narrow, crowded road towards Sultankeh, a small village close to the Sundar Industrial Estate in Lahore. Through some of his friends in East Punjab, Iqbal Qaiser had found out that Rehmat Ali's grandchildren were living in this village. Upon inquiring, we found ourselves in front of an old dilapidated haveli next to the village mosque.

Escaping the Partition riots in East Punjab, Baba Mulle Shah Fakir, Rehmat Ali's father, had moved to Montgomery (later the name was changed to Sahiwal) city in south Punjab with his family, including Fateh Shah, his orphaned grandchild, the father of these two men in front of us. Perhaps Mulle Shah Fakir wanted to be close to his son's grave. He could not be with him when he was hanged. The family was informed of the date of execution on 24 March 1915, only a day prior to the hanging. Rehmat Ali was hanged on the appointed day and his body was buried in the graveyard outside the jail. A few years later, the family moved to this haveli, a part of which was allotted to them.

The architecture of the haveli appeared as if it had been encroached upon. Walls had been constructed, dividing unequally the grand arches, windows, doors and the veranda. The family received a small portion of the division, a couple of rooms with a small courtyard. We were greeted warmly and taken into a small room with three charpoys. Underneath the hospitality there was a sense of unease, awkwardness.

Before us, no one in Pakistan had asked them anything about their grandfather, Rehmat Ali. So they had never had to confront how the legacy of their grandfather fit into the Pakistani historical narrative. They knew he was respected in India, which brought a sense of pride, but this was not India any more. India was our enemy, and we, the visitors, were Pakistanis. We had fought three wars with India. Our heroes were their villains and vice versa. Where did Rehmat Ali fit in Pakistan, a pre-Partition freedom fighter who gave up his life for his ideals of achieving freedom for India?

Rehmat Ali was based in Manila, Philippines, when he first came across *Hindustan Ghadar*, a revolutionary magazine set up by Hardayal in San Francisco, USA. He, along with many other Indian migrants, was inspired by the revolutionary literature of *Hindustan Ghadar*.

Hardayal had moved to Lahore from Delhi in 1903 after he earned a government scholarship to study at Punjab University. Here he completed his master's in English followed by history, in which he broke the university record.[77] He then travelled to England after securing a scholarship at Oxford. A few months prior to the completion of his degree, he left the programme. He had become a committed nationalist. He had also by now abandoned Western attire in favour of Indian clothes.

Economic compulsions eventually led him to move to Paris, where he first established contact with Egyptian nationalists fighting British imperialism in their country, as well as Russian revolutionaries. This was to become the most important feature of the Ghadar movement. Its global outreach resulted in close collaborations between different groups, all fighting a common enemy—Britain. Contacts were established with Egyptian nationalists, Russian revolutionaries and the German and Japanese governments to assist the Indian national struggle.

Local groups of Indian migrants sympathetic to the Indian nationalist cause were set up in Panama, Manila, Tokyo, Shanghai, Canton, Bangkok, Rangoon, Singapore, Penang, Borneo and Berlin.[78] In its outreach, therefore, the movement inspired by Hardayal was a remarkable one that placed the Indian national struggle in a global framework. Many Indian migrants who actively supported the cause had experienced racism in their host countries, which for them was a result of the subjugation of India by the British.

This was also the biggest weakness of the movement. Its supporters, hordes of Indian labourers and students living in all quarters of the world, felt passionately for the cause and were willing to sacrifice for it, but lacked an organization that could bring them all together and present them with a structured plan. *Hindustan Ghadar* was their only point of reference. While the magazine published passionate literature extolling the use of violence to emancipate their country, arousing the emotions of its readers, it failed to organize any systematic plan that could have channelled the sentiments of thousands of people.[79]

Perhaps one reason was the political ideology of Hardayal. A widely read intellectual, he was inspired by Russian anarchists, who diverged from Marxist ideology in their belief that it was not just one class, the proletariat, which had the potential to bring about revolutionary change.[80] It is for this reason that after moving to California, Hardayal was able to bring together Punjabi migrant workers along with Indian students to the same platform. He was also sceptical of any one particular party leading the revolution, for he felt that eventually that party too becomes a privileged class. For the Russian anarchists, the individual was the society and hence there was a focus on individual spontaneous heroic acts, as opposed to any organized systematic effort. Without any coherent structure this became the central feature of the Ghadar movement.

Hardayal was of the opinion that it was essential to lay the ground prior to any revolution, which is why *Hindustan Ghadar* was launched on 1 November 1913. Right from the inaugural issue, there was a romanticization of 'martyrdom'.[81] He was a man of words who was more comfortable writing about revolution than actually drafting a plan to achieve it. The revolution was to be somewhere in the distant future, when the opportunity was right. For now, the people needed to be prepared. The popularity of

Hindustan Ghadar exploded and its subscription ran into several thousands. It was read wherever there were any Indian migrants.

Soon after, in 1914, clouds of the First World War began roaring across the skies of Europe. Hardayal and his compatriots felt that the opportunity was ripe to strike against an occupying imperial authority. Contacts were established with the German and Japanese governments. Weapons and other logistical support were secured. Leaders of the movement made passionate speeches around California urging migrants to return to India to emancipate it from the shackles of slavery. Fiery essays, poems and stories were published in *Hindustan Ghadar* that reached out to thousands of Indians around the world, exhorting them to do the same. Indians serving in the imperial army were encouraged to switch sides. One of the success stories was the Singapore Mutiny of 1915, when 850 Indian sepoys rose up against the British officers in Singapore and virtually controlled the city-state for over a month. The uprising was finally crushed in the last days of February 1915 followed by an inquiry and the public execution of forty-seven sepoys.[82]

Ships began leaving for India from Canada and USA in August 1914. These were further augmented by supporters from other ports. It is believed that by November 1914, about 3000 men from different ports left for India.[83] There was a sense of euphoria on these ships. These revolutionaries talked openly about their plans, singing songs of freedom. Their bravado was contagious.

While the revolutionaries were intoxicated by a sense of purpose, larger than their individual lives, there was no fixed plan as to what was to be done when they reached India. British intelligence had already become aware of their plans in California. Their proselytizing and singing on ships did not help in keeping their plan discreet. Many of the revolutionaries were captured as soon as they landed in India.[84] Others who evaded arrest went to their ancestral villages. There was no central authority guiding the movement, with each individual or small group deciding its own fate.

Having been fed the propaganda that India was ripe for revolution, the revolutionaries were disappointed when they reached their villages. Not only were most of the Punjabi villagers apathetic to their cause, many were overtly hostile to their agenda.[85] With lucrative employment in the army and the improvement of economic conditions thanks to advanced agricultural technologies and connection with the global market, many Punjabis, especially in the rural areas, remained strongly pro-Empire.

A semblance of direction was provided to the movement, now being called the Ghadar Mutiny by the British, when, in January 1915, Rash Behari Bose, a radical Bengali nationalist who had earlier masterminded the assassination attempt on Lord Hardinge, the British viceroy, took over the movement's leadership in India.[86]

Ghadari revolutionaries, who in the meantime had been making contact with Indians within the army and the police to revolt, assured Bose that army units in Lahore, Ferozepur, Meerut, Agra, Benares and Lucknow were ready to defect. On the template of the revolt of 1857, a revolt was planned for 21 February 1915. However the British, through their spies, had already learnt of the plan. Special tribunals were arranged in Lahore, Benares, Mandalay and Singapore. The Lahore Conspiracy Case trial was held in Lahore which resulted in the hanging of forty-six people and life imprisonment of 194.[87] This eventually came to be known as the First Lahore Conspiracy Case after a Second Lahore Conspiracy Case trial was held in 1931 which resulted in the deaths of Bhagat Singh and his comrades.

Inspired by the movement, Rehmat Ali had landed on the shores of India from Manila, where he had migrated to work. Upon observing the disorientation within the ranks, he decided to return to his ancestral village where he, along with other comrades, began working on his own. They established contact with Indian soldiers within the army and police to try to woo them over to their side.

After one such meeting in Ferozepur district, Rehmat Ali and twenty other people were travelling in a tonga when they were stopped by an Indian police inspector. Two of his comrades had pistols, which became a source of argument between the inspector and the party. They tried convincing the police inspector to join their nationalist cause but he was adamant. The resulting scuffle led to one of the constables slapping Rehmat Ali, resulting in a full-blown fight. The constable and the inspector were shot dead as Rehmat Ali and his party escaped the scene. However, not long after, all of them were caught. Their case was heard in the Ferozepur sessions court where they were ordered to be hanged. Twelve of them were sent to Lahore Camp while Rehmat Ali, along with the rest, was transferred to Montgomery Camp where he was executed on 25 March 1915.[88] All of them became martyrs of the Ghadar Movement.

While the Ghadar Movement failed to achieve its purpose, its ripples were felt across the political landscape of India. The valour and sacrifice of these young men, romanticizing martyrdom, willing to give up their lives for the nationalist cause, became a source of inspiration for future revolutionaries. Bhagat Singh, for example, held one of these young revolutionaries, a nineteen-year-old boy who was hanged in the First Lahore Conspiracy Case, Kartar Singh Sarabha, in high esteem. Bhagat Singh always kept Sarabha's picture in his front pocket, while a portrait of him was garlanded and placed on a dais during the Naujawan Bharat Sabha's meetings.[89]

The failure of the movement also led to a reorientation. Many of its supporters who had watched the movement collapse from abroad, moved to Moscow and aligned the party with the communist agenda, which was not the case in 1915. Eventually, many of these Marxist revolutionaries moved to India and formed the Kirti Kisan Sabha, a Marxist organization based in Punjab that focused on labour and peasant agitations. They formed a crucial alliance with the Naujawan Bharat Sabha under the leadership of Bhagat Singh in 1928.[90]

The blue sky had become tinged with grey as we exited the house. The sound of the azan blared from the neighbouring mosque. The elder brother, after seeing us off, headed in the direction of the mosque. Early Monday morning he would return to his school, where young children would be taught that Pakistan was created due to the unrelenting efforts of the Muslim League. There would be no mention of the anti-colonial movement, no explanation of why the British rule needed to be overthrown— just a justification of why Pakistan was needed to solve the problem of perpetual antagonism between Hindus and Muslims. There would be no mention of Lala Lajpat Rai, Bhagat Singh or Rehmat Ali. Yet another generation of Pakistanis would grow up without ever having heard their names or their connection with the city of Lahore.

5

THE IMPERIAL SYMBOL

There had been scattered news about sepoys of the army upset about the cartridges they had been given for a new rifle. Rumoured to be smeared with pig and cow fat, both Muslim and Hindu soldiers were refusing to use them. While most of the discontent remained far away from Punjab, in the cantonments of Barrackpore, Agra, Allahabad, Ambala and Meerut, there were also a few cases of Punjab-based sepoys refusing to handle the cartridges. John Lawrence, the chief commissioner of Punjab and the ultimate authority in the province, did not give much credence to these rumours.

John Lawrence had replaced his brother Henry, who had earned much respect in Punjab, particularly with the Sikh aristocrats who always had his sympathy, especially in the aftermath of the annexation of Punjab in 1849. John, on the other hand, ruled the province with an iron grip. Much of the groundwork had already been done prior to his appointment.

Before the formal annexation of the province, while Henry Lawrence served as the resident of the East India Company in

Lahore between the two Anglo-Sikh Wars of 1846 and 1849, he had already established himself as a de facto ruler of the province, the last major empire left in India to be gulped down by the Company. Young British officers, officially known as 'assistant to the resident', had spread out all over the province, which included Peshawar at that time, and taken up key administrative roles sidelining the governors appointed by the Lahore Durbar being run in the name of the child king Duleep Singh, the youngest surviving son of the legendary Maharaja Ranjit Singh.

These assistants to the resident, who came to be known as 'Lawrence's men', included some of the most extraordinary officers of the time, including James Abbott and John Nicholson, who not only ensured the establishment of the Company's writ over Punjab, but also made Punjab its symbolic fort. Many of these men were still in place when John took up the newly created post in 1853.

It had also helped that John had been one of the three members of the board that had governed Punjab from 1849 to 1853. The board was presided over by Henry, who had been assigned the duty of raising new regiments, disarming the population and improving relations between the Company and the deposed but still-powerful members of the abolished Durbar; John had been assigned revenue and finance. A third member, Charles Mansel, was responsible for police and justice.[1] He was soon replaced by Robert Montgomery who, under John, emerged as the second most powerful man in the province.

The board in fact had been created after the annexation of Punjab by Governor General Lord Dalhousie, to weaken Henry and empower his younger brother, John. Henry had been close to Dalhousie's predecessor, Hardinge. The resident of Punjab had expressed his reservations about the annexation and had exhibited sympathy to the ruling elite of the Durbar, exhorting the governor general to maintain some of their privileges in exchange for their loyalty to the Company. Dalhousie was an expansionist. He also saw himself as a modernizer of India, which had no room for landed gentry. His view of the aristocrats was shared by John, who too thought of them as parasites and believed that their era was about to end.

Upon the annexation of Punjab, it was widely believed that Henry would run the province, given his track record; however his political differences with Dalhousie became an impediment and led to the creation of the board.

In his years on the board, John took some popular steps that earned him much fame in the province. Land tax was reduced by half and even more in some places. Transit and town duties that had been introduced during the reign of the Durbar were abolished.[2] Despite these reductions, the inflow of revenue increased because improved security and the bureaucratic outreach of the colonial state meant that revenue from several regions like Multan, far away from the political capital, began reaching the Lahore treasury regularly. Instead of crop, tax was now collected in the form of money. The British were laying down the perfect bureaucratic machine, setting up a vertical pyramid, with Lahore at its apex. While Lahore was politically significant even prior to the British, under the colonial state, due to better tax collection and infrastructure that connected it with other parts of the province, it was to emerge as the undisputed centre.

In a city that is increasingly vying for space, extending in all directions, ghettoizing historic villages and towns as it takes over their agricultural land, Governor House located on Mall Road, spread over 90 acres, is a rarity.[3] Its white boundary wall, interspersed with bastions, manned by armed guards and security cameras, forms a circumference of several kilometres. Guarded by about a dozen policemen standing behind a picket, the main gate of the house faces Mall Road.

The site of Governor House once contained an abandoned kiln and the tomb of Muhammad Kasim Khan, a cousin of Emperor Akbar. It was appropriated by Jamadar Khushal Singh, the chamberlain of Maharaja Ranjit Singh, and used as the site of a house.[4] The house was taken over by the British, destroyed and reconstructed in its latest incarnation. A white bungalow in the middle of a sprawling garden with all kinds of trees from India and beyond, this house was initially used by Deputy Commissioner Major MacGregor. In 1859, it was converted into Governor House for the residence of Robert Montgomery upon his appointment as the lieutenant governor of Punjab after John Lawrence left for Britain. Home to the lieutenant governor, it became the seat of power of the colonial state in the province.

Facing Governor House is Lawrence Garden. At the centre of this garden are two colonial structures, now serving as the Quaid-i-Azam library. The Montgomery and Lawrence halls were constructed in the latter half of the nineteenth century to serve as a focal point for social gatherings of the British establishment in the city. They also served as the Lahore Gymkhana before it was eventually moved to its present location a few kilometres away, in 1972, while these halls were converted into a public library.[5]

Though its official name is Bagh-i-Jinnah, the park is still popularly referred to as Lawrence Garden, named after John Lawrence. One of the most popular gardens in Lahore, it was the first public park in the city open to its residents. In a distinct departure from the Mughal garden tradition, with its focus on symmetry and fountains and the garden serving as a symbolic representation of heaven on earth, Lawrence Garden was designed to be a horticultural experiment.[6] The plants that were grown here were also sold. After the establishment of Government College and Punjab University, and the introduction of botany as an academic course, this garden also became a botanical garden. In

1912, a part of the garden was taken over by Government College for academic purposes.

At a little distance, next to Lahore High Court, was a statue of John Lawrence holding a sword in one hand and a pen in the other. Inaugurated in 1887, the base of the statue read, 'Will you be governed by the pen or sword?' It was removed in the 1920s at the peak of the nationalist movement.

The early colonial administrators of Punjab, as in other parts of the country, sincerely believed in the benevolent nature of their government. They were convinced that it was their duty, as more 'civilized' and 'developed' people, to 'modernize' India, for which it was essential to rid it of its evils. For John Lawrence, one of the biggest impediments to India's progress was feudalism. Already disempowered after the annexation of the province, the former aristocrats, members of the Durbar and the feudal lords continued to suffer when John took over the reins of the province in 1853 after his brother resigned upon developing differences with him, resulting in the dissolution of the board.

Within six months of the annexation, jagirs worth Rs 12,57,000 were confiscated by the state, while only Rs 58,300 was paid in compensation. While land belonging to the 'rebel' chiefs who did not side with the British during the Second Anglo-Sikh War was immediately seized, even those who supported the British did not fare much better. Their incomes were reduced and assured only during their lifetimes, not to be automatically passed on to their descendants. In addition, they were stripped of administrative and magisterial authority.[7] The aim was to strengthen the peasants, the direct tax payers.

With improved security, an increased amount of land had been brought under cultivation. Even at the peak of Maharaja Ranjit Singh's rule, the rural areas were frequently subjected to bandit raids. The situation improved drastically with the arrival of the British. The Muslims particularly felt a sense of relief, since under the Lahore Durbar, some religious practices, for example, the calling of the azan from minarets, had been banned. The colonial state projected itself as a neutral protector of all religions.

The province was divided into six divisions, each headed by a British commissioner. These were further divided into districts, each governed by a deputy commissioner. Most of the British officers came from the military.[8] A few consecutive years of good agricultural produce immediately after annexation heightened prosperity in the province.

John Lawrence, the man who was certain he had brought law and order to a wild society, had every reason to believe that Punjab had agreed to be governed by the pen. And so, without giving much thought to rumours of unrest, he left along with his family for the hill station of Murree in early May of 1857. He handed over the reins in Lahore to his trusted aide Robert Montgomery, who was appointed the judicial commissioner after the disbanding of the board. However a telegram received in Rawalpindi on 12 May jolted him out of his complacency.

It is a small structure in the middle of an open courtyard. There is a wide mosque on one side of the shrine and a few trees on the other. On a warm afternoon, several devotees laze around on the cool marble under the shade of the trees. At the centre of the shrine is the grave of Mian Mir, a sixteenth-century Sufi saint, who rose to prominence after Dara Shikoh, the Mughal crown prince, became his follower. The support of the prince made it one of the most popular Sufi shrines in the city.

There is a vast residential settlement behind the shrine which gets its name from the occupant of the tomb. Bordering this settlement on one side is the Mian Mir Cantonment. Manned by an army check post, the cantonment was established in 1852 after the annexation of Punjab. At a distance of about 7 kilometres from the walled city, the cantonment was deliberately established away from the city to avoid the intermingling of soldiers with civilians. Today, as the city expands, it has engulfed the cantonment and a large section within it has been converted into a residential area, open to civilians.

On the morning of 13 May 1857, the 'native' regiments at Mian Mir Cantonment stood in formation. 'Pile arms!' they were ordered. The soldiers were confused. Their hesitation quickly changed to alarm as a long line of artillery composed of British soldiers appeared before them, with ramrods in their hands.[9] One by one, all weapons were laid down in a pile.

Robert Montgomery oversaw the proceedings. He could not afford to take any chances. The day before, a telegram had found its way to Montgomery's table. Indian sepoys who had rebelled against their British officers and gathered in Delhi were burning down houses and killing Britishers in the city. The same telegram also reached Lawrence in Rawalpindi.

The telegraph line between Lahore and Rawalpindi was down. Montgomery was still in the process of consultation with his fellow officers when Richard Lawrence, younger brother of the chief commissioner and commander of military police, was informed by a Brahmin clerk that the native regiments stationed in Mian Mir Cantonment were on the verge of revolt.[10] The information was enough for Montgomery to make up his mind. Some reservations were expressed by British officers posted at the cantonment, but Montgomery was adamant.

Discretion was required lest the sepoys became aware of the imminent disarmament and acted pre-emptively. The fall of Lahore, after Delhi, would have been a huge victory for the 'rebels'. A scheduled ball was organized as planned to give the impression that everything was normal. In the morning the sepoys were caught off guard by the order to surrender their weapons. The plan had worked.

Immediately after, Lawrence from Rawalpindi and Montgomery from Lahore sent telegrams and messages to all British officers to transfer the contents of their treasuries to the nearest military station, escorted by the Punjab police. They were instructed to distrust 'Hindustani' guards and were ordered to read all sepoys' letters.[11]

Sitting in Rawalpindi, a journey of four days from the provincial capital at the time, John Lawrence was aware of the significance Delhi held for the rebels. He understood that the Mughal king, even though a figurehead, had the potential to bring together diverse groups. Similarly, he also understood the importance of Lahore and Punjab. Less than a decade ago, the British had fought some of the most ferocious battles they had ever engaged in, with the Sikhs in Punjab. The capture of Lahore by Punjabi sepoys could have reignited a flame of revenge within the members of the Lahore Durbar, recently disempowered and stripped of their financial resources. With the fall of Punjab, Lawrence understood, it would be impossible to salvage the Empire in India.

The 'rebels' too understood the importance of winning over Punjab. Several letters were written to sepoys in different regiments and to deposed aristocrats and rajas of independent kingdoms by Bahadur Shah Zafar, Nana Sahib and Azeemullah Khan, who had emerged as the prominent leaders of the rebellion. Montgomery reported that the Muslims of Patna were in correspondence with a regiment in Peshawar, urging them to revolt. The Mughal king sent several messages to the raja of Patiala in vain, asking him to join their cause. When the raja failed to respond, he wrote directly to his subjects. All these letters were intercepted by the raja.[12]

There were some crucial successes in the province to the chagrin of the chief commissioner. An infantry regiment stationed at Ferozepur rebelled and joined the 'mutineers' in Delhi. Three native regiments in Jalandhar rebelled and headed to Delhi. There were further acts of defiance in Sialkot, Jhelum and Rawalpindi.

The most potent opposition came from a place south of Lahore, led by Ahmad Khan Kharal. It seemed as if emissaries from Delhi had reached him, inspiring him to bring together other chiefs and initiate a rebellion. An extra assistant commissioner was killed. The towns of Jhamra, Harappa and Kamalia were 'burnt' and 'plundered', claimed British sources.[13] British troops led by Major Chamberlain marched in from Multan but were besieged at Chichawatni. It was not until reinforcements arrived from Lahore, followed by Multan, Jhang and Gurdaspur, that the tide began to turn in favour of the British. Kharal was killed along with his sons, but the rebellion continued, led in turn by other prominent chiefs. It was finally quelled in November, six months after it had begun.

The chiefs who had supported the British in Punjab during the revolt were rewarded with vast tracts of lands and honours, even as the memories of Kharal slowly faded away. Songs of his bravery and sacrifice remained limited to the Sahiwal district, where the rebellion had taken place. There was obviously no official sanctification of his memory. On the other hand, the memory of colonial administrators who had helped put an end to the rebellion of 1857 was enshrined and preserved through the names of roads and institutes. The area where the 'rebellion' broke out was renamed Montgomery, after Robert Montgomery. While it made sense for the colonial state to do so, ironically, a lot of these names continue to live on in Lahore, even as Kharal, the leader behind the only major rebellion against the British in 1857 in Punjab, has almost been erased from popular memory.

Only the facade of the building survives. 'Allah-u-Akbar' is written in elegant calligraphy on the top of the building to ensure that no confusion is caused by its name—Laxmi Building. Even as the rest of this pre-Partition edifice crumbled, somehow its beautiful facade survived. Not so long ago the local government realized its historical and architectural significance and decided to renovate it. A pale yellow with a blue border replaced the iconic white paint. The building lends it name to this junction, Laxmi Chowk, one of the most important connectors in the city of Lahore. Even though officially the name of the chowk has been changed, no one seems to remember what it was changed to.

Hand-painted hoardings of movies inhabit the tops of all the buildings around the chowk. Flaring nostrils, the stare of death, a raised finger, oiled moustaches, voluptuous seductresses in shiny kurta-dhotis thrusting their hips. Even as Punjabi cinema, loud, violent, lascivious, lay on its deathbed, struggling for a final breath of air, somehow these repositories of tradition have survived. Laxmi Chowk, from before Partition, when Lahore was a major centre of the film industry along with Bombay and Calcutta, till a few years ago, was the hub of the Pakistani film industry, which is also called Lollywood, its 'L' coming from Lahore.

The abandoned buildings of numerous cinemas, taken over by the land mafia or drug addicts, are some of the last remaining vestiges of that world. Desperately clinging to an era long lost, producers, distributors and others from the industry have still retained their offices at Laxmi Chowk, their walls an archival collection of long-forgotten popular movies that once ran in these cinema halls.

On the ground floors of these buildings are some of the most iconic restaurants of Lahore, dispensing haleem, biryani, payee, nihari, chanay, halwa puri. No other locality in the city offered a wider range of traditional food items before the introduction of Food Street next to Badshahi Masjid. Even today, those looking for authentic Lahori cuisine flock to Laxmi Chowk.

A few years ago, a member of the city's Hindu community told me that the largest gathering for Diwali and Holi in Lahore used to take place at Laxmi Chowk. 'On the occasion of Diwali, Laxmi Building was lit with lamps,' he reminisced. It was Laxmi Chowk that people had in mind when they repeated the famous Lahori proverb, 'If you haven't seen Lahore you haven't been born.'

All the four roads that converge at this junction retain memories of colonial rule. It is here that Abbott Road—named after James Abbott, one of Henry Lawrence's men stationed in the region of Hazara between 1846 and 1849, who effectively 'subdued' the 'wild' population of this region[14]—merges into McLeod Road—'Maclore' in the vernacular, named after Donald McLeod, commissioner for revenue under John Lawrence. Dissecting Abbot Road is Montgomery Road, a reminder of the man responsible for disarming the regiments in Lahore.

McLeod Road, as it heads towards the railway station, gives birth to a short road, only a few kilometres long, named after the most crucial colonial administrator of 1857. It is widely believed that it was John Nicholson's timely support to the British forces in Delhi that allowed them to recapture the city. While the capture of Delhi by the rebels in May inspired sepoys in other parts of India to pour in with their support, its fall in the month of September changed the momentum in favour of the British. Just before the capture of Delhi, John Lawrence is believed to have warned that if Delhi was not retaken by 20 September, he might not be able to maintain peace in Punjab.[15] But Delhi was secured and the man whose role had been pivotal to this was Nicholson.

Nicholson, who had become one of Lawrence's men in 1847, was serving as the deputy commissioner of Bannu when the rebellion broke out. In his long years of service, he had earned quite a reputation for himself as a ruthless tyrant, known for his insolence towards the locals. He had become a legend by the time he died during the battle for Delhi.

Telegraph wires were down between Delhi and Calcutta in the days following the outbreak of the rebellion, with Governor General

Lord Canning, seated in Calcutta, virtually cut off from the rest of the Indian Empire. In the absence of the highest authority, John Lawrence, still in Rawalpindi, assumed an increasingly important role. Even as he sat with his advisers in the early days, discussing ways to secure Punjab, he was also planning to launch an attack on Delhi to take it back from the rebels. With further uprisings in Oudh, the British forces became increasingly occupied, thus leaving the fate of Delhi to John Lawrence's Punjab regiments.

In the days to come, John was to emerge as the de facto leader of the British counter-attack. For all practical purposes, he was to serve as the governor general during the War of 1857.[16] In a meeting in Rawalpindi, presided over by him, it was decided that a movable column would be sent towards Delhi from Punjab which would not only assist the British forces camped outside the city but also put down rebellion in different parts of Punjab. The process of disarming native regiments had already begun in cantonments across the province soon after Montgomery acted pre-emptively in Lahore.

Nicholson, who had by now been promoted to the rank of brigadier, was given the task of commanding this column. Fresh reinforcements were on their way from Britain, but would take some time, while other British regiments were busy fighting 'rebels' in Lucknow and Kanpur. Even before Nicholson reached Delhi with his column, stories of his bravery and brutality reached the ears of the dispirited soldiers stationed outside the city. On their way they had disarmed numerous units and crushed several rebellions.[17] Recruiting as they went along, the column was 4200-strong when it reached Delhi, with a majority of Sikh soldiers.[18] Reinvigorated by the movable column and heavy guns and ammunition from Punjab, the British were finally able to attack Delhi on 14 September, with Nicholson leading one of the four columns that entered the city from different points. He was hit by a bullet during the assault, which claimed his life a few days later.

The entire British establishment understood that it was due to John Lawrence's single-mindedness and quick thinking that Delhi was back in the British fold. Only a decade earlier, the British were on the verge of being defeated in Punjab. Despite ruling the province directly after the Second Anglo-Sikh War, there was a deep sense of fear in some segments of the administration of another ferocious uprising. The War of 1857, however, completely turned the tide for the British in Punjab. After the fall of Delhi, John's Punjab reinforcement went to help British forces regain parts of Oudh and the Rohilla areas.[19] Lord Canning, the governor general, was quick to point out that Punjab was no longer a weakness but a source of strength for the British Empire, thanks to John Lawrence.[20]

In February 1859, Delhi was made one of the districts of Punjab after it was ceded to it. Punjab had emerged as the military backbone of the Empire, a colonial police-state. The position of the chief commissioner was raised to the coveted post of lieutenant governor. Key officers who had managed the turn of events were generously rewarded. Montgomery was appointed the lieutenant governor of the province while John Lawrence returned to England to a hero's welcome. He was to come back a few years later, in 1864, as the viceroy of India.

The golden dome of the smadh of Guru Arjan looks pale in comparison to the regal white smadh of Maharaja Ranjit Singh. Protected by a boundary wall, both these structures are in a compound facing Lahore Fort. This area is strictly off limits for Muslim tourists. Only Sikhs and tourists from other parts of the world are welcome.

In the seventeenth century, the river used to flow right at the base of this fort located on top of a mound. It was to this river that Guru Arjan Singh had decided to give his life, instead of his executioner. In his diary, Emperor Jahangir claimed that he had got Guru Arjan, leader of the growing Sikh community, assassinated for his alleged support to the rebel prince Khusrau who was leading a rebellion against his father. About seventy years later, on the orders of Emperor Aurangzeb, grandson of Emperor Jahangir, Guru Tegh Bahadur, grandson of Guru Arjan, was executed in Delhi.

These two events symbolize the tumultuous relationship between the Sikh Gurus and the Mughals. Many battles were fought between these two unequal parties in the years between these two Gurus and after. In Sikh iconography, Mughal authorities became a symbol of atrocity, bent upon curbing the message of the Gurus.

John Lawrence and other colonial officers, caught unexpectedly in the whirlpool of 1857, were aware of these historic events and their sentimental impact on the Sikh community. Desperate to cling on to Punjab and use its forces to 'rescue' Delhi, they were willing to exploit this historic animosity.

Thousands of Sikh soldiers were recruited from Punjab to fight on behalf of the colonial state with the promise of avenging the honour of their Gurus by attacking the Mughal capital and its king, Bahadur Shah Zafar. Deliberately, a prophecy was spread throughout the Sikh community in Punjab that the time had come for the Sikhs to attack Delhi and avenge the insult with the help of the white man.[21] They were given a free rein by British officers after the conquest of the city. With the intention of ingratiating himself to the Sikh soldiers, Captain Hodson, a British officer responsible for the arrest of Bahadur Shah Zafar and other Mughal princes, shot and killed two Mughal princes after he had assured them of safety.[22] He then ordered their bodies to be taken to Delhi and placed at the same spot in Chandni Chowk where, in 1675, on the orders of Aurangzeb, the decapitated head of Guru Tegh Bahadur had been placed. Henceforth, he came to be regarded by the Sikh soldiers as an 'avenger of the martyred Guru'.[23]

In many ways, the War of 1857 laid the foundation of the British policy of 'divide and rule'. John Lawrence's model for the Punjab regiment was to serve as the basis for new recruitment policies across the Empire in India. His experience with the Sikh soldiers highlighted how historical, religious, cultural, social and geographical biases could be accentuated between India's diverse communities to play them against each other for the benefit of the Empire. The Sikh–Mughal conflict was hyped up in 1857 to rile Sikh soldiers against a 'Mughal-led' rebellion. Similarly, prejudices between Punjabis and 'Hindustanis' of eastern India were played up so as to reinforce the differences between these communities.[24]

The first sign of these policies manifested in the army recruitment procedures following 1857. While the earlier recruitment was from one particular group from one region, immediately after 1857, the need for recruiting diverse groups within a regiment was felt so that a sense of kinship between individuals was more difficult to establish.[25]

However, in the 1880s, a new theory for recruitment was taking root, one that continues to cast its shadow upon military recruitment in India and Pakistan. This was the myth of the 'martial races'. Charles Darwin's *On the Origin of Species* was published in 1859, and captured the imagination of British society. The pseudo-science of eugenics came into being, premised upon a hierarchal classification of human races with the Europeans on top. In Indian society, those who looked more European—fair-skinned with sharp noses—were higher on this scale than those who were darker complexioned with flatter noses.[26] This concept was further reinforced by the Indo-European languages spoken in the north-western part of India, much of which is part of Pakistan today. These communities were believed to be superior to the Dravidian-speaking people of southern India.[27]

It was believed that due to their superior racial nature, the martial races understood concepts of honour and duty better than other races. This was seemingly borne out by their loyalty to the British during the War of 1857, while the high-caste Brahmins who had been part of the British army and had rebelled in 1857 had done so because of their 'devious' and 'treacherous' mentality.[28] Punjabis, by virtue of being categorized as a martial race, composed more than half the British Indian army by the end of the nineteenth century,[29] whereas in 1857, their numbers had been negligible.

It is due to this disproportionate representation of Punjabis that Pakistan inherited one-third of the British Indian army in 1947, thus sowing the seeds of a civil–military imbalance right at its inception.[30] Punjab still constitutes the largest recruiting ground for the army in Pakistan, with the organization covertly continuing to believe in the myth of the martial races inherited from the colonial masters. This overwhelming representation in the army, and a sense of racial superiority, is the primary reason why other provinces resent Punjab.

With the institutionalization of the concept of martial races, the policy of intermingling soldiers from various areas within a regiment eventually gave way to 'class company', which meant a company was composed of ethnically homogenous groups.[31] The martial races were encouraged to retain their religious, cultural and ethnic purity.[32] These attitudes were internalized by these ethnic groups, who started viewing themselves through the lens of their colonial masters.

The policy of dividing people along religious, ethnic and caste lines was further institutionalized by the introduction of separate religious electorates as well as through census reports, which categorized people into different ethnic groups. The colonial education system promoted a communal interpretation of history that exploited historic grievances. It is these 'historical injustices' that were 'avenged' during the riots of Partition and continue to be evoked during incidents of communal violence in both India and Pakistan.

The fundamental shift that the British colonial state underwent after the War of 1857 was of power being transferred from the East India Company to the British government, thus making India a direct colony of Britain.

There was another paradigm shift, once again initiated by John Lawrence, and later adopted by the colonial state, to continue on to the political life of contemporary Pakistan.

The condition of the haveli bears testimony to its lost glory. It used to be a three-storey structure with a basement, but all the rooms have been lost. Only the ruins of the haveli survive, with the courtyard occupied by a handful of buffaloes. When I visited the village of Padhana in 2010 to see the condition of the haveli of the legendary Jawala Singh, the family was living in an adjacent compound. It was still a comfortable dwelling, but a far cry from the multi-million-rupee jagir the family once owned under Sardar Mith Singh in the early years of the nineteenth century. Sardar Mith Singh had joined Maharaja Ranjit Singh's camp and helped him with the occupation of Lahore in 1799, and later during expeditions to Kasur and Kashmir, among others. He accrued great wealth during his time with the maharaja.[33]

He was succeeded by his son, Sardar Jawala Singh, who, like his father, distinguished himself in Ranjit Singh's army, particularly in the campaigns of Malwa, Multan and Mankera. His bravery and loyalty to the maharaja led to an increase in his estate. He was married to the elder sister of Maharani Jind Kaur, the Maharaja's youngest wife.[34] The haveli I was visiting had been constructed by him.

Located on the outskirts of Lahore, the village of Padhana skirts the international boundary between India and Pakistan.

Standing at the entrance to the village, I could see Nowshera Dhala across the fields in Indian territory. Farmers worked in their fields in the middle of the two countries. A little boy sat on a milestone that marked the international border, and which looked out of place in this lush green landscape. The fence meant to protect cross-border activity is deeper within the Indian side. The boy sat mockingly on the milestone in no-man's land. It was hard to tell if he was Indian or Pakistani.

In the middle of the village rose a whitewashed gurdwara with multiple domes. From behind these domes the long pole of Nishan Sahib bore witness to the presence of a Sikh community. There was a gurdwara behind me as well, in the village of Padhana, in complete contrast to the gurdwara in front. It was a triple-storey building with a single white dome at the top, blackened from weathering. There was a boundary wall around the gurdwara, its gate locked. There was no Nishan Sahib within the premises but behind it was a black pole with a palm on top, signifying the presence of the Shia community.

The gurdwara was constructed in the seventeenth century to commemorate the visit of the sixth Sikh Guru, the warrior saint, Guru Hargobind. It was initially a modest structure but was later renovated by the Sikh rulers of Padhana, the family of Jawala Singh. The gurdwara was taken over by refugees from the other side of the border following Partition. Not far from the gurdwara is the smadh of Jawala Singh, who died in 1835. This too was taken over by refugees.

I sat in the guest room of the family with Sardar Amanullah Khan sitting across from me. He was a tall, bulky man in his eighties, sitting on a chair, clutching his walking stick with both hands. He had a long, white beard and a trimmed moustache. This is what distinguishes the style of the Sikh beard from the Muslim one. While Sikhs allow their moustache to grow along with their beard, Muslims tend to keep their moustache trimmed even when they let their beard grow long. There was a skullcap on his head. His grandson, a young boy of about twelve, sat on the sofa next to me, playing with my camera.

'My father, Sardar Harcharan Singh, converted to Islam a few years before Partition,' said Sardar Amanullah Khan. 'He changed his name to Nasarullah Khan, while I became Amanullah Khan. My Sikh name was Hardhayan Singh.' I wanted to confront him, ask him if his father had converted to Islam at the time of Partition to retain his ancestral property.

'Did he convert at the time of Partition?' I asked him, pretending to have missed his last comment.

'No,' he said firmly. 'He converted a couple of years before Partition. My father's other brothers did not and left for India. I still have Sikh cousins there, all of whom rose to prominent positions. One of them, Sardar Gurdial Singh, even became a lieutenant general in the Indian Army. I am still in touch with some of my family members in India.'

While Henry Lawrence was sympathetic to the aristocracy after the annexation of Punjab by the British in 1849, his brother John was particularly resentful of them. Numerous former aristocrats were stripped of their lands during his tenure. John earnestly believed that he was empowering the ordinary people by removing the landlords, which would result in people realizing the benevolence of the colonial state. He hoped this would eventually make the people staunch supporters of the Empire, as opposed to supporting their former rulers who he believed did nothing but live off the toil of the ordinary folk.

This was an attitude shared by many other colonial administrators such as Governor General Lord Dalhousie. This illusion was soon shattered by the events of 1857. The colonial state realized that by disempowering landed aristocrats, they had made powerful enemies who still commanded respect amongst the common people. The colonial state quickly calculated that it could strengthen its control over India if it won former aristocrats over to its side. Immediately after the recapture of Delhi, John Lawrence's strategy of recruiting the Sikh gentry against the 'rebel' soldiers became the blueprint of colonial state policy, followed rigorously right up to Partition.

In the early days of the rebellion in 1857, heeding the advice of his Sikh aide, Nihal Singh Chachi, John Lawrence wrote directly to several Sikh chiefs urging them to join hands with the British to redeem their situation.[35] The sardars were asked to raise horsemen and fight for the British, and in return the state promised to return their lands. The Sikh sardars responded favourably, eager to improve their economic and political condition. Even those landlords who had fought against the British in 1849 were now fighting on their side.

The policy of pampering the local aristocracy became an important feature of the colonial state after 1857. Montgomery, after becoming the lieutenant governor of Punjab, described the aristocracy as 'a great bulwark for the state'.[36] Besides reinstating their estates, there was a realization that the aristocrats should be given respect. While earlier, junior colonial officers were dismissive of them, in the years following 1857 they treated aristocrats with 'consideration and courtesy'.[37] They were included in the local administration and given magistrate powers with judicial control over people of a defined jurisdiction.[38] Furthermore, they were given titles such Rai, Rai Bahadur, Sardar, Sardar Bahadur and Khan Bahadur.[39] Oftentimes there was much competition amongst the nobles for these honorary titles.

The history of the Padhana chiefs in this context is no different from many of the Sikh aristocrats during the time of Maharaja Ranjit Singh. Their property and wealth too declined with the ascendance of the British. Sardar Hardit Singh, who became the head of the family in 1849, lost large portions of his jagir.[40] The situation began to improve following the change in British

Chauburji seen beyond pillars being constructed for the Orange Line metro track

This structure is believed to be the tomb of Zeb-un-Nissa

The remains of Jain Mandir next to Chauburji

Entrance to the enclosure where Habib Jalib is buried

Ahmadiyya Buildings now rechristened Muhammadiyya Buildings. The old name is visible on the side.

Bradlaugh Hall

Protest at Bhagat Singh Chowk on 23 March 2011

Rehmat Ali's grandchildren holding his photograph

The smadh of Ganga Ram

Entrance to the haveli of
Jawala Singh at Padhana

The grave of Bamba Sutherland
at the Gora Qabristan

The smadh of Jawahir Singh

The smadh of Ranjit Singh, with the minaret of Badshahi Masjid in the background

The mausoleum of Mian Mir

The mausoleum of Nadira Begum next to the shrine of Mian Mir

The mausoleum of Empress Nur Jahan

The mausoleum of Asaf Khan

The grave of
Shah Hussain next
to that of his beloved
Madho Lal

The grave of
Dulla Bhatti
at Miani Sahib

The mausoleum of
Qutb al-Din Aibak

The tomb of Malik Ayaz at
Shahalami Bazaar

Azad Chowdry and his son, Yashwa, at the Valmiki Neela Gumbad Mandir

policy after 1857. Sardar Hardit Singh's grandson, Sardar Atma Singh, who became the head of the family in 1868, was made an honorary magistrate with jurisdiction over fifty-two villages. He was also given the title 'Sardar'.[41] His son, Sardar Bahadur Sardar Jiwan Singh, who became the head of the family in 1897, was a civil judge and honorary magistrate with jurisdiction over the entire district of Lahore. He was awarded the title 'Sardar Bahadur' in 1915.[42] His son, Sardar Sardul Singh, became the head of the family in 1933 and was also an honorary magistrate.[43]

For the Muslim chiefs in Punjab, the situation did not change much following 1947. Many quickly aligned with the new state and retained their jagirs and honorary judicial powers. While the half-hearted land reforms of Zulfikar Ali Bhutto's government in the 1970s stripped a few such landlords of their property, in southern Punjab and Sindh a majority of the families empowered by the British continue to exert political influence. Several joined the Parliament and formed the ruling class. Their influence on the state of Pakistan, whether civilian or military, continues till today.

For example, despite having the lowest GDP to tax ratio in South Asia, the Parliament continues to block any bill to pass agricultural tax, the burden of which would directly fall on the landlords. It is able to do this because many of these landlords are part of the Parliament. Several of them have deep ties with the military establishment as well, with members of their families serving in high-ranking posts. No government following Bhutto's has contemplated land reforms that would reduce the size of landholdings. It remains perhaps one of the biggest ironies of Pakistan that a social class propped up by the colonial state to serve as a buffer between itself and the masses continues to determine the fate of millions of people in the postcolonial nation.

It's a single-storey structure painted yellow, with a white dome on top. It looks more like a Mughal mausoleum than a Hindu smadh. The wide courtyard appears at odds with the encroaching buildings around it. Standing at the entrance, I bring out my phone to take a picture but a security guard jumps off his seat and tells me not to with his finger. He has been appointed by the ETPB, responsible for the maintenance of non-Muslim properties in Pakistan, which has been in charge of this building since the 1980s. The board has removed encroachments and renovated the structure, which has meant filling up an adjacent pool and constructing a courtyard on it, while also replacing the original architecture with a 'modern' version.

On a quiet Sunday morning, Lahore slowly stirs from its sleep and the shops begin to open. Restaurants serving breakfast, however, have been functioning since early morning. The small roads leading up to the smadh of Ganga Ram, which are otherwise congested, look wider without the onslaught of cars and other vehicles. Just off the main Ravi Road that skirts around Iqbal Park, the smadh is located within a dense community, not far from Gol Bagh, where the statue of Lala Lajpat Rai once inspired young revolutionaries.

The story of modern Lahore is the story of Ganga Ram. Lahore would not have been the city it became under colonial rule but for this man. With ingenuity, he transformed the city's physical landscape to reflect the glory of the modern colonial state. Lahore, due to the efforts of Ganga Ram, became an icon of colonial power, its prestige, its magnificence and its 'superiority' to preceding native cultures.

Born to a police officer two years after the annexation of Punjab, Ganga Ram was a graduate of the prestigious Thomason College of Civil Engineering, located in Roorkee. There was no engineering course in Punjab at the time, with the first one starting in Punjab University in Lahore the year Ganga Ram graduated.[44]

Like many aspiring migrants, Ganga Ram turned to Lahore after his education. In the years following the annexation of Punjab, Lahore had emerged as a major economic centre of not only Punjab, but also the entire country.

From 1849 to 1901 its population had grown from an estimated 1,20,000 to 2,00,000,[45] overshadowing neighbouring Amritsar which, till the year 1881, was slightly more populated than Lahore.[46] With the development of the cantonment for the army and Civil Lines for colonial administrators, the city needed human power which came in the form of migrants. The census of 1911 identified that 463 out of every 1000 residents of the city were born outside the district.[47] In the 1920s it was recorded to be the fifth-largest city in British India.[48] In the late nineteenth and early twentieth centuries, the colleges and universities of the city were seen as a gateway to a better life.[49] A degree from any of its prestigious universities or colleges was enough to secure a government job with all its perks.

At the top of this pyramid was Government College, located a little distance from the walled city, in Civil Lines, at the junction of Upper Mall and Lower Mall. A minaret with a small clock at the top is visible from afar. The building points towards the sky, the ultimate expression of neo-Gothic architecture in British India. Moved to its current location in 1877, and affiliated with the neighbouring Punjab University, Government College became Lahore's premier liberal arts institution in British India and after.[50] Amongst its alumni are two Nobel laureates, Abdus Salam and Har Gobind Khorana, poets Allama Iqbal and Faiz Ahmed Faiz, politicians Muhammad Zafarullah Khan, Nawaz Sharif and Yousuf Raza Gillani, writers Prakash Tandon, Bano Qudsia and Khushwant Singh, and the famous Indian film star Dev Anand.

Within walking distance of Government College, located on Mall Road, is Punjab University. Founded in 1869, it offered a number of degrees in not only Indian languages and literature but also English, modern science and humanities.[51] It was regarded as a university where 'oriental' knowledge interacted with 'English' education. Even its architecture reflected an amalgamation of these two worlds. With its balconies, domes, columns and a watch tower, the building is a perfect specimen of Indo-Saracenic architecture.

A distinct form that developed in British India in the late eighteenth and early nineteenth centuries, the Indo-Saracenic architectural tradition sought to combine the British Gothic tradition with Mughal and traditional Hindu architectural techniques. It grew from the realization that the colonial state needed to express its authority in India through traditional Indian symbols.[52] Exploring the colonial architecture in Lahore, one can see the evolution of this thought. The earliest colonial structures in Lahore—the Lawrence and Montgomery halls— were constructed in neo-colonial traditions and almost appear as an anomaly in the landscape of the city. A transition can be noted in later constructions that began adapting traditional architectural techniques to colonial sensibilities.

Aitchison College, originally called Punjab Chiefs' College, is one of the earliest examples of Indo-Saracenic architecture in Lahore. Constructed in the late nineteenth century, it includes features such as pre-Mughal *chattri*s, shallow-relief patterns in the brickwork taken from the Mughals, interwoven arches and screens incorporated from Umayyad Spain and a clock on a tower rising from the centre of the building.[53]

Around the same time, the Punjab Chief Court was designed, later known as Lahore High Court. The building too adopted influences from diverse architectural traditions, much like the laws upheld by the court, which were an amalgamation of British and local traditions.[54] Part of a similar tradition were the buildings of the post office, Lahore Museum and Mayo School of Industrial Arts that eventually came to be known as National College of Arts. Lahore was being transformed by the colonial state, modelled into a symbol of ascendant British authority. They wanted to leave a mark on this ancient city which had once been the seat of Mughal power, so it would bear the mark of the strength of the colonial state that had raised a new city, a better city, out of the ashes of its lost glory.

Ganga Ram was one of a handful of Indians who were able to help the colonial state create this narrative through architecture. When he arrived in Lahore, he was offered the position of assistant engineer, which led him to oversee the construction of some of these iconic buildings, including the high court, the Anglican Cathedral and Aitchison College.[55] Due to a lack of trained architects, engineers like Ganga Ram were also expected to help design the building.

After the completion of Aitchison College, he was promoted to the post of Lahore's executive engineer, a position he retained till his retirement. During his tenure, he oversaw the construction of some of Lahore's most iconic structures, including the museum, Mayo School of Arts, the post office, the Albert Victor Wing of Lahore's Mayo Hospital and the Government College Chemical Laboratory.[56] His time in government service earned him considerable wealth.

He set up the Ganga Ram Trust that oversaw the construction of a hospital in the city in his name with a medical college next to it. The trust also established girls' high schools and a Hindu widows' home and school.[57] Ganga Ram Hospital, just behind Lawrence Garden, still functions under its original name. It is one of the signifiers that continues to remind the city that there was a past to Lahore that was different from what is envisioned and desired today. For his services to the colonial state and his charitable work, Ganga Ram was awarded the title 'Rai Bahadur' and knighted by the order of the British Crown in 1922.[58]

Like an anomaly, a statue of Queen Victoria sits in the middle of the Islamic gallery in Lahore Museum. Guns, swords and shields are displayed on walls behind glass enclosures around her. The statue doesn't belong here; rather, it would seem out of place anywhere in the museum. It is a forced inclusion, the result of a lack of options, a commitment to the preservation of 'our history', a history that we would rather preserve in museums than on the streets of Lahore.

A few kilometres from here, at a point on Mall Road that is still popularly referred to as 'Charing Cross' even though officially its name has been changed to Faisal Chowk, under a marble pavilion with a small dome reminiscent of Mughal architecture, is a sculpture of the Quran. The colonnaded Punjab Parliament stands behind it. It was under this pavilion that the bronze statue of Queen Victoria was once placed. With the changing sensibilities of the city, in a culture of increasing Islamization in which the art of sculpture is looked down upon, the statue was removed in 1951, and replaced by a sculpture of the Quran during the Zia years.

The image of a British regent sitting under a Mughal-style marble dome was meant to symbolize a continuation of the imperial history of India, with Queen Victoria meant to be portrayed as a successor of the Indian royals. The technique was aligned with the colonial state's strategy of using local architectural traditions to depict British symbols of power.

The pavilion was designed by another prodigal son of Lahore, whose imprint on the city, much like his contemporary Ganga Ram, continues to survive in a Lahore that is eager to forget its past. There was no doubt that for Bhai Ram Singh, designer of this pavilion, Queen Victoria held a special place. During his long and prestigious career as an architect, arguably, the highlight was a commission which came from the Queen herself, to design and fabricate, in 'Indian' style, the banquet at the Osborn House on the Isle of Wight, her palatial holiday home.[59] In 1891, Bhai Ram Singh was sent to England to oversee the construction of the 'Durbar' room. Throughout his life he enjoyed the patronage of the queen and the prince regent.

Born in Rasulpur, a village in district Gurdaspur, Bhai Ram Singh studied carpentry at the Mission School in Amritsar. He became a student of Mayo School of Arts in Lahore, a college set up by John Lockwood Kipling, who also served as the first principal of the college, to promote 'indigenous' art traditions. John Lockwood was the father of the famous writer Rudyard Kipling. After his graduation, Bhai Ram Singh started working at Mayo School of Arts and, along with his mentor, Kipling, designed several structures around the city including Lahore Museum and Aitchison College.[60]

In 1909, he became the first Indian principal of the college.[61] On many projects Bhai Ram Singh and Ganga Ram had the opportunity to work together. Perhaps their most important collaboration was the design and construction of DAV College, which today serves as the Islamia College.[62] The purposeful use of Hindu motifs in the design of the building reflected the revival of Vedic philosophy followed by the Arya Samaj, the patron of the college.

Together, Ganga Ram and Bhai Ram Singh represent the transition of Lahore into a colonial metropolis that became an ultimate symbol of British 'modernity'. In many ways, Lahore today is a descendant of the colonial city. The institutions and infrastructure laid down by the British still function and shape the city's political and social milieu. It is still regarded as the educational capital of the country. The colleges and universities established during the British era are still regarded as the premier institutes of the country. Along with them, the city is now home to hundreds of new private colleges and schools that have sprung up in recent years following the privatization of education.

Migration has only increased after the creation of Pakistan. Lahore still serves as a major economic hub, with numerous industries functioning on its outskirts. Given the political uncertainty in Karachi, Lahore has in recent years emerged as the prime choice for several investors.

Much like how the colonial state used architecture and the development of infrastructure in the city as a tool to construct a certain narrative about its benevolence, the 'development' of Lahore and its infrastructure continues to be used as a political statement. It boasts of the best roads and public transport system in the country. While law and order remain a perennial concern in the administration of Karachi, Lahore, despite its massive size, seems to be in a much better situation, apart from petty crime. Lahore is a model city, used by the state and competing political claimants to express their ambitions.

The British completely transformed Lahore by imposing their definitions of modernity, progress and development on the people of the city. But in the 100 years of British rule over Punjab, not only was the British framework accepted, it was also internalized by the local populace in such a manner that it paved the way for the death of existing pre-British institutions, some of which had evolved over centuries. The 'development' of Lahore had a price: the destruction of indigenous institutions and traditions—a price that the city continues to pay.

The turret of a Hindu temple rises unexpectedly from somewhere amidst the shops. A black corrosive powder has settled over the structure. The turret is the last remaining evidence of the temple. The rest of the building has been transformed into a government school while other parts of the property have been taken over by shopkeepers. The turret remains visible as one drives around the circular market in D-Block in Model Town.

It is among the best preserved of the temples that were once constructed in Model Town—a planned residential scheme in Lahore. The man responsible for its construction outside the walled city of Lahore, the first of its kind not just in Lahore but also in all of British India, was Diwan Khem Chand, a barrister who had studied law in England. There, he had come across the ideas of Ebenezer Howard, founder of the garden city movement, which aimed to combine open gardens within residential schemes and to have a decentralized civic society with industries, shops, professional services, schools and other facilities. In his book, Howard included diagrams of the garden city with a circular geometry, and a community garden at the centre. Additionally, there was a park at the centre of each block which would have buildings of public use. Established in 1921, Model Town was based on the plan published in Howard's book, with gurdwaras, mosques, schools, temples and churches constructed alternately at the centre of each block.[63]

While schools, mosques and some churches have survived, the temples and gurdwaras have been transformed, with traces of their original structures slowly removed. In B-Block, for example, I unexpectedly came across a Sikh gurdwara, a single-storey building, without any dome or mark of religious identification, standing in the middle of the park where children play cricket. The gurdwara had been converted into a residence. Only the older members of the residential complex were aware of the building's history.

Similarly, on the western edge of the complex, there was a *shamshan* ghat. A vast ground, it was converted into a graveyard after Partition, a function it continues to serve.

Constructed with funds collected through private subscriptions, Model Town till the time of Partition was dominated by wealthy Hindu capitalists who owned about two-thirds of all the properties.[64] Retired provincial and municipal government employees who were accustomed to living in bungalows were the initial residents of the society.[65] The first houses in Model

Town followed the British bungalow style, with shaded verandas, axial symmetry, open spaces around the construction and other smaller constructions to serve particular purposes, such as vehicle parking and servants' quarters.[66] All houses had to conform to strict planning restrictions.[67] Incidentally, Model Town was the first residential scheme in the city to introduce the flush toilet system.[68]

In many ways, the construction of Model Town in the 1920s was a culmination of the city's adaptation to British residential sensibilities. The process of course had begun soon after annexation. While a majority of the population in 1849 lived within the confines of the walled city, in multistorey houses, the British introduced a new model of living in Civil Lines and the cantonment with their wide avenues, spacious bungalows and compartmentalization of rooms for different uses, in a stark departure from the traditional houses in the walled city. There, hardly any compartmentalization of rooms existed and each floor was one big room, with the pattern replicated on higher floors. Even the houses of the elite were no different. Many of these houses within the walled city also had shops on the ground floor that opened on to the street.[69]

Sensibilities began to change as the affluent class took to emulating the lifestyle of the British, as the state also adopted a paternalistic attitude. In 1862, the Lahore Municipal Committee was established, laws for which were revised in 1884, allowing the committee to regulate construction policies. This involved beginning the inspection of building plans, comparing the construction of the structure with the alignment of the street and also inspecting the drainage system, which was lacking in traditional houses constructed within the walled city.[70] In 1922, the Town Improvement Act was passed, which planned the growth of Lahore's suburbs.

Influenced by the British concept of space, the influential residents of the city started moving out of 'congested' localities in the walled city and into the suburbs, preferring to live in British-style bungalows. The first to adopt this new lifestyle were the educated elite, the doctors and lawyers, who began moving into Civil Lines. Soon, new suburban localities sprang up, such as Nisbet Road, Sant Nagar, Krishan Nagar, Ram Nagar and Gowal Mandi.[71] Like Civil Lines, these suburban communities had wider roads and spacious houses compartmentalized into different functional rooms. Most of these houses were multistorey structures, with shops on the ground floor, amalgamating Indian architectural techniques with British sensibilities.[72] However, with Model Town, the bungalow became the preferred way of living for the educated Indian elite. While there was hardly any space between residential units in the walled city, there were vast empty spaces between bungalows.

Model Town was the ultimate expression of aspiration for the growing educated elite. This was also made possible with the advent of motor vehicles in Lahore which changed the way people conceived distance and time, thus allowing suburban communities to develop further away from the walled city. The distance between the walled city and Model Town is more than 10 kilometres. From 1943, a regular bus service started between Model Town and the Shah Alami market in the walled city.[73]

It wasn't, however, just architecture that changed under the colonial state. Several local institutions quickly eroded as the society experienced seismic shifts. Perhaps the biggest loss was of indigenous educational institutions. A remarkable report detailing the different kinds of local models of education in Punjab was compiled by G.W. Leitner thirty-three years after the annexation of the province. It contains a scathing indictment of the devastation of the indigenous education system following the introduction of the British education system.

The various kinds of schools identified by Leitner included Persian, Quranic, Sanskrit and Gurmukhi. There were also specialized schools for the children of merchants. At a higher level, students were encouraged to seek the guidance of specialists in their fields. Leitner points out how rigorous the syllabus was for certain subjects such as astronomy, mathematics, medicine, philosophy and theology.

The colonial state completely ignored these indigenous models of education when it introduced its 'modern' education system. Education, along with infrastructural development, became a tool of propaganda to highlight the benevolence of the colonial state. Any form of education that did not emerge from the European system was derided and looked down upon. The Indian elite, trained in institutions set up by the British, internalized these colonial attitudes. The present education model of Pakistan (and India) is a direct legacy of the colonial system, where indigenous systems and methodologies have all but disappeared.

A wide gulf opened up between 'educated' children and their 'uneducated' parents. Urdu, a foreign language until then in Punjab, was imposed as a medium of education, along with English. The knowledge that the older generations possessed through the indigenous education system became irrelevant, and an entire culture and its traditions came to be looked down upon.

On 20 October 2016, about a dozen protesters gathered outside the head office of Pakistan's largest private school network located on Guru Mangat Road in Lahore. The name of the road is derived from the hamlet Guru Mangat, now completely surrounded and ghettoized by Gulberg Housing Society. Somewhere in the middle of the community are also the remains of an old Jain temple. The temple was constructed to commemorate the visit of another saint, Shri Chandrasuri, a prominent Jain monk, whose

smadh is located in Mehrauli in Delhi. The buildings of the
temple were taken over by the local populace, their little domes
the last remaining signs of the historic structure. There was also
a massive pool next to the temple, now the site of residences. It
is believed that Shri Chandrasuri undertook an extensive tour of
Punjab, trying to retrace the journey of Lord Mahavira. One of
these journeys brought him here to a hamlet now at the centre
of Lahore.[74] Was it the footsteps of Mahavira that brought him to
Guru Mangat?

The gathering of protesters was depressingly small. The
situation would have been different had this been Sindh or
Khyber Pakhtunkhwa but it was not. This was Lahore, the
capital of Punjab, where colonial policies had changed the fabric
of society.

The group of protesters, led by Punjabi nationalist and literary
organizations, were protesting against the school for 'disrespecting'
their language and culture. The principal of the school's branch in
Sahiwal in south Punjab, about 170 kilometres from Lahore, had
issued a circular stating the school's policies. One of the rules was
that foul language was not permitted on campus. It explained the
point thus: 'Taunts, abuses, Punjabi and hate speech.'[75] Punjabi
had been declared a foul language. The circular was shared on
social media by one of the parents from where it went viral.
Online petitions began. Exacerbating the situation, the head office
defended the principal saying on its official social media page that
no parents would like their children to use foul language. They
had completely missed the point.

While this unfortunate school was the one that came into
the limelight and was rightly reprimanded, this attitude is not
particular. Punjabi as a language and culture is looked down upon
by most private schools and colleges around the province. While
Urdu is a compulsory subject and English an avenue for social
mobility, Punjabi is considered the language of the uneducated,

the unruly. It is seen as a language of curses. The educated, the cultured, speak either Urdu or English.

Young children in private schools are exposed at an early age to the literature of Dickens, Shakespeare, Dante, Yeats in English and Allama Iqbal, Meer Taqi Meer and Faiz Ahmed Faiz in Urdu, but there is absolutely no mention of Punjabi literature. Children with elaborate formal education spend their entire lives in the cities of Punjab without any knowledge of Ghulam Farid, Waris Shah, Bulleh Shah, Shah Hussain, Guru Nanak and Baba Fariduddin Shakarganj, all classic Punjabi poets. Devoid of their language and literature, these young adults spend an entire lifetime alienated from the culture of their land.

The root of the problem lies in British education policy. Urdu, as opposed to Punjabi, served as the medium of education. With complete ignorance of Punjabi and its literature, the language was labelled unruly and unsuited to 'scientific' education by colonial officers. Urdu, on the other hand, was promoted as the state language, to be used as a medium of instruction by government schools along with English. This was in contrast to the educational policy of the British in other parts of the country. For example, in Bengal, Bengali continued to serve as the medium of education. The promotion of Urdu over Punjabi further aggravated the communal issue in Punjab, with the Muslims embracing the language, while the Hindus demanded the introduction of Hindi as the medium of education. Punjabi became associated with the Sikh community. This attitude continues to exist in contemporary Punjab.

In independent Pakistan, the situation of Punjab was somewhat of an oxymoron. On the one hand, Punjab became a symbol of the Pakistani state, a hegemonic power that overshadowed the smaller provinces. On the other hand, the unique Punjabi culture, expressed in language and festivals and rituals, began to be associated with a non-Muslim heritage. The hegemonic province was fine with giving up its distinct identity. Perhaps this was even required to a certain extent. Punjab was now the symbol of the Pakistani state, defined through its Islamic identity, represented through the Urdu language. Punjab could not afford to be Punjabi any more, for it had to be Pakistan.

The situation in the smaller provinces was the opposite. With an overarching state eager to dictate what their culture and heritage would be, there was a heightening of nationalist identity, resulting in a stronger claim to one's distinct, indigenous identity. This is a phenomenon that was experienced in East Pakistan and now in Sindh, Baluchistan and Khyber Pakhtunkhwa.

Small as the gathering of protesters was, their voices were loud. A case against the school was filed at Lahore High Court for insulting 'Punjabi culture'. Representatives of the institute were summoned to court, reprimanded publicly and made to apologize. The Punjabi nationalist organizations hailed this as a victory. But this was only a small battle. The culture and the education system that has given birth to this antagonistic attitude towards Punjabi still exists in Punjab, more deeply rooted in its soil than ever before.

Perhaps a greater catastrophe was the linking of education with the job market. Education, for the first time under the colonial state, came to be associated with economic advancement. This completely altered the way students interacted with education. While education in the indigenous model was seen as a tool to refine one's personality, in this new model, it became a ladder to climb the steps of economic success.

One, however, has to be careful not to romanticize the indigenous model of education. The system was far from perfect, dogmatic in certain disciplines and in fact could have learned immensely from European scholarship. But that was not to be. Leitner suggested how, instead of completely replacing the indigenous education system, a product of the history and culture of this society, the colonial education system could have revamped it and inculcated aspects of it. This would have no doubt resulted in a healthier system instead of creating a people embarrassed of their own culture.

The intellectual growth of the people was of course never the agenda of the colonial state. Its education system was premised upon the 'civilizing' role of education. The locals were seen as uncivilized people who could be civilized and made to appreciate the benefits of the colonial state through education.[76] While one of the advantages of the colonial education system was the creation of a political class that began opposing the colonial state and took a leading role in the anti-colonial movement, it continued to share the colonial attitudes of the 'civilizing' aspect of the education system.

With the death of the indigenous education system, the society also experienced a fading away of other intellectual pursuits. With the advent of European science, the traditional knowledge of medicine, astronomy and philosophy was slowly supplanted by colonial fields. In only a couple of years, the society experienced fundamental shifts and lost knowledge and culture that had been accumulated over generations. While British education, science and medicine opened for us avenues that would otherwise have remained shut, it also managed to cut us off from our traditional knowledge which could have benefited from exposure to European systems of knowledge.

6

THE CITY OF NOSTALGIA

Holding a wreath of flowers in one hand, the angel, wearing a flowing gown, her curly hair scattered around her shoulders, rests an elbow on the cross. Her eyes are closed and her expression is forlorn. The tops of her wings have broken off. Another angel, decapitated, rests on a small slab at the base of the cross. With one hand she is tying a piece of cloth across the cross, and with the other, placing a wreath on it. A sculpture hangs on the back of a cross, waiting for eternity, like several others whose forms gradually wither away.

The other graves are not as elaborate, just sombre reminders of death with religious inscriptions. Some have been recently visited and are covered with fresh flowers. Others haven't had any visitors for decades. Located on Jail Road behind the Lahore Gymkhana golf course, Gora Qabristan was built in the 1920s for the British population of the city. Initially reserved for the British, it eventually began admitting anglicized Indian Christians. Several colonial officers whose bodies could not be returned to England were laid to rest here, never to be visited by their loved ones.

After the creation of Pakistan, the graveyard was taken over by the local Christian community.

Some of the most elaborate graves, the ones with statues, are also the oldest, from the 1920s to the 1940s. A walk through the graveyard gives one an idea of changing sensibilities—statues replaced by simple crosses, crosses eventually replaced by just tombstones. Located in the heart of Lahore, it is a tiny oasis of Christian sculptural and artisanal work. Perhaps it was due to this that it was attacked in 1991 by a mob protesting American involvement in the Gulf War. The graves, with their ostensible Christian features, became a symbol of American imperialism. Many of the heads, hands and wings of the angels guarding these graves were destroyed at the time by the mob, with the graveyard's guards looking on helplessly.

On 10 March 1957, a modest funeral was held here, arranged by the deputy high commissioner of the UK in Pakistan. In the presence of a handful of mourners, the last living descendant of Maharaja Ranjit Singh, Bamba Sutherland, was consigned to the earth. She had spent the last several years of her life in Lahore, the city of her ancestors, in a bungalow in Model Town. She had moved to Lahore in the early 1900s, and continued to live there with her husband, Dr David Waters Sutherland, who became the principal of the famous King Edwards Medical College in the city. After his death she remained in Lahore. Even the hurricane of Partition could not dislodge her.

Perhaps she was fulfilling the unrequited yearning of her father, Duleep Singh, and grandmother, Maharani Jind Kaur. Both of them died with Lahore on their lips. During their lifetimes, they had been forbidden from returning to the former capital of the Khalsa Empire, a city which in their eyes had no rival in the world, whose charm not even London, the seat of imperial power, or Paris, the City of Light, could rival. Aware of her grandmother's desire, Bamba had orchestrated the removal of her ashes from Bombay in 1924, to be placed next to the smadh of her grandfather, Maharaja Ranjit Singh, in Lahore.

Her father, the deposed boy-king, Maharaja Duleep Singh, before he died in a rundown Paris hotel still dreaming of Lahore, was convinced that his loyal subjects would rise up in arms against the British upon his return. He had no doubt that just a glimpse of his face would suffice as a call to action.[1] Memories of an evening at Spence's Hotel in Calcutta were imprinted on his mind, when hundreds of Sikh soldiers had encircled the hotel upon learning that he had returned to India and was at the hotel with his mother, Rani Jind, in the year 1861. Veterans of the Second Opium War, the Sikh soldiers had shouted slogans in favour of the Khalsa Empire, the lost empire of his father, which the British had snatched from him through deceit.[2]

At least ostensibly, before the Spence Hotel incident, the deposed maharaja had not shown much interest in regaining his empire. In fact, ever since his 'adoption' by the colonial state at the age of ten, he had gone out of his way to convince it of his loyalty. At fourteen, in 1853, he had converted to Christianity while living in Fatehgarh, UP, under the protection of Dr Spencer John Login, a Scottish surgeon, and his wife. At fifteen, he was permitted to travel to England where he quickly won over Queen Victoria, began living as an aristocrat with a vast estate, and regularly featured at the court. Behind closed doors, a maternal bond is believed to have developed between the queen and Duleep Singh. When shown the famed Koh-i-noor diamond for the first time after it was forcibly taken away as a 'gift' by the British following the annexation of his empire, Duleep Singh presented it to Queen Victoria, as a gift from a humble servant to his sovereign.[3] The queen regularly wore the Koh-i-noor from that day on.

The charm of the imperial court and a royal lifestyle began to fade away, however, as the deposed maharaja came of age.

He began wondering about his mother, from whom he had been separated as a child. The regent of his empire, Rani Jindan, the youngest wife of Maharaja Ranjit Singh, had been imprisoned by the British resident for conspiring against British rule. Initially imprisoned within Lahore Fort, she was moved to Sheikhupura Fort, from where she was transferred to Chunar Fort, close to the city of Benares. She escaped to Nepal, where the colonial state, using its influence, had kept her as a virtual prisoner. Painting her as a sexual predator, the British administration made the decision to keep her 'corrupting' influence away from the young maharaja, who had hitherto shown all the signs of a perfect loyal prince.

At the age of twenty-one, the deposed maharaja wanted to re-establish contact with his mother. Reluctantly, the British allowed communication between them and gave permission for a meeting, the first since she had been whisked away from him in 1847, when the boy maharaja had been taken to Shalimar Garden for a 'recreational' tour. As far away from Punjab as possible, Calcutta's Spence's Hotel was chosen, for the British were aware that her imprisonment had turned Rani Jindan into a rallying cry for the 'rebels'. The Second Anglo-Sikh War, which had established British hegemony over Punjab, had seen some fierce battles, causing the British unexpected losses. Even with an iron grip over Punjab, the British state was paranoid about the potential significance of the return of the maharaja and the regent to the land of the five rivers.

For the British, at least, the meeting did not go as expected. Once united with her son, Rani Jindan refused to be separated from him. Upon Duleep Singh's insistence, the British authorities allowed her to return to England with her son.

The deposed maharaja quickly transformed under his mother's influence. Soon after his return to England, the loyal subject began showing signs of rebellion. The British even contemplated sending Rani Jindan back and imprisoning her, but she died on 1 August 1863. Her last wish was that she be returned to Lahore, and her ashes buried next to Maharaja Ranjit Singh, but that was unacceptable to the British. She was temporarily interred in London but Duleep Singh was allowed to take her body back to India to be cremated. With Lahore or any other part of Punjab out of bounds, he was given permission to cremate her in Bombay where her ashes remained until they were removed by her granddaughter, Bamba Sutherland.

Despite the short period of time she spent with her son, Duleep Singh was completely transformed under Rani Jindan. He began questioning the terms of the settlement that took his empire away from him. He turned down a deposed princess suggested by Queen Victoria and instead chose to marry Bamba Muller, the sixteen-year-old 'illegitimate' daughter of a German merchant and an Abyssinian slave.[4] Duleep Singh knew that she, with her background and lack of education, would invoke the displeasure of his aristocratic circle, but perhaps that was what he wanted.

Soon after his marriage, he took to drinking heavily and associating with dancing girls much more than he had as a bachelor. Embarrassed by his antics, the British government in 1877 threatened to stop his pension if he didn't change his lifestyle. Duleep's response was to spend even more extravagantly, while demanding that his family jewels, worth half a million pounds, be returned to him along with over a million pounds worth of ancestral lands.[5] These, he claimed, were never part of the treaty he had signed as a child. When his demands were refused, he began writing in newspapers, trying to win the support of the British people, but only managed to reduce his situation to a farce.[6]

In desperation, Duleep Singh decided to return to Punjab, harbouring dreams of regaining a lost empire by inspiring a rebellion just with his presence. He also hoped the Russians coming in from Afghanistan would help him in this endeavour.[7]

Selling off all his properties in England, he sailed for India with his family. On the way, he also reverted to Sikhism in a modest ceremony. Even before his ship could reach the Suez Canal, however, he was arrested by British authorities at Port Said. He was eventually released but coerced to return to Europe.

On 2 April 1893, Duleep Singh passed away in a cheap Parisian hotel. His last wish, for his body to be returned to Punjab, was rejected by a paranoid colonial state, which felt his funeral would bring together nationalists and serve as a rallying force against the state. His body was moved to Britain, where he was buried in accordance with Christian rites.

Sitting across the Sutlej, which was the agreed-upon boundary between the Khalsa Empire and the British territories, the British were convinced that the former was beginning to implode. Local chieftains empowered by a weakened central authority had risen up in revolt against the Durbar. Two sons of Ranjit Singh, Peshaura Singh and Kashmira Singh, had refused to acknowledge the sovereignty of the boy-king, Duleep Singh. The Khalsa army, after years of appeasement and a taste of political power, was beyond the Durbar's control.

In the summer of 1845, less than two years after Maharaja Duleep Singh's coronation, the strength of the army had increased to 1,20,000, by more than 50 per cent of what it had been at the time of Ranjit Singh's death. Power within the army had been wrested by the *panchs*—soldiers appointed to put forward their 'grievances' and 'concerns' to protect the sanctity of the Khalsa Empire, on the model of the indigenous panchayat system in the villages of Punjab. With the increasing strength of the army, the hold of the Durbar had weakened, as competing claimants to the throne bribed panchs to further their claims.

Between 1839 and 1844, three descendants of Ranjit Singh had succeeded him one after another, all of whom had lost their lives either through assassination, as in the case of Sher Singh, or under mysterious circumstances, like Kharak Singh and his son Nau Nihal Singh. Local chieftains who had sworn allegiance to Maharaja Ranjit Singh, seeing the weakening of the Durbar, had stopped paying tributes as they sought greater autonomy. Within the Durbar, powerful lobbies had emerged which began reaching out to British authorities across the river as well as to the panchs to strengthen their position.

Rani Jindan, cognizant of the precarious condition of the Durbar, understood the threat posed to her and her six-year-old son. Many, the British included, thought the situation was beyond her and would soon spiral out of control. Almost four decades younger than Ranjit Singh, Jindan Kaur, the beautiful daughter of the kernel-keeper of the maharaja, was only seventeen when his eye fell on her and he decided to marry her. Soon after her marriage, she bore the maharaja's youngest son. Court gossips that had earlier tried to diminish the reputation of another son of the maharaja began a whisper campaign that Duleep Singh was not the maharaja's son but that of a poor Muslim water carrier, Gulloo.[8]

Maharaja Ranjit Singh put an end to these rumours through a public declaration where he acknowledged Duleep Singh as his legitimate child and heir. Hence, six years after the death of his father, Duleep Singh's elevation to the throne of the Khalsa Empire could not be challenged, while Rani Jindan became the regent.

Actual power, however, lay with the wazir, Hira Singh, the son of Maharaja Ranjit Singh's wazir, Raja Dhian Singh, who had played a crucial role in the succession struggle and had eventually lost his life when Maharaja Sher Singh was assassinated. Hira Singh, whom the maharaja had been fond of during his lifetime, took up the dangerous but powerful post of wazir after his father's death.

With the support of his Brahmin mentor Pandit Jalla, Hira Singh swiftly took charge of the situation and stabilized the political unrest, much to everyone's surprise. The wazir, with the help of his uncle, Raja Ghulab Singh, put an end to the rebellion of Kashmira Singh and Peshaura Singh, and moved against Attar Singh Sindhianwala, another claimant to the throne, whose family had earlier rebelled against Maharaja Sher Singh and sought the support of the British against the maharaja. Rumoured to be supported by Dhian Singh, his brother Lehna and their nephew, Ajit Sindhianwala, had assassinated Sher Singh after he had welcomed them back to Punjab and then subsequently lost their lives at the hands of the Khalsa army, after they were incited by Hira Singh. The sentiments of the Khalsa army were effectively manipulated by Hira Singh who reminded them of the treachery of Attar Singh Sindhianwala when he sought the support of the British against the Durbar. Attar Singh and Kashmira Singh both lost their lives in the fight for the throne.

With the opposition crushed, the army under his perceived control and the boy-king and regent powerless, Hira Singh and his mentor, Pandit Jalla, appeared invincible. However, the duo finally crossed a line when they publicly began criticizing Rani Jindan and her ambitious brother, Jawahir Singh.

Already aggrieved by Hira Singh's apathy towards the maharaja, Rani Jindan grabbed the opportunity and used the insult as a rallying point against the powerful wazir and his mentor. Would the protectors of the Khalsa, an empire that was bestowed upon them by their maharaja, her husband, allow Hira Singh and Pandit Jalla to insult the heir of Ranjit Singh? In her campaign against Hira Singh, Rani Jindan revealed her true self, emerging from the shadows of the harem into public life. She would no longer hide behind her veil but show her face in public, defying all norms.

Years later, the British, when in control of Lahore, found this flaunting of feminine 'modesty' by the rani to be scandalous. In the years to come, she would show all the signs of an efficient political leader who successfully balanced the power groups in the Durbar, kept the army satisfied, was defiant to the British, and finally made a rebel out of Maharaja Duleep Singh.

Hira Singh and Pandit Jalla anticipated the winds of change and made a sudden dash to save their lives, heading towards Jammu where Ghulab Singh, even though nominally under the influence of the Lahore Durbar, was for all practical purposes running an independent kingdom. On 21 December 1844, they fled Lahore but were intercepted by the Khalsa army that, after killing them, impaled their heads on spears and marched back to the city.

Jind Kaur had successfully wrested control back from the Jammu lobby and, together with Jawahir Singh, and her alleged lover, Lal Singh,[9] emerged at the helm of the Lahore Durbar. It was a weakened durbar, though, with several provinces refusing to pay tribute to the central authority, including Jammu and the powerful province of Multan in the south.

Immediately after Jawahir Singh's ascension as wazir, Peshaura Singh, egged on by Ghulab Singh from Jammu, rebelled and made another bid for the throne. Like the previous time, his rebellion was short-lived and he soon surrendered upon being besieged at Sialkot Fort. He was to be moved to Lahore but on the way, upon Jawahir Singh's order, was put to death.

The Khalsa army, which already resented their wazir, interpreted this act as an insult to the legacy of their beloved maharaja.[10] The panchs convened and it was decided that the insolent wazir needed to be put to death. The maharani could only look on helplessly as her brother was killed in front of her eyes.

It was evident that despite the titles and the constant appeasement through salary increments, it was the Khalsa army that was the true power behind the throne.

For some time afterwards, no one was willing to put himself at the head of such a ferocious army, which had, in less than a year, killed two of its commanders. Eventually Lal Singh was appointed the wazir, and Tej Singh became the head of the army.

While the rani could not save her brother from the wrath of the soldiers, she decreed the construction of a smadh to commemorate him. At a short distance from the fort, visible from its windows, a tall structure was raised that contained Jawahir Singh's remains. His smadh was constructed with a turret on top that made it look like a temple. The Guru Granth Sahib was recited without a break at Jawahir Singh's smadh for as long as the rani was in power.

Parking the car next to the railway track, I walked into a congested locality close by in search of the final resting place of Jawahir Singh. The colony was built after the laying of the track, in order to house railway workers. Once, the turret atop Jawahir Singh's smadh was visible from the main road; now its remains are hidden somewhere within the ever-expanding neighbourhood.

Soon enough, I noticed a tall, decrepit turret. I headed in its direction. Turning into a narrow street hemmed in by several tall houses, I discovered the smadh of Khushal Singh, the chamberlain of Maharaja Ranjit Singh, at the end of the road. Constructed with small bricks, its outer wall was covered with political posters. A staircase led into the smadh, which had a small dome at the top. This was once a spacious complex. It wasn't a smadh any more, though. It had been converted into a residence, divided amongst several families.

At a little distance, in another narrow street, I found the smadh of Jawahir Singh. Only the turret remained of the original structure, the rest having been converted into residential quarters.

Once while looking at a map of India, Maharaja Ranjit Singh is reported to have said, 'One day it will all be red.' He meant the British would overrun India.[11] While the two empires maintained a cordial relationship during his lifetime, war became inevitable soon after his death.

The British, who had been observing the situation since the maharaja's death, were convinced that the overgrown and overpaid army, despite its impressive numbers and weaponry, lacked discipline and was nothing but a rabble. They knew that in the imminent battle between the two forces, the Sikhs would be no match for the far better disciplined British army. They would soon find out that they could not have been more wrong.

Over the years the British had been building up their army across the Sutlej, preparing to go to war against the Khalsa army. The British forces in Punjab had increased from 2500 to 8000 men immediately after the maharaja's death. The city of Ferozepur, which abutted the Sikh territories and had been a bone of contention between the two empires during Ranjit Singh's lifetime, was converted into a British cantonment. In subsequent years, the number of men was increased to 14,000 as new cantonments came up in Ambala, Kasauli and Shimla. With a reserved force of 10,000 at Meerut, the number of men in Punjab was further increased to 32,000, with sixty-eight guns. In 1845, 30-ton boats built in Bombay were transported to Ferozepur to be used as a bridge.[12]

The situation worsened with the appointment of Major Broadfoot as the agent for the affairs of the Sikhs. One of his first acts was the declaration that the Cis-Sutlej territories (on the eastern side of the Sutlej) which had been guaranteed to Maharaja Ranjit Singh under the Amritsar Treaty of 1809, would fall under British protection after the death or deposition of Maharaja Duleep Singh.[13]

Jawahir Singh, who was the wazir at the time, was infuriated when he came to know of this.[14] The sense of outrage did not die with him but was rather used by other powerful chiefs for their own political agendas. It was suggested that what was being planned for the Cis-Sutlej territories would eventually be extended to all the possessions of the maharaja.

Aware of their increasingly precarious position, Lal Singh and Tej Singh thought that the ideal way to weaken the army would be by pitting it against the British. It is reported that the two convinced Rani Jindan, grieving the death of her brother, to accept their plan.[15] She wanted to avenge her brother's death, and was also aware of the sword of Damocles that dangled over not just her own head but also that of her son. Rani Jindan might have thought that a weakened or defeated army, and the arrival of British troops in Lahore, could bolster support for the disempowered Durbar.

On 11 December 1845, about 35,000–40,000 Sikh soldiers[16] crossed the river and attacked a small British contingent of 7000 at Ferozepur.[17] Even before the war began, Lal Singh and Tej Singh had written to the British, telling them of their plans to deliberately lead the army into a catastrophe. In exchange, they wanted their interests to be protected when the British took over Lahore.

Unaware of these machinations, the Khalsa army threw itself into battle. The panchs had been temporarily abandoned for a unified command structure. There were many examples of individual bravery, taking the British, who had consistently underestimated the Khalsa army in their correspondence, completely by surprise. On several occasions, when the army was at a vantage position and a decisive victory seemed at hand, Tej Singh and Lal Singh would pull back, leaving their army unprotected. During the battle of Sobraon, for instance, after bringing thousands of his soldiers across the Sutlej, Tej Singh receded across the river and even destroyed a portion of the bridge of boats so that the soldiers had no way to return.[18]

Increasingly disillusioned, the Khalsa army reached out to Ghulab Singh in Jammu to take over the reins of the army. Ghulab Singh, however, had other plans. He had already been in deliberations with the British to protect his interests. Rani Jindan, for whom memories of Hira Singh's ministry were still fresh, was reluctant to allow Ghulab Singh to return to Lahore and take over the army. Eventually she ran out of options when the Khalsa army pressurized her to allow him to take up the ministry.

Ghulab Singh played both sides masterfully. He rebuked the Khalsa army for its impulsive decision to wage war against the British, while also maintaining contact with the British and positioning himself as the sole arbitrator between the two sides. He even held back provisions for the army to break their spirit so as to coerce them to accept him as an arbitrator without any conditions and with complete authority. Despite their success on the battlefield, the British were also willing to negotiate because of the heavy causalities they had suffered. They were afraid that a prolonged war with the Sikhs might inspire similar 'rebellions' in other parts of north India.[19]

On 9 March 1846, the Treaty of Lahore was signed between the British and the Khalsa Empire, bringing the First Anglo-Sikh War to an end, placing stringent conditions on the Durbar. All territory between the Sutlej and the Beas was retained by the British, while the Durbar was stipulated to pay 1.5 million pounds as war indemnity. The treasury was completely empty. Thus it was decided that Ghulab Singh would pay the indemnity from his personal treasury and would, in return, retain the lands of Jammu and Kashmir, becoming its independent ruler.

This had, of course, been his agenda all along. The British too were happy to weaken the Khalsa Empire, while maintaining a buffer between their territory and Afghanistan.[20] A separate treaty, called the Treaty of Amritsar, was signed between the British and Raja Ghulab Singh, making him the king of Jammu and Kashmir—another can of worms that would play out a century later during the Partition of India and Pakistan.

The Lahore Durbar had achieved its purpose. The Khalsa army had been defeated and the British forces, for the first time, entered the capital to 'protect' the maharaja. It was meant to be a temporary arrangement, with the Durbar independent to look after its affairs. It soon became clear, though, that the newly appointed resident, Henry Lawrence, was the ultimate authority, while the Durbar and its governors would be nominal heads. Tej Singh, one of the chief architects of the war, benefited through British presence, while the other two accomplices, Lal Singh and Rani Jindan, would soon pay the price for their folly.

By the end of the year, it had become clear that the British were here to stay. At the 'insistence' of the Lahore Durbar, on 26 December 1846, the Treaty of Bhyroval was signed between the British and representatives of the Durbar, requesting them to stay on till the maharaja turned sixteen, with full authority and control over the state. The regent was removed from her post with a hefty annual pension, as a council of regency composed of influential members of the Durbar headed by the British resident became the head of the government.

Infuriated at being removed from her politically powerful position, Rani Jindan became the focus of 'anti-British' activities soon after. Her influence over the maharaja was seen as corrupting.

Matters took a turn for the worse when, under the rani's influence, Maharaja Duleep Singh refused to anoint Tej Singh, her sworn enemy and an ally of the British, as Raja of Sialkot in front of the entire Durbar.

On 19 August 1847, while the maharaja was taken to the Shalimar Gardens for 'entertainment', the maharani, in the darkness of the night, was escorted out of Lahore Fort with her entourage. She would not be allowed to see the maharaja, her son, till the fateful meeting in Calcutta, more than thirteen years later.

With the appointment of Lord Dalhousie, a passionate supporter of the expansion of the British Empire, as governor general in 1847, it was a matter of time before the British formally annexed the province. The excuse presented itself in April 1848 when two British officers, Patrick Alexander Vans Agnew and Andrew Anderson, were assassinated by soldiers in Multan.

As part of their strategy to appoint allied governors in different parts of Punjab, the British had decided to remove Mulraj from Multan and replace him with Agnew. Despite the humiliation, Mulraj had acceded to the demand and was willing to retire with a pension. His soldiers, however, had different ideas. After killing both Agnew and Anderson, another British officer meant to assist the new governor, the soldiers turned to Mulraj to 'lead' the rebellion. Fearing for his life and out of options, Mulraj became the reluctant leader of a rebellion against the Lahore Durbar in 1848, by now completely controlled by the British. This was the beginning of what came to be known as the Second Anglo-Sikh War.[21]

In another part of Punjab, towards the north-west, in the region of Hazara, Chutter Singh, the nominal governor, also soon found himself in a similar situation. While Chutter Singh was the Durbar-appointed governor, the power lay with James Abbot, who held a particular disdain for the governor. In a similar unfortunate incident, an American officer by the name of Canora, a representative of the British, was killed by Chutter Singh's soldiers. While this was an accident, Abbot was convinced that it was a show of rebellion by Chutter Singh.

Chutter Singh, much like Mulraj, became a reluctant leader of the rebellion, joined by his son Sher Singh, who had earlier gone to Multan with his soldiers to curb Mulraj's rebellion, but owing to the changing situation and state of mind of his soldiers, had returned to Hazara. Mutual suspicion did not allow Mulraj and Sher Singh to join forces.[22] Perhaps this could have been the key to changing the outcome of the war.

While the Sikh soldiers initially had reason to celebrate, the war was eventually lost after massive casualties on both sides. On 12 March 1849, the last battle was fought between the British and the forces of Chutter Singh and Sher Singh on the plains of Gujrat.

Throughout the war, the Lahore Durbar firmly stood behind the British. However, this was not good enough for Lord Dalhousie who blamed the Durbar for the rebellion even though it had no role to play in it, and used it as a pretext to usurp Punjab once and for all.

On 29 March 1849, Maharaja Duleep Singh held court at Lahore Fort for the last time, as he 'renounced on his behalf and on behalf of all heirs and successors, every right, title or claim to Punjab'.[23] All the properties of the kingdom were taken over by the British, which included, among much else, the famed Koh-i-noor.

The garden once extended as far as the eye could see. The baradari of the sixteenth-century Sufi poet stood at one edge of the garden, while the River Ravi flowed behind it. This open ground was far away from the congested streets of the walled city. Its wide expanse allowed enough space for the Khalsa army to gather and exhibit its latest drills, under the command of its European officers, to the mighty Maharaja Ranjit Singh. He took immense pride in his army, the backbone of his empire. Impressed by the discipline of the British army, he had modelled his army on it, recruiting European officers and British renegades to teach his soldiers the same drills the British officers exhibited across the Sutlej.[24] Sipping his wine in the shade of this breezy baradari, the maharaja would frequently monitor his soldiers' discipline and preparedness.

Even if Maharaja Sher Singh lacked the political acumen and military genius of his father, he made up for it through pomp and splendour. He too would inspect the Khalsa army, bigger than it had been at the time of his father, in the wide expanse of the garden of Shah Bilawal. Most of the European officers who had trained the soldiers meticulously were still there. The Khalsa army that had expanded the rule of Maharaja Ranjit Singh from a small fiefdom in Gujranwala to all of Punjab, gulping down areas from Afghanistan to Kashmir and Multan, still looked ferocious.

The borders of the Khalsa Empire would have been even wider had it not been for the British. Even so, it was a remarkable empire that stretched from Peshawar in the west to the Sutlej in the east, and from Kashmir in the north to Multan in the south. Sitting at the head of this mighty army as the sovereign of the empire, through a stroke of luck, deceit, treachery, rebellion and violence, was Maharaja Sher Singh.

He had been away from the imperial capital when his father passed away after a prolonged illness. This had been done deliberately in order to ensure a smooth transition of power to the eldest son, Kharak Singh.[25] Sher Singh, an able general who had proven himself in many battles, was convinced of his superiority but could not find enough support to back his claim. His fortunes turned unexpectedly when both Kharak Singh and his son and successor, Maharaja Nau Nihal Singh, died on the same day.

A scion of the Kanhaiya misl and the Sukerchakia misl (Ranjit Singh's misl), Sher Singh, even before he was born, was destined to be the heir of Maharaja Ranjit Singh. The Khalsa Empire was his prerogative. That is what his grandmother, Sada Kaur, had planned when she assisted a young Ranjit Singh in sweeping through Punjab. But that was not to be. Her daughter, Mehtab Kaur, Ranjit Singh's first wife, was beaten to the post by Raj Kaur (also known as Datar Kaur), the second wife, who gave birth to Kharak Singh five years before Sher Singh was born.[26] Kharak Singh thus became the heir apparent.

Sher Singh and Tara Singh were twin boys born in 1807 to Mehtab Kaur more than a decade after marriage. When the boys were born, gossip spread through the court claiming them to be 'illegitimate'.[27] Another rumour was that Mehtab Kaur had actually given birth to a girl and had replaced her child with two boys, newly born to a weaver and a carpenter.[28] Threatened by the birth of a second son, the rumours were spread by Raj Kaur, Kharak Singh's mother.[29] In fact, so effective were these rumours that Ranjit Singh for some time refused to acknowledge the sons as his legitimate heirs, unlike what he did later on the birth of Duleep Singh.

With the ascension of Maharaja Kharak Singh and his tussle with his son, Nau Nihal Singh, Sher Singh stayed away from the capital, perhaps waiting for an opportune time. Fortune turned in his favour when, after Kharak Singh's death, Nau Nihal Singh died mysteriously. With both rivals gone, there was general consensus among the Sikh aristocracy and the Khalsa army that Sher Singh would be an acceptable choice. Raja Dhian Singh, the cunning wazir who had earlier served under Maharaja Ranjit Singh and then under Kharak Singh and Nau Nihal Singh, now reached out to Sher Singh to prepare to march to Lahore and claim the throne. By this time another powerful group had emerged at the Lahore court and spilt the Durbar and the army right down the middle.

The Sandhawalia clans led by two brothers, Attar Singh and Lehna Singh, and their nephew Ajit Singh, shared familial connections with Ranjit Singh. They were also associated with Kharak Singh through his wife, Chand Kaur.[30] By instigating members of the army, officers, and the Sikh aristocracy against the 'influence' of the Jammu brothers and by once again raising doubts about the paternity of Sher Singh, the Sandhawalias propped up Chand Kaur to take over the affairs of the court as regent. Chand Kaur claimed that her daughter-in-law was pregnant with Nau Nihal's child, the rightful heir to the throne, and that she would be responsible for looking after the throne until the child was born and came of age.[31] With the support of sections of the Khalsa army and the Sandhawalias, Chand Kaur was able to take control of the government, even if temporarily, with Raja Dhian Singh retained as the wazir.

It is believed that Dhian Singh would have continued serving the regent had Chand Kaur not favoured the advice of the Sandhawalias over him.[32] Thus, while feigning loyalty to her, Dhian Singh reached out to Sher Singh to take over the throne. Meanwhile, he also began contacting different sections of the army and bribing them to stand behind Sher Singh in case of a showdown.

Behind the scenes, Sher Singh and Dhian Singh also began reaching out to the British to support them in their claim against Chand Kaur, while publicly Sher Singh accused the regent and the Sandhawalias of colluding with the British. The regent and the Sandhawalias too felt it necessary to ask the British for help.[33] With heightened rhetoric against the British and the politicization of the Khalsa army, a genie had been unleashed: an act that would eventually result in the First Anglo-Sikh War and the imminent end of the Sikh Empire.

The political tension finally erupted when, upon hearing that Nau Nihal Singh's wife had given birth to a stillborn child,

Sher Singh—unannounced and supported by a large section of the army—reached Lahore on 14 January 1841 to snatch the crown from the 'usurper'.[34] However one of his principal supporters, Dhian Singh, was not in Lahore when Sher Singh arrived, while Dhian Singh's brother, Ghulab Singh, present in Lahore, continued supporting the regent. With the gates of the fort locked, its boundary was surrounded by the army now openly supporting Sher Singh.

Without waiting for Dhian Singh, the army wanted to breach the walls of the fort and forcefully remove the regent and her supporters. Ghulab Singh did try with partial success to mediate between the two parties, but things finally settled with the arrival of Dhian Singh on 18 January. The regent was convinced to quit her position with a promise of a jagir, while the Sandhawalia brothers managed to flee to British territory. Sher Singh was pronounced maharaja and Dhian Singh retained his position as the wazir. As a reward for their loyalty, the soldiers were given a permanent increase in salary.[35] A little more than a year later, on 11 June 1842, Chand Kaur was murdered by her maids, who were later killed on the orders of the wazir, Dhian Singh.[36]

With the former regent dead and the Sandhawalias away from Punjab, there was no ostensible threat to Maharaja Sher Singh. The situation turned again when, convinced by the British and his wazir, he allowed the Sandhawalias to return to Lahore. Soon after his ascension to power, Sher Singh distanced himself from his wazir and began relying on his 'priest', Bhai Gurmukh Singh.[37] With the Sandhawalias back in Punjab, Dhian Singh began to conspire with them to weaken Maharaja Sher Singh's hold on the throne. They were told that they had been invited back to Lahore as part of a ruse and that their life was under threat.[38] Unbeknownst to Dhian Singh, Ajit Singh and Lehna Singh were making plans of their own. The three had decided to get rid of the maharaja, though what Dhian Singh did not know was that the brothers were also planning his death so that they could usurp the throne for themselves.

On an empty ground next to the baradari are the remains of the smadh of Maharaja Sher Singh. When I visited it in 2008, the entire structure, ringed by an outer wall, was in ruins. Facing the smadh, sitting on the floor outside a single room, a young man was grinding bhang leaves. A few older men stood next to him. At some point after Partition, the smadh of Maharaja Sher Singh had been converted into a Sufi shrine.[39]

The condition of the baradari was even worse. The roof had collapsed, the floral and geometric patterns on its walls had faded away. Where once the Ravi flowed behind the baradari, now there was a small enclosure for solid waste management put up by the district government. It was overflowing with garbage, with some of it spilling into this sixteenth-century structure. All traces of the garden which, along with Shalimar a few kilometres away, was one of the most famous in the city, had disappeared as the area around the smadh and the baradari were taken up by a congested locality.

On 15 September 1843, Maharaja Sher Singh was sitting at this baradari with his son Kanvar Pratap Singh, inspecting the Khalsa army, when his cousin Ajit Singh Sandhawalia asked him to look at a new English gun he had procured. Ever since his return, Ajit Singh had made efforts to grow close to the maharaja. Sher Singh, unaware of the plot, walked towards his death. Ajit Singh shot him and severed his head with his sword, while Lehna Singh killed the maharaja's twelve-year-old son.

They subsequently marched towards Lahore Fort along with the wazir who, until that moment, thought they were executing a plan crafted by him. On the way to the fort, Dhian Singh was separated from his guards and also killed. The situation had by now spiralled out of control. A segment of the Khalsa army led by Hira Singh, Dhian Singh's son, laid siege to the fort. The brothers were caught and killed by the army, their severed heads exhibited at the gates of Lahore as revenge for killing their maharaja.

The walled city of Lahore was said to have twelve gates and one *mori*, or small hole, that allowed entry into the city. After the gates were locked in the evening, the mori allowed visitors in. The primary function of Mori Gate, as it came to be known, was to allow the removal of garbage from the city. The dead would be taken through this exit for cremation on the banks of the Ravi. A little ahead of the gate, across from the grain market, there is a vast open ground called Maidan Bhaiyanwalla. This is where people congregated before taking the body for cremation.[40]

To one side of this ground stands one of the most splendid havelis of Lahore, that of Nau Nihal Singh—a four-storey structure, with wooden *jharoka*s, false windows and frescoes on the external walls, adorned with floral and geometrical patterns. Next to its wooden door is a blue board that reads 'Government Victoria Girls Higher Secondary School'. This remarkable haveli, the most exquisite specimen of Sikh heritage in Lahore, was converted into a government school under British rule, a role it continues to serve.

The frescoes inside the haveli are even more breathtaking. One notices Hindu motifs, drawings of Ram, Sita, Krishna and Radha, sharing space with pictures of Sikh Gurus, reminiscent of a time when there was no rigid distinction between Hinduism and Sikhism. The exclusivity was propped up during the colonial era when, similar to Hindus and Muslims, the Sikh community experienced a sharpening of communal identity.[41]

As various political intrigues unfolded after the death of Maharaja Ranjit Singh, gradually leading to the disintegration of his empire, this haveli became host to two such plots. It is here that Kharak Singh was sent to 'recover' by his son Nau Nihal Singh as he became the de facto ruler. Kharak Singh breathed his last in this haveli. Maharani Chand Kaur too was sent here after she was deposed by Maharaja Sher Singh, to be killed by her maids.[42]

While drugs, alcohol, orgies and parties had always been a weakness of the crown prince, the situation did not improve much after he became the maharaja. Many of his generals and advisers quickly became frustrated with Kharak Singh's inability to concentrate on matters of state.[43] Leading the pack was Dhian Singh, who perhaps would not have been too bothered by Kharak Singh's distractedness had the maharaja left the control of the administration completely to him. That was not to be. Soon after coming to power, Kharak Singh became close to Chet Singh, his relative by marriage.[44] Aware of the ambitions of the young prince, Nau Nihal Singh, and the support he could muster, Dhian Singh began corresponding with him, urging him to return to Lahore and take over the reins of the kingdom.

An alleged process of slowly poisoning Kharak Singh ensued.[45] As the small doses of poison mixed in his food began to affect the maharaja's health, Nau Nihal Singh, with the help of the wazir, took charge of the Lahore Durbar. Over the next six months, as Kharak Singh's organs began shutting down because of the poison, he became bedridden. In another five months, he was dead.[46]

During his short tenure as the head of the state on his father's behalf, the young prince showed signs of promise. Given the political uncertainty, much of the kingdom suffered from a lack of law and order, while the army was beginning to show signs of disturbance which would soon have an effect on the political sphere. Not only was Nau Nihal able to manage law and order, he also utilized the army's energy for further conquests. The areas of Mandi and Suket were appropriated under the leadership of General Ventura, while Ladakh and parts of Baltistan were included in the empire by Ghulab Singh.[47]

While Nau Nihal Singh worked with Dhian Singh to oust his father, it is also claimed that he eventually wanted to sideline Dhian Singh and his brothers who shared between them the administration of the Sikh Empire.[48] Dhian Singh, astute as he was, is believed to have been aware of these plans, and is therefore suspected of orchestrating Nau Nihal's death.

As Nau Nihal was returning from his father's cremation, a gateway under which he was passing mysteriously collapsed, injuring his head. There are several conflicting reports about the exact nature of his injuries. Some claim that the injuries were brutal and the young maharaja lost his life soon after. Others claim that the injuries were only minor and that the maharaja was seen standing without support and even talking after the incident. He was taken to Lahore Fort, where he is believed to have died a little while later from severe injuries to his skull, which, if one were to go by some of the reports, did not exist at the time of the accident.[49] In this way, the young maharaja, perhaps the only one who was worthy of walking in the shoes of his ancestor, died mysteriously on the same day as his father.

There were many who benefited from Nau Nihal's untimely death, including his mother, Chand Kaur, who took up the role of regent. According to one narrative, she was about to perform sati with the body of her husband when she witnessed the accident and escaped, going on to head Lahore Durbar.[50]

It is an unusual situation. The mosque's loudspeakers are silent as the sound of the recitation of the Guru Granth Sahib echoes in the air. Gathered around a small palanquin, hundreds of Sikh men listen with their heads bowed as two Granthis recite from the sacred text. There is not a single woman in sight. Typically, this is not the case; almost as many women as men cross over the border to Lahore during various Sikh religious festivals around the year. This event, however, was an exception—the death anniversary of Sher-e-Punjab Maharaja Ranjit Singh was perhaps much more masculine an occasion than any other.

It was a Wednesday morning, 29 June 2011, and I had acquired special permission to attend the prayer ceremony for which a few hundred Sikh pilgrims had arrived in Lahore, an event that was otherwise shut off for Pakistani Muslims.

Located next to Badshahi Mosque, facing Lahore Fort, the smadh of Maharaja Ranjit Singh adds to the historicity of this area. Behind Badshahi Mosque and the fort is the walled city of Lahore, with the Ravi in the opposite direction, acting as an unofficial boundary for the contemporary city even though there are parts of it that have spread to the western side of the river.

The smadh is a multistorey building, a beautiful amalgamation of Hindu and Muslim architectural traditions. While there are cupolas and window balconies adorning its facade, there is a small dome at its apex. The smadh of Guru Arjan with its golden dome stands in the shadow of this smadh, paling somewhat in comparison.

Still preserved, the intricate artwork inside the smadh depicts court life. Similar to the haveli of Nau Nihal Singh, paintings of Hindu deities are dominant. On any regular day, a picture of Maharaja Ranjit Singh is placed at the smadh at the centre of the hall, along with the picture of the last maharaja of Punjab, Duleep Singh. Just behind the smadh is the last resting place of the eleven women who performed sati during Maharaja Ranjit Singh's cremation, more evidence of how interconnected Sikhism was with Hinduism at the time. Four of them were his wives, the other seven his concubines.

The congregation dispersed at the conclusion of prayers and headed to the langar hall. On the way I got hold of Amanpreet Singh, a thirty-five-year-old trader from Ludhiana, who had travelled to Pakistan for the first time. 'The maharaja was a great leader. People were happy during his time. There was justice, education, wealth and prosperity. There was no crime. People would leave their shops unattended as there was no concept of stealing,' he told me.

Ranjit Singh was a truly remarkable ruler. Politically astute, he would use diplomacy to expand his empire wherever military action could be avoided. Setting up a system of patronage and alliance, along with military conquests, he was in a short period of time able to conquer the entire region of Punjab as well as parts of Afghanistan, Bahawalpur, Multan and Kashmir.

His dream of a pan-Punjabi empire that also brought parts of East Punjab into its orbit could not be achieved due to the presence of the British on the eastern front, who quickly took the independent Sikh fiefs of eastern Punjab under their protection and forbade Ranjit Singh from expanding beyond the Sutlej. For a while Ranjit Singh contemplated defiance, but the memories of the humbled Marathas were too recent to ignore and so, in 1809, he signed the Treaty of Amritsar with the British. It promised perpetual friendship and an acknowledgement of Ranjit Singh's sovereignty over his kingdom.

With the east beyond his reach, Ranjit Singh eyed Sindh in the south. Given his military superiority, there was no doubt he would have been successful, but once again the British swooped in and prohibited him from doing so. Many historians believe that without the constraints of the British, Ranjit Singh would have reached Calcutta in the east and Mysore in the south, making himself the supreme ruler of the entire Indian peninsula.[51]

Barred from expanding eastwards or southwards, Ranjit Singh turned to the west, the land of the Afghans. It is this westward expansion of the Khalsa Empire that is allotted much symbolic significance in Punjabi historiography.

With the weakening of the hold of the Mughal Empire in the eighteenth century, Punjab was up for grabs. Afghan rulers, one after another, beginning with Nadir Shah and ending with Ahmad Shah Abdali, eyed the fertile land across the Indus with envy. Raids were launched into the province, causing havoc. Small Sikh misls or groups sprang up in different parts of the province, playing the role of scavengers in the wake of these raids.

Towards the late eighteenth century, two of the twelve misls emerged as the most powerful—Sukerchakia (founded by Ranjit Singh's grandfather that controlled territory around Gujranwala) and Kanhaiya (which included parts of Kasur, Gurdaspur and Amritsar). A political alliance was forged between these groups when Ranjit Singh, the boy-scion of the Sukerchakia misl, was betrothed to Mehtab Kaur, daughter of the chief of the Kanhaiya misl.

With the merger of these two misls, Ranjit Singh, under the guidance of his mother-in-law, Sada Kaur, chief of the Kanhaiya misl after the death of her husband and father-in-law, found himself at the head of the most powerful Sikh army in all of Punjab. With the backing of the Kanhaiya misl, Ranjit Singh had every reason to believe he could achieve his goal of the first Sikh Empire. He wanted to be like the mighty Mughals. But before he could acquire an empire, he needed a capital.

Lahore, by the end of the eighteenth century, was far from the city of gardens the Mughals had fashioned. It was a city in decline, a city of relics, a city of nostalgia. A sense of lost glory lingered in its air through the remnants of its monuments, most of them occupied by squatters. It was no longer the economic or cultural hub it had been at the time of the Mughals but it was still Lahore, the eternal political capital of Punjab, a city that could, unlike any other, transform Ranjit Singh from the chief of a misl into a maharaja overnight.

While its walls are gone, the gateway still remains. At a distance of about 4 kilometres from the walled city of Lahore, close to the famed Laxmi Chowk, the name of the locality 'Qila Gujjar Singh' still keeps alive the memory of one of the three Sikh rulers of Lahore before Ranjit Singh. All of them belonged to the Bhangi misl which was once a powerful group with its centre at Amritsar, but had lost much of its might due to a prolonged power struggle with the Sukerchakia misl.

The walled city and Lahore Fort fell under the sway of Lehna Singh who was for official purposes recognized as the governor of Lahore, ruling on behalf of the Afghan king Ahmad Shah Abdali, but in practice exercising free reign. After the conquest of Lahore, he was incorporated into the court of Ranjit Singh, where he was able to distinguish himself.

Suba Singh, the third of the triumvirate rulers of Lahore, controlled parts of southern Lahore with his base at Nawan Kot, while Gujjar Singh controlled this part of the city, where he constructed a fort in a jungle and invited people to inhabit the region.

Ranjit Singh marched into the city in the year 1799 without opposition. With Lahore under his control, his reputation soared. He could no longer be dismissed as a chief of a misl. He was a king on the rise, a future maharaja of an empire.

Soon after, Ranjit Singh was able to capture Amritsar, the last bastion of the Bhangi misl. While Lahore enhanced his political reputation, it was the capture of Amritsar that added the mystery of religious zeal to his mission. Crowned maharaja, Ranjit Singh was not the king of any earthly empire but of the Khalsa Empire, the culmination of the efforts of the Gurus. It was the completion of Guru Nanak's mission which had been taken forward by all the other Gurus; the reason that the Gurus had sacrificed their lives and those of their children. This is what Guru Gobind Singh had envisioned, a dream that had been fulfilled by Ranjit Singh.

Coins in the new empire did not bear the name of the maharaja but of Guru Nanak, the founder of Sikhism. The government was called the Khalsa Durbar and the army was the Khalsa army. Sikh and Hindu rituals played a prominent role at the Durbar.[52] Historic Sikh gurdwaras commemorating events from the lives of the Gurus were renovated and expanded. Vast tracts of lands were affixed to these religious institutions making them financially independent. A minority that, until a few decades ago, had been brutally persecuted by the proxies of the Mughal and Afghan kings was now the master of a nascent empire.

While Ranjit Singh positioned himself as the maharaja, his Khalsa Empire was far from a theological kingdom. Many Muslims were appointed to important positions in the Durbar and the army. His chief physician, who also assisted him in dealing with the British, was a Muslim, Fakir Azizuddin Bokhari. His descendants still reside in Lahore and take immense pride in the role their ancestors played in the Khalsa Durbar. Muhammad Sultan, Elahi Baksh and Ghaus Muhammad Khan were some of the prominent generals in his army. The kotwal or chief police officer of his capital was a Muslim called Imam Baksh.[53]

Persian remained the official language of the court, while separate courts were reserved for Muslim subjects where jurists decided on their matters in accordance with Islamic law. Unani or Greek medicine, which had been popularised by Muslims in South Asia, was distributed free of cost, while Quranic and Arabic language schools continued to function throughout his empire.[54]

Even so, Maharaja Ranjit Singh is popularly recalled in Pakistan today as a Sikh tyrant who desecrated Muslim buildings. There is some truth to this. The expansive courtyard of Badshahi Mosque, the grandest mosque in the city, was converted into a stable for army horses, while its rooms were used as depots for guns and ammunition. Ranjit Singh is said to have spent a night with his favourite consort, Moran Sarkar, who happened to be Muslim, in the minaret of the splendid Wazir Khan Mosque, another prominent mosque in the city constructed during the tenure of Shah Jahan.[55] The azan was also banned during his rule for the inconvenience it caused the empire's non-Muslim subjects.

Several Mughal-era gardens, buildings and mausoleums were taken over by members of the Sikh aristocracy and other courtiers. Even the iconic mausoleum of Jahangir, on the western edge of River Ravi was not spared. The entire structure was removed and shifted to a small space between Lahore Fort and Badshahi Mosque, and a garden was raised around it. This came to be known as Hazuri Bagh, where the maharaja would occasionally grant an audience to his subjects.

Whereas most of these stories are recalled to show the atrocities and injustices committed by the maharaja against his Muslim subjects, stories of the maharaja or members of his family patronizing Muslim establishments are often ignored, perhaps deliberately, because they do not fit a simplistic narrative. Just behind Wazir Khan Mosque is another Mughal-era mosque, which had been converted into a gurdwara. Upon the intercession of the Fakir brothers, and on the orders of the maharaja, the mosque was renovated and opened for Muslims.[56] A library was constructed at the shrine of Data Darbar on the orders of his wife, Jind Kaur, to which she donated the royal collection of handwritten copies of the Quran, adding to the shrine's stature.[57]

With the weakening of the Afghan Empire and the internecine war, Ranjit Singh turned his attention westwards. For centuries, Punjab and other parts of north India had borne the brunt of invasions from the west. The Mongols, Mughals and Afghans had entered India via Afghanistan. Ranjit Singh seemed to turn the tide of invasion. This was the first time that a Punjabi ruler was heading westward.

Peshawar, one of the oldest cities in South Asia and the summer capital of the Afghan Empire, oscillated between the Afghans and the Khalsa Empire for several years before it was finally secured in 1834.[58] The boundaries of the Khalsa Empire would have extended even farther west but for British interference. They wanted to secure the Afghan throne for Shah Shuja, their puppet ruler, and for that they needed Ranjit Singh to forgo his ambition.

Peshawar and other areas around it, which had been incorporated into the Khalsa Empire despite the resentment of the Afghans, remained a part of it and were later bequeathed to the British. Peshawar and other parts of modern Khyber Pakhtunkhwa became part of Pakistan after Partition; however, even after the creation of the country, it remained a bone of contention between Pakistan and Afghanistan. Afghanistan claimed it as part of its territory which had been forcefully taken away. The boundaries of British India and subsequently Pakistan would have ended at the Indus had it not been for the eastward expansion of Maharaja Ranjit Singh.

7

THE MUGHAL CAPITAL

With its tall minarets made of sandstone brought from Jaipur, and its bright white dome, Badshahi Masjid in Lahore is an inextricable aspect of the identity of the city. Just outside the mosque is the grave of the national poet, Allama Iqbal, the man identified as the ideological father of Pakistan. Facing the mosque is Hazuri Bagh, with its pavilion extracted from Jahangir's mausoleum. Behind the Bagh is the Alamgiri Gate of Lahore Fort, named after Aurangzeb, with a flag of Pakistan fluttering atop. Also in the vicinity is Roshani Darwaza, one of the twelve gateways to the walled city of Lahore. At night, lamps were used to light the way from the gate of the fort to the Roshani Darwaza as the nobility of the Mughal court returned to their havelis in the walled city after a day at the court. Hence the name 'Roshani'—light.

Before the construction of Faisal Mosque in Islamabad, Badshahi Masjid had the honour of being the largest mosque in the country. Usually teeming with tourists, Pakistan's most famous mosque comes to life on the occasion of Friday prayers and during

Eid, when thousands of devotees gather in its vast courtyard to offer prayers. Next to its boundary wall is the recently introduced Food Street, where rooftop restaurants vie to provide the best view of the mosque, illuminated by floodlights at night, with some of the light also falling on the white dome of the smadh of Maharaja Ranjit Singh behind it.

At the entrance of the mosque are some pictures from the colonial era. They show the mosque's dilapidated condition after having served as a horse stable during the Sikh era. Sher Singh is rumoured to have used the tall minarets of the mosque to bombard the thick walls of the fort in an attempt to wrest control from the regent Chand Kaur, wife of Maharaja Kharak Singh.

The pictures narrate the story of the mosque, of the benevolence of the 'just and fair' colonial empire that returned its control to the rightful inheritors—the Muslims of the city. It narrates the story of colonial historiography, the categorization of history into Hindu, Muslim, Sikh and British eras, pitting epochs, communities, religions and histories against one other, and in the process creating new classifications that might not have been there at the start. History used as a political tool, an excuse, a justification for the imposition of colonial rule. The British were needed to rescue the Muslims from the Sikhs, the Hindus from the Muslims, the Dravidians from the Aryans, the Dalits from the Brahmins, the past from the present.

The narrative continues to unfold even today, throughout South Asia, as modern sensibilities are imposed on historical characters making heroes out of them, of imagined communities. The Mughal rule, for example, in this narrative became a symbol of the oppressive Muslim 'colonialism' of India, as foreign to the Indian subcontinent as British rule, while figures such as Chhatrapati Shivaji were representative of Hindu indigenous resistance. Just like the British, everything Muslim was deemed 'foreign', alien to the Indian subcontinent, a coercive historical anomaly that ruptured the Indian, read Hindu, civilization. In this narrative there was room for Jains, Buddhists and Sikhs within the fold of Hindu nationalism, but not for the Muslims, the successors of foreign occupation.

At the other end of the spectrum, the Muslims too looked back to a 'glorious' past when this infidel land was ruled by one true force. This imagined memory became the basis of laying down future plans, with one group determined to uproot all vestiges of foreign influence, and the other wanting to take inspiration from the past to reclaim lost glory. The British, in the meantime, were more than eager to perpetuate this communalization of history for it provided them with a justification to govern as arbitrators, as correctors of historical injustices.

In this communalization of history, Emperor Aurangzeb (1618–1707) bears the dubious distinction of being blamed for the downfall of the mighty Mughal Empire due to his intolerance, a product of his puritanical interpretation of religion. It is believed that during his long rule, which saw the expansion of the Mughal Empire to its zenith, Aurangzeb isolated several of his key Hindu allies because of his religious policies. Ever since the time of Emperor Akbar, *jizya*, a tax levied on non-Muslim subjects in a Muslim Empire for their protection, stood abolished. It was reintroduced by Aurangzeb, adding to the grievances of his Hindu subjects, including his Rajput allies, whose support to the Mughal throne had been crucial to its stability throughout Mughal history. Also, Aurangzeb's protracted campaign in the Deccan was perceived as his vainglorious attempt to expand his autocratic rule, which put such a burden on the state that it quickly unravelled after his death.

As evidence of Aurangzeb's intolerance, it is argued that he demolished several Hindu temples. Sikh history notes how he ordered the assassination of the ninth Sikh Guru, Tegh Bahadur, for his sympathy to the Kashmiri Brahmins. The Mughal-Sikh conflict continued with Guru Tegh Bahadur's son, Guru Gobind Singh, who waged several battles with the powerful Mughal army. The staunchest opposition to Aurangzeb came from the Marathas in the south, under the leadership of Shivaji.

Aurangzeb's treatment of his father and brothers is also depicted as a testimony of his cruelty. After usurping the throne from his father, Shah Jahan, Aurangzeb is believed to have imprisoned him in Agra, where he was rumoured to have been deprived of luxuries he had grown accustomed to, including music. It is cited that since Aurangzeb adhered to a puritanical interpretation of Islam, he was of the belief that music was not allowed, and had it banned throughout the empire. A much-narrated popular story has it that traditional musicians who had been part of the profession for generations were rendered unemployed and took out a funeral procession of their musical instruments. When Aurangzeb heard of it, he reportedly ordered that the instruments should be buried so deep that they may never be heard again.

The third of four brothers, Aurangzeb is accused of having had all his brothers murdered. He is also alleged to have sent his captive father the decapitated head of his eldest brother, Dara Shikoh, Shah Jahan's favourite son. Thus having forcefully snatched the crown from his father and his brother who had been appointed crown prince, Aurangzeb, in popular history, is depicted as a usurper who had no right to be at the head of the Mughal Empire. The subsequent weakening of the empire is presented as proof of his unsuitability for the throne.

Just a little more than thirty years after his death, Delhi, the Mughal capital and the symbol of its authority, was ransacked by the Persian army of Nadir Shah. Between 1707 and 1719, the Mughal Empire had lost most of its vitality after a series of weak emperors, wars of succession and machinations of members of the nobility. Aurangzeb was the last effective emperor of the Mughal Empire.

In the Pakistani narrative, Aurangzeb is presented as a hero who fought and expanded the frontiers of the Islamic empire. He is depicted as a pious Muslim who reintroduced Islamic laws by banning music and levying jizya. While Akbar in the Indian discourse is depicted as a tolerant ruler who treated his Hindu subjects with respect, encouraged interfaith dialogue and also abolished jizya, in the Pakistani narrative, he is viewed with scepticism because of his experiments with different religious philosophies and his attempt to forge a religion of his own, Din-i-Ilahi, which is considered a human's attempt to intervene with the word of God.

In contrast, Aurangzeb is imagined to be a true believer who removed corrupt practices from religion and the court, and once again purified the empire. The Indian narrative abhors him for the same reason, for abandoning the syncretic, and even politically expedient, practices of his predecessors in favour of a more puritanical interpretation of Islam, eventually resulting in the disintegration of the empire.

While Aurangzeb becomes a villain in this narrative, his eldest brother, the crown prince Dara Shikoh, becomes a tragic prince, the tolerant scholar-king, who could have steered the fate of the Mughal Empire in a different direction. Dara Shikoh was drawn towards the mystical interpretation of Islam, Sufi, which is eclectic in nature. Writing several years after his assassination, Niccolao Manucci, a former associate of the crown prince, recalled how Dara had no religion—when he was with Muslims he adopted their religion, when he was with Hindus, he praised Hinduism. It is for this reason, Manucci believed, that Dara Shikoh was declared a *kafir* by the puritan Aurangzeb and beheaded.[1]

During the reign of Shah Jahan, while the other princes took up military assignments and political roles in different parts of the empire, the eldest prince remained close to the emperor. Under his influence, the Mughal court, similar to the court of Akbar, became a site for religious debates, where scholars from various religions were invited to expound on philosophical doctrines.

While Aurangzeb antagonized the Sikhs by assassinating their Guru, Dara Shikoh is believed to have had close ties with Guru Har Rai, the seventh Sikh Guru. According to some narratives, Guru Har Rai had been asked to assist the prince during the war of succession against his brothers; however, Dara Shikoh was captured before the Guru could mobilize his forces.[2]

Dara Shikoh had a particular association with Lahore, the city of his spiritual mentor, Mian Mir. He served as the governor of Lahore before being drawn into the battle of succession. In Lahore, Dara Shikoh undertook several building projects and brought back imperial funds to the city, which had dried out after Akbar moved his capital out of the city in 1598.

Young boys played cricket in the vacant ground in front of the mausoleum. Behind it and on the side of the structure were the remnants of the royal garden that surrounded the grave. Originally there was a water tank around the mausoleum, similar to Jahangir's famous Hiran Minar at Sheikhupura, a city neighbouring Lahore. In the nineteenth century, when the British built the Mian Mir cantonment, they dismantled the tank and used its bricks for construction.

Covered in green cloth, the grave of Nadira Begum, the sole wife of Dara Shikoh, is housed in this monument. Several men, most of whom appeared to be drug addicts, were asleep under the shade of the building, next to the grave of the princess. A couple of boys prepared a hashish-filled cigarette in a corner.

On the southern side of the mausoleum is the fortification that protects the shrine of Mian Mir from puritans who regard the religious practices at such Sufi shrines to be un-Islamic. On the shrine's walls, posters of its competing guardians were pasted. A giant billboard next to the wall had a picture of one of the guardians next to Nawaz Sharif. These posters perfectly captured the feudalization of such Sufi shrines, which is exploited by puritans, giving a class framework to their religious struggle.

Nadira Begum died when Dara Shikoh had already lost the war of succession and was on his way to Iran. Even though they had abandoned the city, it was her last wish to be buried in Lahore, the city of Mian Mir. The mausoleum was constructed by a prince in exile, fighting for his life, yet attached to the city by a spiritual bond. The site of this mausoleum was chosen on purpose, so that she remained under the shadow of the Sufi saint even after her death. The architectural alignment of the mausoleum is such that it begins where the shrine ends, so that symbolically the head of the princess lies at the feet of the saint.

The most iconic building funded by Dara Shikoh in Lahore was the shrine of Mian Mir. He was for long considered the city's patron saint, before the title shifted to Data Sahib during the colonial era. Mian Mir was a Sufi of the Qadriyyah *silsila*, an order established by the twelfth-century Islamic scholar Abdul Qadir Gilani. While some claim that Dara Shikoh was a devotee of Mian Mir, others suggest that he was a follower of Mulla Shah, who happened to be a disciple of Mian Mir and a successor to his spiritual seat.[3] The pluralism and syncretism of Mian Mir can be gauged from the fact that he was believed to have been a close friend of Guru Arjan, the fifth Sikh Guru. It is popularly believed that when Guru Arjan laid the foundation of Sri Harmandir Sahib (the Golden Temple) in Amritsar, he invited Mian Mir to place the first brick.

Guru Arjan was assassinated in Lahore at the behest of Emperor Jahangir. Before his execution, he was tortured and placed in a cauldron of boiling water as burning sand was poured on his head. Some narratives suggest that Mian Mir met Guru Arjan and offered to intercede on his behalf with the emperor, which the Guru refused. Another narrative suggests that Mian Mir, looking at the atrocities committed on the Guru, offered to destroy the mighty Mughal Empire through his spiritual power, which the Guru rejected. Mian Mir is believed to have enjoyed cordial relations with the Mughal court and some historical evidence suggests that it was through his intercession that Guru Hargobind, the sixth Sikh Guru, was freed from Mughal imprisonment.[4]

Another interesting character who illustrates Dara Shikoh's syncretism is Sarmad, the naked fakir. An Armenian Jew, Sarmad is believed to have fallen in love with a young Hindu boy on a trading trip to India. Consumed by the ecstasy of love, he shed his clothes and let his hair grow, living like a mendicant in various cities and towns of the Mughal Empire. While in Delhi, stories of this strange mystic reached the ears of the crown prince who, impressed by his philosophical exposition, became his disciple. Sarmad too, like Dara, was declared a heretic and executed by Aurangzeb, soon after Dara Shikoh's death.

Not only did Dara Shikoh associate with Sufi scholars and other religious philosophers, he is also reputed to have been an eminent poet and intellectual. Some of his best-known works include *Safinat-ul-Auliya*, which documents the lives of about 400 mystics along with the essence of their teachings. His book *Sakinat-ul-Auliya* is a biography of Mian Mir.[5] In his ambition to find some common ground between Hindu and Muslim philosophies, he wrote *Majma al-Bahrain* (confluence of two oceans) that sought to reconcile Vedantic and Islamic metaphysical doctrines.[6] He also translated several Hindu texts into Persian, including the Bhagavad Gita, the Ramayana, the Yoga Vasistha and the Upanishads.[7] In fact, it was his translation of the Upanishads that was first translated into Latin, through which European scholars gained access to the texts.[8] He also commissioned the translation of several other prominent Hindu texts into Persian, including his dialogues with a Punjabi Hindu mystic from Lahore, Baba Lal.[9]

These dialogues provide an interesting insight into the mind of a prince struggling to reconcile his political ambition with his spiritual goals. This is a theme that forms the basis for much of Dara Shikoh's original work.[10] It also lends itself to a simplistic narrative—a Sufi Dara Shikoh up against a fundamentalist Aurangzeb, one tormented by the burden forced upon him, the other politically shrewd and willing to do whatever it took to capture the throne. The implication is that Dara Shikoh was too 'good' for the ugly world of politics, destined to lose even before the battle had begun.

Perhaps the most memorable structure that Dara Shikoh wanted to raise in Lahore was one that was never completed. Sandstone had already been brought from Jaipur and plans had been prepared to lay a splendid pathway connecting Lahore Fort with the shrine of Mian Mir. This was to be Dara Shikoh's ultimate expression of devotion to his spiritual mentor. Before work could begin on the project, the war of succession broke out and the sandstone remained untouched.

When Aurangzeb came to power, he wanted to put the sandstone to some use. He decided to construct a splendid mosque, on the pattern of the glorious Jama Masjid of Delhi built by his father, the dethroned Shah Jahan. Thus Badshahi Masjid of Lahore came into being, on the orders of Emperor Aurangzeb, at a cost of 5 lakh rupees, with the sandstone procured by Dara Shikoh to honour his Sufi mentor.[11]

These two structures, one that was planned and the other that was constructed, are reflective of the divergent religious sensibilities of the two princes—Dara Shikoh, a Sufi at heart, for whom the shrine of Mian Mir was the ultimate expression of his religiosity, and Aurangzeb, the puritanical Muslim, for whom it was not the shrine but the mosque that was a gateway to the Divine. The story of Badshahi Masjid of Lahore is the story of Dara Shikoh and Aurangzeb, of a shrine and a mosque and competing interpretations of religion.

Dara Shikoh's death was lamented in Lahore, just as it was in Delhi. This grief, for a little while at least, took the form of resentment against the new structure, Badshahi Masjid. The mosque seemed a reminder of the fallen prince and the 'usurper' brother. Some local narratives suggest that for several years after its construction, people refused to offer prayers there.[12] The memory of the unconstructed pathway gradually receded but some memories of Dara Shikoh remained alive. This narrative remains popular even today in certain intellectual circles in Lahore.

While in the popular narrative, Aurangzeb's 'usurpation' of the throne from the crown prince is depicted as a sign of his treachery, there are a few historians who counter this simplistic account. For them, Dara Shikoh's appointment as crown prince was part of the problem. However, all of these narratives agree that Aurangzeb was perhaps the most politically astute and battle-hardened of his brothers, while Dara Shikoh, despite being the crown prince, was the least prepared in statecraft.

Primogeniture was not really part of the Mughal ethos. Shah Jahan himself was Jahangir's third son and much like his own sons, had rebelled against his father. By the time Shah Jahan became emperor, it was quite clear that ascendancy to the Mughal throne would be contested, with sons rebelling against fathers, and brothers killing brothers. Even within the Timurid tradition, from where the Mughals traced their descent, the concept of competition between princes for the throne was an accepted convention.[13] In this context, the title of crown prince did not hold much significance. Aurangzeb's challenge to Dara Shikoh was therefore almost a part of Mughal heritage.

While Aurangzeb and the other princes were given important military assignments far away from the capital, Dara Shikoh, being the favourite son, was kept close. Despite holding political and military posts, he lacked the actual field experience that his brothers had. This was to play a crucial role during the battle of succession.

When Dara Shikoh had been given a crucial military assignment—to secure the region of Kandahar—he had failed miserably. Historical records suggest how, instead of listening to the advice of his commanders, he heeded the advice of soothsayers and spiritual leaders, making decisions that turned out to be catastrophic for the Mughal forces. Not many in the Mughal nobility were convinced of Dara Shikoh's ability to transform into an effective ruler.

This was compounded by the fact that Dara Shikoh had managed to rub several noblemen the wrong way with his haughty behaviour and lack of interest in their advice. In 1658, at a crucial point in the all-important Battle of Samugarh fought between Dara Shikoh on one side and Aurangzeb and Murad, the youngest brother, on the other, Khalil Allah, a commander of Dara's, betrayed him for his alleged intimate relationship with his wife.[14]

So while Dara Shikoh had religious views that were beyond doubt much more tolerant than his brother's, it does not necessarily mean that Dara would have made a more effective ruler or that the Hindu nobility would have unconditionally supported him over his brother. Several factors other than religious ideology determined the formation or rupture of political alliances. Even before Aurangzeb had secured the throne, many members of the nobility, Hindus and Muslims included, believed that given his military background and political shrewdness, he was the most able heir to the Mughal throne. It doesn't seem as if Aurangzeb's puritanism deterred his potential allies or that Dara Shikoh's appreciation of Hindu philosophy won him much support during the crucial war of succession.

Given Dara Shikoh's lack of political and military acumen, there is no reason to believe that the Mughal Empire would have lasted longer than it did had he succeeded to the throne. The campaign of Kandahar had clearly proven that while Dara shared Akbar's intellectual curiosity, he lacked the military and administrative skills that made his forebear such a successful sovereign.

Assured of their political and economic interests, Aurangzeb formed an alliance with the Rajputs during the war of succession.[15] Subsequently many members of the Rajput nobility, such as Jai Singh and Jaswant Singh, were accorded higher positions in the court of Aurangzeb, higher than any Hindu since the days of Emperor Akbar.[16] The reintroduction of jizya was opposed more by the working and trader classes in urban centres than the Hindu nobility.[17] The latter's association with the Mughal court actually increased after 1679, challenging the conventionally held belief that the reimposition of jizya put Aurangzeb at odds with his Hindu allies.[18]

Popularly, the reimposition of jizya is seen as evidence of an attempt to convert the majority population of his empire to Islam. While it is true that Aurangzeb justified the tax in the name of sharia or religious law, it not entirely fair to see it as an attempt to enforce Islamic law on a non-Muslim population in an effort to convert them. Even though in official pronouncements the tax was explained as a feature of Islamic law, there is reason to believe that there were economic compulsions behind it. The decision to reimpose jizya was taken in 1679, almost two decades after Aurangzeb had secured the Mughal throne for himself. It is suggested that the empire was in dire straits economically at the end of the 1670s due to several conflicts—in the Deccan, the north-east, with Afghan tribesmen, with the Rathors and the Sisodias.[19] Jizya, in this context, would have provided a much-needed infusion into the royal treasury.

Also, the Marathas were exerting their strength and several kingdoms, such as Bijapur and Golconda, were aligning with them. Through his military operations in the Deccan, Aurangzeb wanted to destroy this alliance but it did not go according to plan and the Marathas remained undaunted. In these trying times, the emperor wanted to invoke religious passion among his Muslim subjects and get them to rally behind him. The reintroduction of jizya was an attempt in that direction.[20]

Another problem with the narrative of the tolerant Sufi versus the fundamentalist puritan is the tacit assumption that Dara Shikoh, given his patronage of and interest in Hindu philosophy, was an exception. The comparison between Dara and Akbar implies that other Mughals were not as tolerant or encouraging of non-Muslim philosophy. On the contrary, there is enough historical evidence that Dara Shikoh, rather than being an exception, was a product of Mughal ethos.

While Akbar began the process of patronizing Hindu scholars and artists, the tradition was upheld by his successors. Jahangir patronized Hindu scholars, poets and artists such as Jadrup Gossain, Rai Manohar Lal, Bishnu Das and Buta or Briksha Rai. Shah Jahan's reign is described as a vibrant era in the history of Hindi language and literature.[21] A few prominent writers and poets connected with his court were Jagannath Pandit, Sundar

Das, Chintamani and Kavindra Acharya. This patronage of Hindu scholars writing in Hindi and Persian continued during the reign of Aurangzeb. Some famous poets and writers who received his support were Birdas, Bhushan, Brinda, Wamat Khattri, Rai Brindaban and Ishwardas Nagar.[22]

There is little reason to believe that many, or most, of Aurangzeb's policies were shaped by his religious worldview. For example, Aurangzeb had Dara Shikoh declared a heretic in order to justify his execution. It needs to be borne in mind that Dara was a particularly popular prince and when he was brought to Delhi for his trial, ordinary city folk came out on to the streets to catch a last glimpse of their prince. Dara's alleged heresy was, in this context, a political tool that Aurangzeb used to construct a narrative around the prince to justify his execution and garner some support for himself, at least from the conservative segment of society. It was a way to get rid of his opponent.

Sarmad, the naked fakir, was also executed because of his political support of the defeated prince, rather than his heterodox religious doctrine. At a time when the old emperor was still alive and a popular prince was at the mercy of a new, self-declared emperor, Aurangzeb might have believed that by aligning his politics with religion, he could strengthen his control over the empire.

Most of Aurangzeb's actions can be explained by these political factors. For example, Aurangzeb is accused of destroying Hindu temples, which is correct but needs to be understood in its context. By ordering the destruction of certain Hindu temples, Aurangzeb was following a long-established tradition of the subcontinent that preceded Muslim rule. Historians such as Romila Thapar and Satish Chandra have identified how prominent Hindu temples were political organizations, closely affiliated with the ruling class of the region. Thus, in cases of rebellion against a king or during times of expansion of the empire, these temples, associated with the ruling class of that particular region, were targeted. It was not just Muslim rulers but also Hindu and Jain kings who engaged in this practice.[23] Therefore, to attribute this tradition to the iconoclastic zeal of a fanatical Muslim emperor would not be an accurate historical reading of events.

This perception is reinforced by the writings and the orders of the kings themselves, who seem to justify the destruction of the temples in the name of Islam. Recent scholarship has dismissed these sources as rhetoric, part of a state-building process, seeking to establish justification for an autocratic ruler's actions.

Analysed in this context, it becomes easier to comprehend why the emperor would order the destruction of certain temples, ignore others, appreciate some and even provide grants to others. While Aurangzeb sought to demolish the temples in Marwar to punish the rebellion of its rulers, he ordered no such thing in the Deccan even when he conquered new areas.[24]

This shows that there were political considerations at play, and there was no indiscriminate destruction of non-Muslim shrines and temples to satisfy some sort of fanatical religious zeal. There is documentary evidence to suggest that Aurangzeb renewed land grants held by Hindu temples in Mathura, the Jangam Bari Math in Varanasi and Balaji's temple in Chitrakoot.[25] There is also evidence of him offering gifts to temples, as also a Sikh gurdwara in Dehradun.[26] He is sometimes falsely accused of destroying the temples at the caves in Ellora. This is not only untrue, but he in fact praised them in his writing, attributing them to the graciousness of Allah.[27] Barbara Metcalf, a contemporary historian with a specialization in South Asia, has pointed out that during his reign Aurangzeb built more temples than he destroyed.[28]

Aurangzeb's attitude towards music and his 'banning' of all performances is identified as a manifestation of his puritanical zeal, reflected in the increasing Islamization of the Mughal Empire, laying the seeds of its imminent destruction. Some historical evidence suggests that Aurangzeb's revulsion towards music began with a youthful affair with a famed singer, Hira Bai Zainabadi. Tragically, Hira Bai died within nine months of their association. It is falsely argued that Aurangzeb gave up listening to music after the sudden death of his lover.[29]

While there is historical evidence to suggest there was some sort of a ban on music, what the ban meant and why it was implemented is open to competing interpretations. First, it needs to be borne in mind that the 'ban' was ordered around 1668–69, almost a decade after Aurangzeb's ascension to the throne. Before this, musical performances were a regular feature of court life, much like they had been throughout Mughal history. Second, there is enough evidence to suggest that the ban applied only to the court of the emperor and not the entire empire. Several close associates of Aurangzeb, including his family members such as his father-in-law Shah Nawaz Khan Safavi, his sister Jahanara, and his daughter Zeb-un-Nissa, continued to patronize musicians and dancers. While Aurangzeb was away in the Deccan, Delhi, due to the patronage of Mughal nobility, became an important centre of the performing arts.[30] Powerful allies of the emperor who remained in close proximity to him during his campaigns continued to enjoy music as well.[31]

Despite the ban on music, Aurangzeb did not render his court musicians and performers unemployed. They received court patronage even though music no longer featured in the royal court. In the rest of the empire, the patronage and performance of music continued unabated. So it can be argued that Aurangzeb's banning of music was a personal decision, part of his notions of piety, a process of exhibiting 'self-control' for the fulfilment of his political ambitions.[32]

While there is no doubt the Mughal Empire went through a process of 'Islamization' during the reign of Aurangzeb, this process cannot be attributed to the iconoclastic, missionary zeal of the emperor as is popularly imagined. There were political reasons behind the implementation of several religious laws, even when the rhetoric was religious.

Aurangzeb was a crafty politician who used religion when it suited him and became 'tolerant' when needed. Perhaps Dara Shikoh, had he succeeded the Mughal throne, might not have reimposed jizya, but his lack of military and administrative skills would have hardly ensured that the Mughal Empire survived longer than it did.

A group of men sat under the shade of an old tree next to the mausoleum. For a moment they paused their conversation and looked towards me. I walked inside, stopping in front of a board that recalled its story, 'Noor Jahan's Tomb', with a faded picture of the empress in the background.

The mausoleum, a single-storey structure with no minarets or domes typical of Mughal architecture, was in one corner of a garden, protected by a boundary wall. Raised on a small platform, a heap of bricks lay at its base to be used in its renovation. Several masons worked in and around the mausoleum. The fresh tiles of the facade of the building shone in the bright sun as the government officials supervising the renovation lost interest in me soon enough and resumed their conversation.

This was once a vast garden, merging into an accompanying garden that contained the mausoleums of Asaf Khan, her brother, and Emperor Jahangir, her husband. Behind the web of electrical wires, the oval dome of Asaf Khan's mausoleum is still visible, separated from the grave of his sister by a railway line laid during the colonial era. The garden of the mausoleum, in perfect symmetry with bricked pathways running down its middle, must have once been a sight to behold, with its fruit trees, flowering plants and waterways, an imperfect attempt to replicate the Garden of Eden. It was now struggling to retain its grass. Only a few trees remained.

In the last years of her life, when the empress was completely divorced from the Mughal political life of which she had once been a central figure, even overshadowing her alcoholic husband, Nur Jahan had vast financial resources at her disposal, granted to her by Jahangir, inherited from her powerful father and raised through her own system of taxation and duties as she single-handedly ran the affairs of the Mughal court.

During the last seventeen years of her life, as her stepson, her sworn enemy during the final years of Jahangir's reign, Shah Jahan, sat at the head of the Mughal Empire, using all the resources at his disposal to discredit Nur Jahan's legacy, she was granted permission to stay in the city and regularly visit her husband's grave. While Jahangir died far away from Lahore, in the foothills of Kashmir, he had expressed the desire to be buried here.

As the battle of succession hastily unfolded in the aftermath of Jahangir's death, Nur Jahan, despite her years of planning and manoeuvring, was quickly outsmarted and imprisoned by Asaf Khan. With various forces looking to secure the throne for themselves, including Jahangir's youngest son, Prince Shahryar, with a concubine who had been backed by the empress, Nur Jahan was cut off from the events and forced to travel to Lahore from Bhimber with her husband's body. With the defeat and subsequent death of Shahryar, Nur Jahan's political influence died as well.

It is believed that the mausoleum of Emperor Jahangir was built by Nur Jahan, who took an active role in its design and construction just as she had in the building of several other gardens and monuments during her reign as empress. Another opinion is that while Nur Jahan may have been involved in the initial planning, the structure was raised by Shah Jahan, for whom the mausoleum might have been a way of legitimizing his ascension after his earlier falling out with his father.[33]

While tension had been brewing between father and son for years, Prince Khurram openly rebelled against the emperor in 1621 upon hearing of his father's illness and anticipating his imminent death. Jahangir survived and Khurram, despite his initial success in Bengal, was eventually left high and dry, with his army routed. He had to go into exile with his family to the Deccan.

Relations between the two remained fraught till the spring of 1626, when Khurram, defeated and stripped of his political support, sought his father's mercy and was granted it, on the condition of abandoning a couple of forts in his possession and sending his young sons, Dara Shikoh and Aurangzeb, to the Mughal court. As the princes travelled to the court, Khurram, utterly dejected, remained in the Deccan which had for years served as his power base.

It was the Deccan that had once raised the prince to the penultimate position, outgrowing his other brothers in stature and establishing firmly his position as the favourite to succeed his father. Even though the prince had already proven himself to be a successful military commander in campaigns to Mewar and Gujarat, it was his success in the Deccan in 1616, when others before him had failed, that was the decisive feather in his cap. For this, he was given the title of Shah Jahan, king of the world, by Emperor Jahangir upon his return. It was the title he would adopt when he ascended to the Mughal throne. He was also awarded the right to sit next to his father during the emperor's assemblies.[34] However, what should have cemented the authority of the young prince eventually resulted in undermining it.

Prince Khurram's rise had been engineered by powerful allies, often referred to as 'junta' in the Mughal court. It is believed that soon after his marriage to Nur Jahan, the emperor handed over the reins of administration to the empress and the junta, happy to spend his days consuming alcohol and opium and enjoying the benefits of his vast empire. His desire was not to further expand the already stretched borders but to simply retain them. Nor was he particularly keen on engaging in the day-to-day affairs of the kingdom, like his father, and was more than willing to allow the empress an active role in its administration, for which she had a flair.

In this, she was accompanied by her father, the charismatic Mirza Ghias Beg, who after migrating from Persia under dire circumstances with his family during the time of Akbar, had risen through the hierarchy of the Mughal bureaucratic administrative structure to secure for himself the position of wazir. He had been awarded the title 'Itimad-ud-Daula', pillar of the state. The third most powerful member of this junta was Asaf Khan, Nur Jahan's elder brother and the father of Mumtaz Mahal, Khurram's wife.

While this alliance of convenience functioned smoothly, there were inherent contradictions which would soon surface. One of the biggest concerns was the question of succession. With Khurram proving his military skills, it was clear that he was the likeliest to succeed the emperor. The eldest prince, Khusrau, had lost his father's support after a failed rebellion, soon after Jahangir's ascension to the throne.

Khusrau's action was in turn the result of another rebellion, of Salim (Jahangir) against his father, Akbar, during the last years of his life. With Salim defeated and already showing signs of alcoholism, a powerful lobby gathered around the young Khusrau. It was even rumoured that Akbar was planning to bypass his son for his grandson, Khusrau. Akbar did eventually forgive Salim and appointed him his successor. Perhaps it was Salim's own rebellion against his father that led him to understand Khurram's revolt and forgive him in the aftermath of his defeat. During Akbar's lifetime, the relationship between Salim and Khusrau remained tense.

After he became emperor, Jahangir had Khusrau 'jailed' at Agra Fort. However, the prince, using the excuse of an excursion, escaped and, gathering his supporters, rebelled against the rule of his father. He was defeated soon after and brought to the emperor in Lahore.

Every evening, dozens of boatmen gather on the banks of the Ravi, offering to take tourists to a little island in the middle of the river, upon which stands a Mughal structure, believed by many to be the oldest building in the city of Lahore. Known as the baradari of Kamran Mirza, the structure is an open room surrounded by a little garden. Originally constructed on the western bank of the river, the baradari eventually found itself in the middle, as the whimsical Ravi changed its course.

Kamran Mirza was the younger brother of Emperor Humayun who too rebelled against his brother for the throne. Soon after his ascension, Humayun turned his attention to Bengal, the eastern frontier where unrest was brewing, handing over the western frontier to his brother. With the emperor away, Kamran established his suzerainty over Punjab. He is believed to have constructed this baradari in Lahore around this time.

With the temporary overthrow of the Mughal Empire and the rise of Sher Shah Suri, a commander who had accompanied Babur to India, Kamran is believed to have reached out to him to grant him control over Punjab for his support against Humayun. He was turned down by the Afghan king. The conflict between the brothers continued as Humayun sought refuge in Persia while Kamran found his way to Kandahar. Kamran was eventually defeated by Humayun, blinded and exiled to Mecca.

Perhaps it was to remind Khusrau of the fate of Kamran Mirza that Jahangir set up court at the baradari as he waited for the arrival of his defeated son. While Khusrau's life was spared, his allies were not as lucky. Mounting him on an elephant next to himself, the emperor marched towards Lahore with the bodies of his allies impaled and hung along the way.[35] In fact, the fifth Sikh Guru Arjan also lost his life for his alleged sympathy towards the prince. Despite his defeat and a lenient punishment, almost a year later, Khusrau is believed to have planned an assassination attempt while imprisoned in Lahore. When his plan was disclosed, Jahangir had the prince blinded and incarcerated under a stricter watch.[36]

While Khusrau was incapacitated, the second son, Parvaiz, was 'dull and incompetent'[37] and, like his father, fond of drinking. Shahryar, the fourth son, had earned the nickname 'good-for-nothing' and is believed to have been easily manipulated.[38] It was therefore not a surprise that Khurram emerged as the likeliest candidate. He understood that if he wanted to rise to the top, he needed powerful allies close to the seat of power. Who could be better than Nur Jahan and her family! Thus Khurram became the fourth and final member of the powerful junta that was in complete charge of the functioning of the Mughal state.[39]

Soon enough, fissures in the junta were visible as Nur Jahan became aware of the increasingly independent power of Khurram. Within the junta he was firmly backed by Asaf Khan, his father-in-law, to whose daughter, Mumtaz Mahal, Khurram was completely devoted. Nur Jahan realized that in the new political dispensation that would arise after Jahangir's death, her role would be particularly diminished as her brother's fortunes would increase exponentially. She thus made a move that would change the nature of Mughal battles of successions, making them bloodier.

Mehr-un-Nissa or Nur Jahan married Emperor Jahangir in 1611 after his gaze fell upon her during the Nauroz festival in the palace, which she had attended with her patron, Ruqayya Begum. She was given the title of Nur Jahan by the emperor after marriage. Ever since the death of her first husband, Sher Afghan, a few years ago, Mehr-un-Nissa had moved to the royal court to serve Ruqayya Begum, the chief consort of Emperor Akbar. Sher Afghan was serving in Bengal when he was killed during a skirmish with the Mughal forces. Even though he had been appointed on the orders of Emperor Jahangir, he was later accused of negligence and asked to present himself at the royal court. When Mughal forces were sent in to arrest him, he sensed foul play and attacked and killed Qutbuddin Khan Koka, who had been tasked with bringing him in. He was killed subsequently by Qutbuddin's soldiers.

Years later, when Emperor Shah Jahan was secure on the Mughal throne, historians would note how Sher Afghan was killed on the orders of Emperor Jahangir so he could marry his wife. She had one daughter from her first marriage, Ladli Begum, who would remain her only child. Ladli Begum is buried in Nur Jahan's mausoleum, next to her.

There are rumours that Nur Jahan wanted Ladli Begum to marry Prince Khurram to attach her fortune to the rising sun, but the prince turned down the offer. The empress is even believed to have approached Khusrau in imprisonment with the offer of marriage and an incentive of freedom if he agreed, but he too turned it down. The empress then approached the youngest son of Jahangir, the easily manipulated Shahryar. The two were married in 1621.

With this marriage, Nur Jahan's intentions became obvious to the other members of the junta. The battle for the throne had begun. The relationship between Asaf Khan and his sister worsened. Keeping a lid on this tension was their father, Mirza Ghias Beg. But with his death in 1622, the relationship quickly deteriorated.[40] What aggravated the situation was when, upon his death, the emperor turned over all his possessions to Nur Jahan instead of his eldest son, as was the convention. To Asaf Khan it was clear that the emperor had done this at the behest of the empress to undermine Asaf Khan's authority.

The single greatest blow to the junta came with the worsening of the situation in the Deccan in 1620. On the basis of his past success, the emperor asked Khurram to head south to handle the matter, but the latter was aware of the changing circumstances at the court and was also cognizant of the emperor's failing health. Khurram had noticed the growing leniency of the emperor towards Khusrau, whose terms of imprisonment had been relaxed over the past few years. He realized that being far removed from the seat of power, he would be in the least advantageous position in case of the emperor's death.

Thus Khurram decided to march to Deccan but on condition that Khusrau be handed over to him. In this demand he was supported by both Asaf Khan and Nur Jahan who understood that with Khusrau and Khurram away, she would be in a better position in case of the emperor's death. She was also aware of the fact that if any harm were to befall the eldest son of the emperor while in Khurram's custody, he would be isolated from not only his father but also his powerful allies.

The expedition down south, as expected, was a success and within six months the unrest was subdued. Khurram, while still in the Deccan, was gifted awards and properties for his accomplishments.

Soon after, on 29 January 1622, Jahangir received a message from Khurram that Khusrau had died of colic pain.[41] Initially receiving the news without scepticism, the emperor began doubting Khurram's intentions when he heard an official who was present with both brothers blaming Khurram for Khusrau's murder. It is likely that upon hearing the news of Jahangir's failing health, Khurram acted pre-emptively to remove the eldest prince from his path. But now his position had been compromised. The emperor ordered the prince to report back to him in person, an order that Khurram refused to acknowledge.

While these events were unfolding in the Deccan, there was unrest on the eastern front of the empire as well, with the city of Kandahar under siege. It is believed that it is during these last few years of Jahangir's life that Nur Jahan acquired unprecedented power. With the junta dismantled and Asaf Khan still serving in the court of the emperor but with his loyalties attached to the rebel prince, Nur Jahan ran the show single-handedly. It is she who is believed to have convinced the emperor to order Khurram to move eastwards to subdue Kandahar, thus making it difficult for him to capture the throne when the moment came. Khurram could hardly refuse to obey the command of the emperor, else he would be declared a rebel.

Khurram, realizing the empress's intention, refused to head to Kandahar, forcing the emperor to order Shahryar to address the issue, which met with little success. As a punishment to Khurram, the emperor ordered the confiscation of certain properties of the prince to fund the expedition to Kandahar. Even as Jahangir took away some properties from Khurram, he awarded a few others as compensation, which shows that the emperor at this point still had no intention of completely isolating the most competent of his sons.

Open conflict erupted soon after, when Khurram was informed about the royal treasury being removed from Agra. Capturing the treasury would mean a shift in the balance of power. It is believed that it was once again Nur Jahan who engineered this move with the intention of bringing to the fore the cold war that was being fought between father and son. Strategically, it was Asaf Khan who was given the responsibility of removing the treasury from Agra, thus making sure that the news reached the rebel prince.

Khurram fell for the bait and marched towards Agra to capture the royal treasury.

Mughal forces led by Mahabat Khan, an old friend of the emperor's, and Prince Parvaiz routed the rebel prince's army, forcing him to retreat to the Deccan. With the success of Parvaiz under the guidance of Mahabat Khan, a new player had entered the battle of succession, where each of the contestants was supported by powerful allies. Parvaiz's triumph was short-lived as Nur Jahan, now threatened by the growing power of Mahabat Khan, raised doubts about his loyalty, forcing him to rebel against the emperor. As a result, both the emperor and the empress were captured by Mahabat Khan's forces.

Once again it was the genius of Nur Jahan that came to the rescue. Despite being under watch, she managed to reach out to her allies, asking them to prepare a force that would rescue them from Mahabat Khan. The latter was defeated and eventually joined hands with Khurram, abandoning his former protégé, Parvaiz. Isolated and left in the wilderness, Parvaiz died of excessive alcohol consumption in 1626. Some accounts suggest he was poisoned by Khurram. The final battle was to be played out between Prince Shahryar and Khurram, or between Nur Jahan and her brother, Asaf Khan.

Security officials at the entrance to Jahangir's mausoleum, just outside the city of Lahore, ensure that no visitor enters without a ticket. Within the complex, there is a *sarai*, a royal inn, flanking which are the mausoleums of Jahangir and Asaf Khan. While most of the visitors entering with me headed to the mausoleum of the emperor, located in the middle of a vast garden, with four tall minarets at each end of the rectangular building, I headed in the opposite direction, towards the mausoleum of Asaf Khan, who in all practicality ensured Prince Khurram's ascension to the Mughal throne.

While the garden around Jahangir's mausoleum was neatly trimmed, the grass at Asaf Khan's was overgrown. The mausoleum itself had a dome at its apex, though it had lost the tiles and mosaic that had once covered its facade. Built for the most powerful person in the Mughal court after the emperor, this building once depicted wealth and power. While the mausoleum of Jahangir was regularly looked after, and renovation was under way at the mausoleum of Nur Jahan, the mausoleum of Asaf Khan remained untouched. The kingmaker is not the same as the king.

Events unfolded quickly following the death of Emperor Jahangir in the hills of Kashmir, from where he was returning after having failed to recuperate from his illness. The empress quickly summoned a meeting of all the powerful nobles, perhaps to garner support for Shahryar to succeed his father. Asaf Khan refused to attend the meeting. Instead, he had her 'imprisoned' within her tent. The empress was thus rendered powerless. Despite the surveillance, she is believed to have leaked a message to Shahryar in Lahore urging him to collect soldiers and come to her rescue.

Hearing about his father's death, Shahryar declared himself the emperor in Lahore. His greatest advantage at this point was his strategic location—in Lahore, where the royal treasury was located. Taking over, he began distributing wealth to garner support for himself. It is estimated that the prince gave away 70 lakh rupees.[42] However, despite his frantic and desperate efforts, he was able to win over only a few nobles. Perhaps if the empress had been close to him, the situation might have turned out differently.

Meanwhile, Khurram was in the Deccan and at least three months away from Lahore.[43] Asaf Khan quickly sent a rider informing him about the emperor's death and asking him to seize the Mughal throne. Asaf Khan realized that with multiple contestants, he would not be able to hold the Mughal throne without the prince for much longer. It is here that he made his master move.

On 29 October 1627, Dawar Baksh, Khusrau's eldest son, was declared emperor of the Mughal empire, supported by Asaf Khan and his allies. They headed towards Lahore where, at a little distance from the city, they confronted the forces of Shahryar and routed them. Shahryar was subsequently captured and blinded. The path was now clear for Khurram to declare himself emperor of the Mughal Empire.

Having been assured of his imminent coronation, Khurram passed an order to his father-in-law that changed the course of subsequent Mughal successions. Still on his way, Khurram ordered the execution of Shahryar, Dawar Baksh, his brother and the sons of Daniyal, a brother of Emperor Jahangir who had died much earlier.[44] Thus, in one blow, all possible claimants to the Mughal throne were eliminated. Never before in the history of the Mughal succession had such an act been committed. A new precedent had been set. It can be said that Aurangzeb was simply following in the footsteps of his father.

I parked the car in front of a small shrine dedicated to Major Shabbir Sharif, a Pakistani solider who had posthumously received the highest military gallantry award, Nishan-e-Haider, for his heroism during the 1971 war. It was a modest structure, where a few visitors had gathered on a Sunday morning as they came visiting their dead relatives.

The graveyard, Miani Sahib, the oldest and largest in the city, extends on both sides of the road. There is an entire network of roads within the graveyard spread over several acres. At the edge of the road where I parked, a vendor of rose petals had set up his stall. The fragrance permeated the air as he sprinkled water on them. There were also incense sticks and chadars with Quranic inscriptions that one could offer at the graves or at one of the many shrines that dotted this graveyard.

Deep within the graveyard, I came across the grave of Dulla Bhatti, a simple cemented structure under an old tree. A board next to it identified its occupant. There was no sign of devotees or visitors, no rotting petals or faded chadars. This was not the grave of a Sufi saint or one of those who, for one reason or another, emerged as Sufi saints after their death, but of a rebel, a landlord from Pindi Bhattian, a town 150 kilometres from Lahore.

Hanged outside the Delhi Darwaza of Lahore on the orders of Emperor Akbar in 1599, much like his father and grandfather before him who were also executed by the emperor, their bodies left hanging, Dulla Bhatti's public execution was meant to serve as an example to the people of the city. However, numerous legends narrate how even in the face of death he stood defiantly, cursing and abusing the emperor residing in Lahore Fort.

Watching the spectacle was the dervish poet of Lahore, Shah Hussain. Many have claimed that he was sympathetic to Dulla's cause and was his associate. At the time of his execution, he is believed to have engaged in a verbal duel with Ali Malik, the Mughal officer in charge of the execution, who threatened him. Prophetically, Shah Hussain predicted that Ali Malik would be killed by the order of the emperor on the same day.

Later, when Ali Malik presented himself at the court of the emperor, Akbar ordered him to recall everything the rebel landlord had uttered before his execution. Giving him a verbatim response, Ali Malik recounted all the profanities Dulla Bhatti had intended for the emperor. Offended, the emperor had him executed the same day for responding literally to his question.[45]

There is no historical evidence to suggest that Shah Hussain and Dulla Bhatti actually knew each other. What relates them is their rebellion. While Dulla Bhatti rebelled against the political organization of the increasingly centralized Mughal kingdom, Shah Hussain rebelled against religious hegemony. He was a Malamati Sufi, belonging to a particular Sufi tradition that challenges conventional normative societal practices. It throws topsy-turvy notions of purity, halal-haram, the sacred and the profane, religiosity and the lack of it.

Shah Hussain is believed to have once abandoned his prayer, which he was leading for a congregation of devotees, after coming across a verse from the Quran stating that God is closer to a believer than one's jugular vein. If God was closer to him than his jugular vein, then He understands his intention better than him, he rationalized. Why then is there a need to express his love for the Divine through ritualistic obligation?

Leaving the mosque, he headed straight to a barber, cut his beard, the symbol of his religion, and went to a tavern and got himself a flask of wine, following which he procured for himself a set of ghungroos and began singing and dancing in the streets of Lahore,[46] all activities deemed 'impure'. His songs were immortalized in his verses as folk singers, musicians and other dervishes sang them, from one generation to another, earning him the status of one of the greatest Sufi Punjabi poets along with Baba Farid, Guru Nanak and Bulleh Shah.

His devotees made him a Sufi saint after his death, turning his grave into a shrine, a symbol of purity, even though he spent his entire life challenging the same notions. In the years to come, he, along with Mian Mir, emerged as the patron saint of Lahore. His annual *urs*, celebrated in spring, is attended by thousands of people. Here they dance, sing and consume hashish, revering the 'Sufi saint' in a non-conventional, non-ritualistic manner, attuned to the philosophy of Shah Hussain.

In precolonial Lahore, where religious boundaries were fluid and the courtyards of shrines, temples and gurdwaras were shared, the adherence to a non-ritualistic devotional form allowed

members of all backgrounds to express their devotion to Shah
Hussain in their own particular manner.

Buried next to Shah Hussain is his beloved Madho Lal,
a Hindu boy to whom he is believed to have been devoted. So
'pure' is their love that their distinct identities have merged and
the shrine is today popularly referred to as 'Madho Lal Hussain'.
This is a popular recurring theme in the Punjabi Sufi tradition,
where the devotee and the beloved, seeker and divine, become
one, if the love is pure. Using the traditional Punjabi symbols of
Heer for the devotee, and Ranjha for the beloved, the divine, Shah
Hussain recited the following:

> Calling upon the name of my beloved
> I myself became Ranjha
> Call me Ranjhan for I am no longer Heer

To devotees who grew up listening to songs of Radha's devotion
to Krishna, Heer-Ranjha appeared as an extension of their own
tradition.

The situation began to change as Lahore 'modernized'
under the colonial regime. With Western education and an
increasingly communal consciousness, the concept of religiosity
also changed. Any tradition that diluted religious boundaries
came to be looked down upon as an 'impure' interpretation. The
educated, burgeoning middle class began moving away from such
Sufi shrines. Also, Sufi saints who upheld a more conventional
interpretation of religion, such as Ali Hujwiri, became prominent
in these changing times. Reflecting the changing sensibilities of
the city, Data Darbar became the most popular shrine of Lahore,
supplanting that of Shah Hussain.

In contemporary Lahore and across Punjab, Shah Hussain has
a unique significance and has been a symbol for leftists critical
of the hegemonic role that Punjab plays and the conservative

interpretation of religion for political ends. He is celebrated by various Punjabi nationalist groups, such as the Punjabi Adabi Board, a conglomeration of progressive Punjabi writers, poets and intellectuals. Every year on the occasion of his urs, along with malangs and dervishes, there is also a small presence of leftist intellectuals at his shrine.

In a similar manner, Dulla Bhatti too has acquired relevance in the contemporary context as a symbol of Punjabi nationalism, which has been overshadowed by a Pakistani identity. Dulla Bhatti is someone who draws together the different religious groups residing in Punjab. Along with Muslims, he is also celebrated by Punjabi Sikhs and Hindus. Much like Shah Hussain, Guru Nanak, Baba Farid and Bulleh Shah, he is a symbol of a Punjabi identity, predating its Pakistani construct. While the latter otherizes, the former brings together distinct religious traditions under one umbrella.

Every winter, on the occasion of Lohri in Punjab (not in Pakistan, though), which is celebrated in the middle of January as the indigenous month of *Poh* concludes and *Maghi* begins, people gather around bonfires in their villages and communities and sing songs of Dulla Bhatti's bravery. These are tales of his exploits—how he robbed the corrupt Mughal nobility and distributed the spoils among the poor. These are tales of how he salvaged the 'honour' of young girls from lecherous powerful men, about how he became their godfather and organized their weddings.

The most popular of these songs tells the story of Sundri and Mundri, two Brahmin sisters. It narrates how a local landlord once caught sight of them and expressed his desire to marry them against the wishes of the sisters and their father. The distressed father approached Dulla Bhatti, who became their godfather and married them off elsewhere. Another popular version of this folk story is that it was Emperor Akbar who fell in love with the beautiful girls and wanted them in his harem. Dulla Bhatti came to their rescue and had them married to suitable grooms on the occasion of Lohri, blatantly defying the emperor.[47]

> Sundri Mundriye
> Who will save you poor one
> Dulla Bhatti is here for you
> The Dulla married off his daughter[48]

There are several such apocryphal folk narratives that talk about how Dulla Bhatti, a landlord from Pindi Bhattian, humbled the mighty Mughal emperor on numerous occasions. Once, it is said, Akbar was passing through a forest in Dulla Bhatti's area and was captured by his forces. He was brought to the landlord's court, but instead of saying that he was the emperor, Akbar insisted that he was only the court jester. Through this pretence, Akbar managed to save his life. On another occasion, it is said, Dulla Bhatti's forces got hold of Prince Salim. Dulla Bhatti let him go, saying that his battle was with the emperor and not his son.[49]

These might be folk tales with little historical credibility, but they do reflect the devotion the people of Punjab felt for Dulla Bhatti and the pride they took in his bravado in the face of the mighty Mughal Empire. A similar folk narrative suggests that he grew up with Salim, raised by his mother, Ladhi. When Prince Salim was born, after a lot of prayers, a soothsayer predicted that for him to become a powerful leader, he needed to be fed milk by a Rajput woman who had given birth on the same day.[50] It turned out that Dulla Bhatti, a Rajput, was born on the same day and hence Salim was handed over to his mother, Ladhi, with several gifts.

Perhaps the emperor was trying to achieve a dual benefit from this arrangement. The landlords of Pindi Bhattian had been in a state of rebellion against the Mughal Empire for two generations. Both Sandal Bhatti and Farid Bhatti, Dulla's grandfather and father respectively, had lost their lives fighting Akbar. In this manner, it seemed Akbar wanted to win the loyalty of this family.

As Salim and Dulla grew up in the same house, Ladhi kept the family's weapons locked away in a room, never letting Dulla know how his father and grandfather had lost their lives. The story further suggests that while Salim thrived in academics, Dulla was better at physical exercise. Sitting on a tree, a young Dulla would aim for the pitchers of women with his catapult. Once, when he broke one, the woman mocked him saying that instead of exhibiting his bravery on these harmless pitchers, he should avenge the death of his father and grandfather. A distraught Dulla reached home, where his mother reluctantly opened the locked door. Thus began Dulla's rebellion.[51]

Folk tales apart, historians have identified the rebellion of the Bhatti clan to be a result of the centralization of the Mughal Empire. The nascent empire, bequeathed to a thirteen-year-old Akbar on the death of his father, was, towards the end of the sixteenth century, expanding in all directions. After throwing off the yoke of his advisers, Akbar embarked upon a process of military expansionism that made the Mughal Empire one of the greatest of its time. He began with extending it over Rajputana, followed by Gujarat and Bengal. After his success in the east he headed west, as Kashmir and parts of Baluchistan fell under his sway. The Deccan was added to the empire towards the end of his life.

As it expanded in all directions, the empire needed a new mechanism that would allow a powerful emperor to control such a vast territory. Akbar opened up the Mughal court to Rajput and other Hindu nobles, much to the chagrin of his Central Asian brethren.[52] He began to patronize the eclectic Chisti Sufi order, paving the way for the religious syncretism that came to define the Mughal court. He abolished the jizya tax and revoked the pilgrimage tax on Hindus. Land grants were awarded to scholars of all religions, while Hindu, Jain, Buddhist and other non-Muslim scholars were invited to the court for discussions.

It is for these reasons that Akbar today is imagined to be a champion of religious tolerance, the opposite of Aurangzeb. There are, however, several recorded events that undermine this 'tolerant' image. The emperor was known to project himself as an orthodox Sunni leader as well. For example, his Rajasthan campaign was referred to as jihad, holy war, to remove 'signs of infidelity'.[53] Throughout the 1560s there were various incidents when the emperor gave permission to forcibly convert certain non-Muslims. Members of a heterodox Islamic sect called Mahdawi were persecuted. Many puritanical Sunni clerics such as Makhdum ul-Mulk Abdullah Sultanpuri and Shaikh Abdun Nabi were patronized. His anti-Shiite sentiment, at least during the early years of his rule, was exhibited when in 1567 he ordered the exhumation of the body of Murtaza Sharif, a Shiite scholar, from an enclosure next to the mausoleum of the famous poet Amir Khusrau in Delhi.[54]

Explaining these contradictions, Munis D. Faruqi, an expert on Mughal history, has suggested that Akbar often resorted to his traditional Sunni credentials when he felt threatened by his half-brother, Mirza Hakim, who had declared a parallel empire in Kabul and posed a threat, if not militarily then ideologically, to the emerging Mughal Empire under Akbar.

While Akbar introduced changes in the administration of the empire to be able to smoothly manage his ever-increasing territory, he alienated many of his former supporters who felt he was betraying his Central Asian heritage. Taking advantage of this, Mirza Hakim began to project himself as the rightful heir to the throne of Babur, adherent of an orthodox Sunni tradition, 'true' to his Central Asian traditions.[55] The court of Mirza Hakim became a refuge for Akbar's political opponents.

Punjab played a particularly important role in this conflict between the two brothers. In 1566, Mirza Hakim invaded Punjab and reached all the way to Lahore. The city refused to yield and he had to eventually return. He made another attempt in 1582, but once again failed to capture the city. This time he had to retreat upon hearing about the arrival of the Mughal army under the emperor's command.[56]

With danger looming on the western front, Akbar paid particular attention to Punjab and Lahore. Lahore under Akbar emerged as a key imperial city, and cast away its parochial-town identity. Lahore became Lahore under Akbar, a title it retains till date. Major infrastructural projects were undertaken. Its boundary walls were strengthened. In 1567, the imperial mint was established in Lahore, making it one of only four centres in the Mughal Empire where coins were minted.[57] Lahore under Akbar was integrated into the Mughal economy. Roads and bridges in other parts of Punjab were also renovated. Parts of Sindh, Baluchistan and Kashmir were brought under Mughal rule to strengthen Akbar's control over Punjab.

It was the increasing control of the Mughal Empire over Punjab that led to the rebellion of the Bhatti clan. Part of the centralization effort was the new land demarcation process and the corresponding revenue system, which was not acceptable to several landlords, including Dulla Bhatti's grandfather, as it ate into their power and resources. The entire empire was divided into *subah*s (provinces), which were further divided into *sarkar*s (districts). The sarkars were divided into smaller units called *pargana*s. Looking at past records, Todar Mal, Akbar's finance minister, devised a taxation system in which the average annual yield of a pargana was calculated and tax was expressed in cash. This was radically different from the previous system in which the emperor relied on a tribute system with no fixed amount, thus giving the zamindar much more control over his economic resources.[58]

Further weakening the authority of the local zamindar, a Mughal administrator called a *faujdar* was appointed in every sarkar, whose job was to help the zamindar collect the stipulated taxes. With the knowledge of the average yield of a particular area, the faujdar would often bypass the local zamindar and go directly to the peasants to collect the taxes.

The faujdar was also allowed to keep a small army, make his own weapons and undertake development projects on behalf of the Mughal authority.[59] As the Mughal Empire extended its control over its territory, the autonomy of the local zamindar was severely compromised. It was to retain this independence that Sandal Bhatti, Dulla's grandfather, first rose up against the emperor, a struggle that continued till Dulla's time.

With the looming threat of his brother on the western front and faced with rebellion from the zamindars, Punjab acquired a special strategic significance for Akbar. Soon after the death of Mirza Hakim in 1585, Akbar abandoned Fatehpur Sikri and established his base in Lahore. Some assert that Akbar had to move his capital to Lahore to directly address the issue of Dulla Bhatti's rebellion.[60] Lahore, in the process, became a principal Mughal city.

Faruqui suggests that after the death of his brother, when there was no other 'rightful successor' of Babur, Akbar once and for all shed his Sunni Muslim ruler image and expressed himself much more freely in religious matters.

The policy of Sulh-i-Kul (peace to all) was formulated around this time.[61] Akbar also initiated his own religious order, which came to be known as Din-i-Ilahi (divine faith), while subsidies for hajj expeditions were withdrawn. Steps were taken to replace the Islamic *hijri* calendar with the *ilahi* calendar, in which the first year was the year of Akbar's ascension in 1556. He also banned the articulation of anti-Shia sentiment in the empire.[62]

His brother's ghost, however, continued to haunt him. In the 1590s, as Salim began presenting a political challenge to his father, many of Mirza Hakim's former supporters, including Mahabat Khan, joined his cause. Like Mirza Hakim, Salim too posed an ideological challenge to his father by casting himself as a religious Sunni alternative.

In these larger struggles of empires and legacies, Dulla Bhatti represents an indigenous movement against an imposing state, a movement to retain autonomy and freedom. While Akbar exhibited a propensity towards religious tolerance, he was still an autocrat, an absolute monarch, whose whims on occasion became laws. Thus, in an era of 'good' Muslim ruler versus 'bad' Muslim ruler, it becomes important to remember other smaller struggles, such as that of Dulla Bhatti, to gain a more nuanced picture of the politics of empire. However, his abandoned grave in Lahore today, visited occasionally by Punjabi nationalists and intellectuals, shows that Dulla's movement is not really remembered in the land of its origin.

8

HUMBLE ORIGINS

Deep within the bazaar, the mausoleum of Qutb al-Din Aibak, founder of the Slave Dynasty, is a lone structure, a yellow building, standing on a little platform. The grave lies within, covered with a piece of red cloth with verses from the Quran printed on it. Facing the mausoleum is a little garden. All around it are tall structures that encroach upon the building from above. These are residential quarters but many are also shops, part of the most iconic bazaar of the historic city of Lahore—Anarkali.

At a short distance from here is the Punjab Civil Secretariat, the centre of provincial bureaucracy, from where the colonial administrators once established their control over the province, a job that has now been taken over by the brown sahibs. The central building here is a specimen of classical European architecture, a bungalow with several colonnades. Constructed in the early nineteenth century by General Jean-François Allard, a French mercenary in the army of Maharaja Ranjit Singh, the building served as the residence of this famous European officer, one among many in the Khalsa army. Allard is buried close by.

Facing this bungalow is a seventeenth-century mausoleum, a typical Mughal structure with a large dome. It now serves as the Punjab Archives, with a vast collection of documents and photographs from the colonial era and earlier. In its past lives, it served as the residence of Prince Kharak Singh, and later of General Jean-Baptiste Ventura, an Italian soldier who joined the Khalsa army along with Allard. It was a church during the early years of colonial rule in Lahore.

Unlike other Mughal structures, the grave of the occupant of the mausoleum is situated in one corner, while the rest of the space has been taken over by a gallery of historical photographs, some hanging on the walls, others put up on boards placed all around the room. Popularly referred to as the mausoleum of Anarkali, the grave is believed to belong to the legendary concubine of Emperor Akbar who fell in love with Prince Salim and had to lose her life for the trespass.

Several historians have reinforced this popular narrative. Syed Abdul Latif, in his 1892 book, *Tareekh-e-Lahore*, claimed that Anarkali, whose original name was Sharf-un-Nissa, was buried alive in a wall for falling in love with Salim. A mausoleum in her memory was constructed by Emperor Jahangir when he succeeded his father. The same narrative was taken up by Imtiaz Ali Taj, a famous playwright from Lahore, who wrote the play *Anarkali* in 1922. This seminal work was to become the basis for many other fictional narratives crafted around the love story of Salim and Anarkali, including the iconic Indian film *Mughal-e-Azam*.

There are historians, however, who present an alternative story. Noor Ahmad Chishti, a chronicler of Lahore, wrote in his book *Tehqiqat-i-Chisti*, first published in 1849, that Anarkali or Sharf-un-Nissa was a favourite concubine of Akbar's who passed away when he was in the Deccan. There is no mention of the love story between Salim and Anarkali, but this happened around the time when Salim rose up in rebellion against his father. On his return from the Deccan, the emperor is believed to have ordered the construction of this splendid mausoleum in the memory of his favourite concubine.

Yet another story is presented by Muhammad Baqir in his book *Lahore: Past and Present* where he asserts that the mausoleum actually belonged to Sahib-i-Jamal, one of the consorts of Jahangir. Since it was located in a pomegranate (*anar*) orchard, it came to be known as the mausoleum of 'Anarkali'. Dara Shikoh in his book *Sakinat-ul-Auliya* also mentions a pomegranate orchard visited by the Sufi saint Mian Mir regularly. Perhaps this was the same garden. In any case, a concubine falling in love with a rebellious prince is highly unlikely. Even in Jahangir's own writings, there is no mention of Anarkali or Sharf-un-Nissa. Whatever the truth behind the story, the mausoleum is today popularly believed to be that of Anarkali who paid with her life for her crime of falling in love with a prince.

In the nineteenth century, as a bazaar developed here, it took its name from the mysterious mausoleum, which is a little distance away. In the years to come, Anarkali Bazaar was to become one of the most prominent markets of Lahore, selling everything from clothes to jewellery and now tyres and bicycles. A walk through the streets of this bazaar is a walk through the history of the city.

A turret rose from behind makeshift shops. Hundreds of people gathered around the clothes shops oblivious to the pre-Partition structure in their midst. It used to be a well, reserved for the Hindus of the area. Several Valmiki Hindus I interviewed from the vicinity told me how they, along with the Muslims, were not allowed to draw water from this well for fear of polluting it. A short distance away, across the street, was a tall white building, with the inscription 'Ram Krishna and Sons Booksellers'. The booksellers moved out of the building after Partition and it was taken over by shoe sellers.

Walking deeper into the bazaar, negotiating this congested space with other pedestrians, cycles, motorbikes, cars, rickshaws and vendors who had laid out their goods on carts, I came across Jia Ram Building, a famous residential building of pre-Partition Anarkali. It was actually a collection of buildings, all interconnected. While the original name was preserved on one of them, on another, Jia Ram had been chiselled off.

Not far from here are the remains of Bansi Mandir, the most exquisite Hindu temple in the area. Its eroded wooden jharoka and windows are covered by a web of wires running haywire, while parts of the facade of this multistorey building are hidden under boards of several shops in the vicinity. On the upper storey, the rooms had been partitioned and divided among several tenants. The temple could have easily passed off as another run-down pre-Partition building had it not been for an intricately designed turret rising from it.

Several such pre-Partition buildings are scattered all over the bazaar, fighting for space with newer, shinier, glass-covered buildings that are gradually replacing the older ones. In sharp contrast to other rundown historic structures is the mausoleum of Qutb al-Din Aibak, the slave king, protected by an iron fence from the shops and houses around it. In one corner of the mausoleum sat an old man, appointed by the government to look after it.

This was not always the case. Like other such structures, this too was a ramshackle old building, occupied by drug addicts, with garbage heaped in the empty plot by the neighbouring shopkeepers. The fate of the building changed in the 1970s when Zulfikar Ali Bhutto, then prime minister, ordered its renovation and regular maintenance. He understood the significance of this mausoleum, of a slave who rose through the ranks of the Ghurid

Empire to become a general in the army of Muhammad of Ghur (or Ghor). After the king's death, he became ruler of the north Indian territories of the Ghurid Empire and founded the Delhi Sultanate, which saw a series of Muslim rulers and was eventually replaced by the Mughals in the sixteenth century.

By selecting this building for renovation while ignoring the other historic structures around it, such as the neighbouring temple, the state was engaging in a process of streamlining history to fit its nationalistic agenda, while discarding aspects that did not fit its narrative. In Qutb al-Din Aibak, the Government of Pakistan had found a perfect candidate. While Muslim invasions of India began in the eighth century with Sindh, and then later with Mahmud Ghazni in the eleventh century, Muslim rule over north India was only established in the twelfth century with the Mamluk dynasty started by Qutb al-Din Aibak.

After establishing his empire, Qutb al-Din Aibak only managed to rule for four years, from 1206 to 1210 CE. These years were fraught with challenges as he spent his time oscillating between Delhi and Lahore, trying to maintain his writ over the areas under his control. He lost his life in a polo accident when he fell off his horse, not far from where his mausoleum is situated. He was buried in Lahore. The Mamluk dynasty saw some powerful rulers after him, including Iltutmish, his immediate successor, and Ghiyas ud-din Balban. Razia Sultana, the only woman to have ever ascended the throne of Delhi, was also a part of the Delhi Sultanate. The Mamluk dynasty was eventually overthrown towards the end of the thirteenth century by Jalal-ud-Din Khalji, who established the Khalji dynasty.

In Delhi, which was serving as Qutb al-Din Aibak's capital, the new king is said to have razed twenty-seven temples at the site of Mehrauli to construct the Qubbat-ul Islam, the oldest mosque in north India, from the ruins of these temples, after he defeated Prithviraj Chauhan.[1] In the process of Pakistani historiography, this represented the triumph of Muslims over Hindus, of Pakistan over India. His origin as a slave also allowed for an opportunity to highlight the 'democratic' nature of Islam, the antithesis to 'caste-ridden' Hinduism. This narrative is still part of official Pakistani history as it is presented in textbooks taught to children in schools and colleges.

This binary view, a dissection of the history of India into Hindu and Muslim, is a product of colonial historiography. In this interpretation, political motives were justified in the name of religion. For example, while it is true that temples were destroyed during Muslim invasions, several other temples were also constructed and protected under the Delhi Sultanate, as Muslim kings began ruling a Hindu-majority region.[2] The destruction of temples therefore may not necessarily have been due to iconoclastic zeal. Rather, it could have been a strategy to de-legitimize the political authority of local rulers, who in many instances drew their power from temples.[3] The looting and destruction of temples, presented as a feature of Muslim rule over India by colonial historians, was never exclusive to Muslim rulers. There are many instances of Buddhist, Hindu and Jain kings looting and attacking temples of their co-religionists during invasions.[4]

In presenting this binary version of the history of India, the British sought to rationalize their own colonization of the country. First, it needed to be underscored that India had been under occupation for several centuries, thus justifying its current occupation by yet another force. Second, by presenting the Muslim rulers as fanatical bigots who oppressed the Hindu population, the British wanted to present themselves as a benign alternative who were needed for the emancipation of the Hindu majority from a Muslim minority.

While it is true that the Muslim rulers of India came from 'outside', there were fundamental differences in the nature of their empires and the one established by the colonial regime. While the goal of the latter was to extract resources from the colony to send back to the home country, Britain in this case, the Muslim empires since Qutb al-Din Aibak became Indian in nature. There was no home country in their context where the extracted resources from a colony were expatriated. Their home was India.

Muslim and Hindu nationalists today, on both sides of the border, share this ideological framework through which history is constructed and understood. For Hindu nationalists, Qutb al-Din Aibak, Aurangzeb and other Muslim rulers are oppressive tyrants who subjugated the Hindus, destroying their temples to build mosques, motivated by a religious zeal. This interpretation has been used to justify events such as the demolition of the Babri Masjid in 1992.

Muslim nationalists interpret these actions as part of their religious devotion, which resulted in the triumph of their religion over others. Nationalists on both sides of the border have thus failed to challenge the simplistic assumptions of this historical point of view. There is thus no difference in their interpretations of history, a product of colonial historiography.

In a post-1971 Pakistan, with the separation of East Pakistan and Indira Gandhi asserting that the 'two-nation theory', the raison d'être of Pakistan, was dead, Zulfikar Ali Bhutto felt that the country faced an ideological existential threat. History, in subsequent years, became a powerful tool in his hand. A historical framework, adopted from the colonial predecessor, was used to contextualize this contemporary conflict between India and Pakistan. In many of his speeches pre- and post-1971, Bhutto referred to a historical conflict between Hindus and Muslims and the war which had been surging for hundreds of years. It is hardly surprising, then, that the mausoleum of Qutb al-Din Aibak, the slave king, was renovated, while a Hindu temple near it completely ignored. It is a narrative through which the Pakistani state continues to imagine history.

There was a tap on my shoulder. I looked at the person standing next to me. I had no idea who he was. I stared at him intently and he stared back. And then, almost like a siren, his voice emerged from the depths of an inexplicable silence, like a shout. 'Do you want this?'

There was a wooden bong in his hand, filled with charas. Just the sight of it triggered a wave of euphoria in my body. I don't know how high I was. Time had ceased to exist. I was beyond the threshold where I should have stopped smoking. The dholwala changed his beat as soon as I took the bong from my benefactor. It was a subtle change. Not many in the audience picked up on it. An extra loop had been added to the beat. It was building up. My benefactor began shaking his head, his long, unkempt hair flying all over his face.

The dervish at the centre of the courtyard next to the dholwala slowed his whirl. He stopped rotating, banging his feet on the ground lightly, accommodating the shift in the beat. His red *chola* danced to the sound of his ghungroo. He beat his foot passionately on the ground. The dholwala recognized the challenge. He added his own signature. They both competed. They both played along. No one was in a hurry. The slower the better. There was a drug-induced patience in the air. Everyone had caught on to the rhythm. Everyone was shaking their heads. Something would eventually give. The dervish, the dholwala, the audience or the beat itself.

The tame beat was now becoming a beast. It could no longer be controlled. The dholwala had to respond. The rhythm sped up. A moment of orgasm, beyond which lay nothing. The dervish too had become a beast. He whirled. He ran. He jumped. He cried. He laughed. The world was his, the moment was his. He longed for destruction. Nothing stood in his path. He alone existed. Nothing else deserved to exist. This was Lord Shiva's *tandava* that had once created the world but would now destroy it.

There are many similarities between the devotees of Shiva and dervishes from the Malamati Sufi school of thought. The Malamati within Sufism represent a group of devotees who do not adhere to any religious law. The *dhamaal* is an integral part of their religious experience. It is a carefree ecstatic dance in which a devotee loses control over himself or herself and is blown away by the rhythm of the music, much like Shiva's tandava, in his form as Nataraja. The dhamaal is only one example of similarities between Sufi dervishes and devotees of Shiva. Like them, the dervishes too sit around a fire in the night consuming hashish or bhang. The ash from the fire in both these traditions is regarded as sacred and is believed to contain healing properties. Shiva, as a *mahayogi*, has dreadlocks piled on top of his head, and it is believed that the River Ganga flows out of his hair, signifying its spiritual powers. The Muslim dervishes too let their hair grow long. Their locks signify life-energy and are believed to contain magical powers.[5]

It was a dance similar to Shiva's tandava that the saint Shahjamal is believed to have performed at this spot to create a giant mound under his feet. We were at the base of this mound. On the top was another musical devotion being performed—calmer, milder and perhaps a little more acceptable to the sensibilities of religious orthodoxy. A group of qawwals sang devotional songs while about 100-odd devotees listened to them patiently. The tomb of this seventeenth-century Muslim saint is located at the top of this mound.

The scene was different at the base. Here, at the centre of the courtyard, a couple of dholwalas played wild beats, improvising accordingly, as hundreds of devotees sat around them in a circle consuming hashish.

The shrine of Shahjamal is a unique island. Surrounded by large bungalows, the shrine is located in the middle of a small, congested community where every Thursday hundreds of devotees arrive to consume psychotropic substances and partake in devotional music. Although smoking hashish is illegal, here the government turns a blind eye, perhaps accepting its consumption as part of the shrine's tradition. It is also here that the secrets of the ancient city of Lahore are buried.

As mentioned in an earlier chapter, several historians believe that it is not the current walled city but the small town of Ichra, about 8 kilometres away, that constituted the ancient city of Lahore. Writing in the eleventh century, a little after the invasion of Mahmud Ghazni and the establishment of his control over Punjab and Lahore, Ali Hujwiri, or Data Sahib, who entered Punjab with Ghazni's caravan, identified the walled city of Lahore as a small village next to the town of Ichra.

Several other narratives strengthen this claim. Some of the oldest temples in Lahore, including the Chand Raat Mandir, were located in Ichra. It is also argued that the Lohari Darwaza of the walled city is actually a misnomer for 'Lahori', and faces Ichra, the original city of Lahore.

This shrine of Shahjamal, located atop a mound, is opposite Ichra, which has now become a congested market consumed by the metropolis of Lahore and devoid of a distinct identity. It must have been an abandoned mound in the seventeenth century when the saint decided to settle here, cut off from civilization.

Like many other archaeological ruins around the country, this one too was incorporated into religious folklore and acquired a particular significance in precolonial Lahore. According to folk stories, a Mughal princess's palace faced the saint's abode. Every morning, when the saint would offer his prayers on a tall building facing hers, she would feel her privacy invaded as anyone standing on the building could look into her palace. When she complained to him, the saint began performing the dhamaal in anger. Such was the vitality of his steps that the building collapsed and was buried under his feet.[6] This story can be viewed as a Muslim version of Shiva's tandava, the angry dance that almost destroyed the world.

While apocryphal in nature, the story may hold the secret to the city's origin. Perhaps an old, destroyed civilization lies buried under the shrine of the saint. Before history became a chronology of events, to be recorded by the colonial state, it was encapsulated, compressed and preserved in names, folk tales, myths and legends. Perhaps the history of Lahore is hidden somewhere in the story of Shahjamal.

Between the Lohari and Mochi Gates once existed the Shahalami Gate, one of the thirteen gateways to the walled city. Only the name survives today. This is also home to Shahalami Bazaar, another iconic bazaar of Lahore, known for its wholesalers, where retailers from all over Punjab come to shop. Deep within the bazaar, inside a mosque, is the mausoleum of Malik Ayaz, Lahore's governor during the Ghaznavid Empire.

While the mosque is imposing, the tomb is nondescript, a small room with a grave and a dome on top. This is regarded as the final resting place of the architect of Lahore, the loyal slave of Mahmud Ghazni.

More is known about Ayaz through legends and tales than recorded history. Historical sources suggest that he was favoured by the king and was raised to the position of the chief of slaves; however, in later poetic and other literary references, the relationship between Mahmud Ghazni and Ayaz acquired a particular significance, of a deep love, even symbolic of the love between a devotee and the divine. In the poems of Saadi, Bostan, Jalaluddin Rumi and even Allama Iqbal, Ayaz is represented as a perfect man, utterly devoted to his master, Mahmud Ghazni, just as a believer is enamoured of God and devoted to him completely.[7] It is these later poets, writers and historians who present a romantic relationship between the two. There are several stories and traditions recording incidents where these two men expressed their love for one other.

Whereas in the Persian literary tradition Ayaz came to signify a true lover, in the writings of Muslim historians, particularly those writing from India, Mahmud Ghazni became the quintessential Muslim ruler, spreading the message of Islam in an infidel land. Every subsequent Muslim king was beseeched to evaluate their achievements in the light of Ghazni's successes, the most widely known of which was the destruction of the Somnath Temple in Gujarat, portrayed as the greatest Hindu temple in India.[8]

It actually wasn't *the* greatest Hindu temple in India; in fact, no one temple could have been given that status. In later Muslim writings, it acquired that particular significance, as if it were the Hindu equivalent of the Ka'aba.[9] This was done to exaggerate the achievements of Mahmud Ghazni.

Legends were crafted about how the idol at Somnath was actually of the goddess Manat, one of the ancient trio of goddesses worshipped in Arabia before the arrival of Islam. It was asserted that when their temple was destroyed by Hazrat Ali, the cousin and son-in-law of the Prophet, the idol was saved and found its way to Gujarat where this temple was constructed in the goddess's honour.[10] Thus, in attacking and looting the temple, Mahmud Ghazni was fulfilling the wish of the Prophet, who had originally asked Hazrat Ali to destroy the temple in Arabia.

While later Muslim writers glorified Mahmud Ghazni and his attacks on Somnath, part of the rhetoric was initiated by the sultan himself. He had succeeded his father, Subuktigin, after deposing his brother. Fighting for political legitimacy, Mahmud desperately sought the patronage of the Caliphate at Baghdad. He began exaggerating his achievements, overstating the significance of the temple and the loot acquired from it, which he pegged at being equivalent to 20 million dinars.[11]

Thapar, in her book *Somanatha: The Many Voices of a History*, identified how contemporary Jain and Hindu sources are conspicuously silent about Mahmud Ghazni's raid on the temple. She points out that it is important to look at these alternative historical sources as opposed to only relying upon Persian sources, for it proves that the 'destruction' of the temple was never as complete and catastrophic as the Persian sources claimed. According to these sources the temple was receiving pilgrims shortly after the attack.[12]

Focusing solely on Persian sources and interpreting them literally, British colonial historians exaggerated the severity of the attack and its impact on the psychology of the 'Hindus'. In 1842, after the debacle of the First Anglo-Afghan War, the British removed what were believed to be the gates of the Somnath Temple from the tomb of Mahmud, which he had allegedly stolen following his attack, and took them back to India.[13] The motive was to restore the honour of the Hindus.

The British interpretation of these events was internalized by the Hindu and Muslim nationalists. The attack on the Somnath Temple became another example of repressive Muslim rule over a subjugated Hindu population. For the Hindu nationalists, the temple's restoration became a way to reclaim lost honour. It was rebuilt in 1951, soon after Indian independence, to signal a new emerging identity. In 1990, when the first rath yatra was undertaken by Hindu nationalists demanding the destruction of the Babri Masjid in Ayodhya and the construction of a Ram temple in its place, it started from the Somnath Temple.[14] For these Hindu nationalists, history in independent India was coming full circle.

While on the one hand, Mahmud Ghazni's attack on Somnath was glorified in Persian sources, there was also a need to augment the prowess of his enemies on the other. They had to be depicted as stronger and mightier, with hundreds of thousands of soldiers and hundreds of elephants so that the victory of the Muslim king with a fraction of the army at his disposal could be better appreciated.

Punjab, before the rise of this Afghan Empire on its western frontier, was ruled by the Hindu king Jayapala. When Subuktigin, Mahmud Ghazni's father, broke away from his Persian patrons and founded an independent empire, the Hindu king is believed to have felt threatened by the rise of this new force right at the border of his kingdom, whose boundaries are believed to have extended within present-day Afghanistan.

Jayapala, the ruler of Lahore, as he is presented in later Muslim resources, is believed to have written to other Hindu rulers, including the kings of Delhi, Ajmer, Kalanjara and Kanauj, and prepared a confederacy to counter the emerging kingdom on the west. With 1 lakh soldiers and hundreds of elephants at his command, he is said to have marched towards the north-west to defeat the forces of Subuktigin pre-emptively. Despite his mammoth force, he was outwitted by the cavalry of the Muslim army and thus had to hand over part of his kingdom to the king of Ghazni. Mahmud of Ghazni is believed to have fought valiantly in this battle.

A few years later, with his ascension to the throne, another battle is believed to have been fought outside the city of Peshawar between a Hindu confederacy and the Muslim forces. This time too, a similar fate awaited the forces of the Hindu king and he was left with no option but to concede the city of Peshawar, one of his most prized possessions, to the Afghans. Defeated and humiliated, the Hindu king is believed to have performed self-immolation along with members of his family outside the city.

In this way, at the turn of the millennium, Punjab opened up to Mahmud Ghazni who repeatedly raided the region and carried his loot back to Ghazni. Mahmud, unlike the Muslim kings of the Delhi Sultanate, had no intention of settling in

Punjab. Ghazni in Afghanistan remained the capital of his empire, with artisans, traders, poets and others migrating from the cities of India to this emerging cultural and political hub. In order to handle the administration of Punjab, governors were appointed by the Afghan king who remained remotely connected with his empire.

Much like the narratives of Somnath, the stories of this ultimate showdown with a Hindu confederacy are also part of the myth-making process, a glorification of Mahmud Ghazni to serve as an example for later Muslim kings in India. The biggest criticism of this narrative is the assumption that there was an overarching Hindu identity shared by the several kingdoms that dotted India at the time of Mahmud's invasion. Another problem with it is the mention of the cities of Lahore, Delhi and Ajmer. While the city of Ajmer had not even been founded at the time, Delhi and Lahore were both relatively insignificant cities.[15] In the early seventeenth century, when these stories were first being written, Delhi and Lahore had become major cities, thus allowing these authors assumptions about their past.

Lahore is falsely cited as the capital of the Hindu kingdom under Jayapala. While Lahore existed as a small settlement at this time, it was never important enough to serve as a capital. It was after Mahmud Ghazni's conquest that the city found its bearings on the political map of Punjab. Acquiring it from Hindu rulers, he appointed a governor for Punjab, with the city as the capital. It is around this time that major construction work transformed the small village into an important city. The greatest benefactor of Lahore is believed to have been Ayaz.

During the battle of succession after Mahmud Ghazni's death, Ayaz supported his son, Masud, who briefly appeared victorious. For his services, Ayaz was appointed deputy governor of Punjab with his base in Lahore, while Masud's young son, Amir Majdud, was appointed the governor. As Majdud was very young at the time, Ayaz, for all practical purposes, functioned as the governor.[16]

It is suggested that Ayaz, during his tenure, raised a new city, fortifying it with a protective wall. While Ghazni served as the western capital, it was Lahore that would be the eastern capital of the empire that lasted almost a century.[17] With royal patronage, several new buildings were added to the city. A mosque was constructed just outside its walls by Ali Hujwiri, Data Sahib. Lavish houses were constructed by the nobles, such as Mas'ud Sad-i Salman, a poet and administrator, who is believed to have constructed three hammams in his house. Sarais and gardens were built and permanent staff was hired for their upkeep.[18] Perhaps the original Lahori Darwaza that later became 'Lohari' was also constructed around this time as a tribute to the older city that the new one was replacing.

After the death of Masud, Ayaz sided with his son Majdud, against his brother Maudad. After Majdud died under mysterious circumstances, Ayaz found himself on the wrong side of history. He is believed to have retired from political life and found refuge in the city he had built. It is here, in 1058 CE, that he is believed to have passed away.[19] Earlier historical records suggest that his mausoleum was situated in a garden. However, all traces of that garden have disappeared and what remains today is a modest mausoleum constructed in a mosque in one of the most crowded bazaars of the city. Inside the mausoleum lies the grave of the architect of the historic city of Lahore.

9

A MYTHOLOGICAL CITY

A huge mural adorned one of the walls of the veranda—Valmiki, with his flowing white beard and his hair in a knot atop his head and a halo in the background, flanked by his two cherubic students, Lav and Kush. A hermitage stood in the background, where Sita, after her banishment from Ayodhya, is believed to have been given refuge by the sage Valmiki. A river flowed behind it, ringed by mountains. While several religious texts believe this was the Tamsa River, a tributary of the Ganga that flows through modern-day Madhya Pradesh and Uttar Pradesh, a few local narratives suggest the site of Valmiki's hermitage as the banks of River Parsuni, an ancient name for the Ravi.

These folk narratives suggest that Lav, Valmiki's disciple and one of the sons of Lord Ram and Sita, founded the city of Lahore. The city came to be known as Lavapuri, the city of Lav, eventually becoming Lahore.[1] The same narrative suggests that his twin brother, Kush, founded the city of Kasur, a twin city of Lahore. At their mythological origin, Lahore and Kasur were tied together in a bond that still holds strong. At Lahore Fort, close to the Alamgiri Gate that faces Badshahi Masjid, there is a little temple dedicated to Lav, the founder of Lahore.

On the opposite wall there is a cross at the centre with a picture of Christ on one side and Mother Mary on the other. Of the two rooms that are situated within the veranda, one is reserved for Valmiki, with his statue covered in a saffron shawl. The other houses several deities of the Hindu pantheon—Shiva, Vishnu, Ganesh, Durga, Kali, Lakshmi, Saraswati.

Facing the veranda is an open courtyard with a berry tree in one corner and a small room at another, used by the temple's caretaker. Overlooking the courtyard are the tall buildings of Anarkali Bazaar. The entrance is a little gate with a saffron flag at the top, identifying it as a temple.

Known as Neela Gumbad Mandir, after a blue-domed, Mughal-era mausoleum that is in its vicinity, the Valmiki temple is the only other functional temple in the city besides the Krishna Mandir at Ravi Road, close to Minar-e-Pakistan. Situated in a narrow street that was once known as Valmiki Street because of the temple and the homes of several Valmiki Hindus before Partition, the street was renamed subsequently. It now serves as the community centre for the descendants of thousands of Valmiki Hindus who stayed back, braving the riots of Partition.

I first went to the temple in 2010, when I was working on a book to document religious festivals of the minorities around Punjab. In the courtyard of the temple, I was greeted by a handful of elderly men, part of the committee responsible for its daily functioning. Every evening they arranged a small puja attended by mostly just them. The temple, however, would transform during a religious festival. For days preceding the event, there would be a group of people in the temple preparing for the festivities. Holi, Diwali, Navratri, Krishna Janmashtami and several other Hindu festivals were celebrated here, but the grandest of all was Valmiki Jayanti, the birth anniversary of the sage.

It was around the time of the celebration of this festival that the true identity of the temple and its significance to its devotees became clear to me. Many of the devotees were Muslims and Christians. Around this time, I met Azad Chowdry and his children, Yashwa and Teresa. While Azad played the tabla, his twelve-year-old son, Yashwa, played the harmonium and sang. Occasionally he was accompanied by Teresa. They were a Christian family but here they were, at a Valmiki Hindu temple, singing bhajans and preparing for Valmiki Jayanti.

Sitting next to them and listening attentively was a professional flautist, Musharraf Ali, a Muslim. He was not a regular visitor to the temple but he would make it a point to attend on Valmiki Jayanti. Despite his religion he also identified as a Valmiki, similar to Azad and his family who were Christian Valmikis.

The religious identity of most of the devotees who visit the temple reflects a certain degree of fluidity, impossible to imagine in a post-Partition environment. Most of them identified as Christian on official documents yet retained their Valmiki association. Many had 'Muslim' names that further complicated their religious identity. Only a handful of them could be identified as Hindu by name.

One of them was Bhagat Lal Khokhar, the priest and the man responsible for the primary functioning of the temple. I had the opportunity to interview him over several sessions, each spanning at least a couple of hours. The priest came across as a prudent man who knew that in order to survive in present-day Lahore, the majority community needed to be appeased. On the occasion of several festivals, Muslim religious leaders and scholars were also invited, and often treated as chief guests. I attended one such festival in 2011 when the priest reached out to invite me for an iftar party at the temple.

There were about a dozen Muslims sitting in the temple's courtyard breaking fasts with traditional items such as dates, pakoras and Rooh Afza that young Valmiki boys served. The event corresponded with Janmashtami, which was celebrated later in the evening once most of the Muslim guests left.

During other religious festivals, when bhajans resonate from the speakers placed in the courtyard, the pandit and other members of the organizing committee ensure that the celebrations do not last late into the night. One needs to be sensitive to one's neighbours, a sensibility that is always expected from a minority religious group, almost never from the majority.

It took several hours of conversations with the priest to peel off the layers of his diplomatic language. Following hours of reiteration of patriotism, the priest finally felt comfortable to talk about discrimination. He told me how the temple's property, which included several shops in its vicinity, belonged to the Valmiki community but had been taken over by the ETPB after Partition and rented out. The rent went to the government as opposed to the Valmiki community. Bhagat Lal argued that the temple was never abandoned by the community and hence rightfully belonged to them.

Even if the community had not physically abandoned the temple during the riots of Partition, it had disappeared, if only temporarily. Deep within the community of Shahdara, on the western side of the Ravi, I interviewed an old widowed woman, Mary. At the time of Partition, she was a little girl living close to the canal. She was a Hindu Valmiki, named Vidya by her parents. She told me how, when they were playing on the banks of the canal, they saw a dead body floating in the water. She immediately ran to her mother to tell her what she had witnessed. Her mother purchased a cross, put a thread through it and hung it around her neck. In that one gesture, she had ceased to be Vidya and became Mary, an identity that she clung to ever since.

Living on the ground floor of the same house was Kamla Kumari, another old widow, who unlike Mary had retained her pre-Partition name but like hundreds of other Valmiki Hindus, changed her religion. Such was the fear of this dual life that the family entirely gave up its religious traditions in the new city. Kamla eventually joined a Christian missionary school in Lahore, where she learned hymns and other forms of Christian prayer, the only prayer she knew. In her home, in one corner of the room she had set up a small mandir with pictures of Hindu deities. Every day she would stand in front of the gods and recite Christian hymns under her breath.

These dual religious identities are in evidence at the Neela Gumbad Mandir where there is a mural of Valmiki on one wall and Jesus Christ and Mary on the other. While Valmiki Jayanti and Janmashtami are celebrated by hundreds of devotees, Christmas and Easter witness an equal number of devotees. The temple of Valmiki swiftly becomes the temple of Christ whenever required.

What brought together these different threads of religious identity at the temple was one common caste identity. Valmiki Hindus are part of the Dalit community, which has experienced social exclusion for generations. At the temple, I interviewed Khem Chand, an old man in his eighties, who had changed his name to Shams Gill after Partition following his conversion to Christianity. He told me how upper-caste Hindus would go out of their way to prevent even the shadow of Valmikis from falling over the well at Anarkali Bazaar. During his youth Khem Chand was a *pehelwan*, a wrestler; however, due to his caste no *akhara* would allow him to practise. Thus, eventually, they set up a small akhara in the vicinity of this temple.

The social exclusion continued after Partition, even though Khem Chand officially became Shams Gill and all the upper-class Hindus from Punjab migrated to India. During our conversations, various stories of untouchability flowed from him. Once, when he, along with several other members of the community, was having a cup of tea at a little dhaba outside Lahore, the Muslim vendor of the stall forced them to pay for the cups as well when he found out about their identities, for they had been rendered impure and would have to be thrown away.

The Muslim converts did not fare much better. Low-caste Hindus who converted to Islam are known as 'Musali' or 'Deendar' in Punjab and are in many ways still treated as untouchable. Many households where they work keep a separate set of utensils for them. While religious identity changed for many of them, their caste identity continued to shade their existence, even as they manoeuvred through a changed environment. I believe that in this context, Valmiki and his temple acquired a particular significance for them. It became an expression of self-identity, a reaction to years and generations of social discrimination.

In the years following Partition when, particularly in Punjab, notions of patriotism were at their peak, any association with a Hindu past was taboo. Dual names and a jettisoning of their religious practices, culture and festivals were the only ways to survive. Bhagat Lal told me how, for years, religious festivals such as Holi and Diwali, which were now much larger affairs celebrated in the courtyard with music and lights, were marked by a brief ritualistic prayer within the confines of the room.

Pakistan's antagonistic relationship with India over the years made the situation even worse. Various Hindus and Sikhs all over the country had to hide their identity or disappear temporarily during the 1965 and 1971 wars. In 1992, as a reaction to the destruction of the Babri Masjid in Ayodhya, hundreds of temples were ransacked, including this one. The pre-Partition idol of Valmiki and Lord Krishna were destroyed and the temple set on fire. The handful of Valmiki Hindus who were part of the administrative team responsible for the maintenance of the temple could only look on, overwhelmed by a mob of hundreds.

With the arrival of Pervez Musharraf and his 'Enlightened Moderation' at the start of the millennium, the situation began to change. Pakistan found itself at the centre of the storm of religious extremism and violence and the state, an ally in the 'war on terror', was desperate to project a softer image of the country. It is around this time that Hindus in many cities across Punjab who had hidden their identities for decades began reclaiming their original names. Religious festivals that had not been observed at a communal level since Partition once again came to be celebrated. The Valmiki temple at Neela Gumbad was also witness to this transition. Many Muslim and Christian Valmikis who had repudiated their connections with it were back, picking up the thread of their identity from where it had been abandoned by their predecessors.

Sage Valmiki, unlike any other Hindu deity, held a particular significance for them. For, more than any other, he was the deity of the Dalits, irrespective of their new religious identity. He himself was a Dalit who defied his caste when he became a sage. He became the most important sage, the *adi-kavi* or the first poet, who composed the Ramayana—its first ever written rendition. Not just that, he challenged caste hierarchy when, in his 24,000 verses of poetry, he described how Sita found refuge in his ashram after she was exiled by her husband. Thus Valmiki mounted an important challenge to caste hierarchy, which attributed only a particular set of activities to each caste and looked down upon the intermingling of castes.

But how could Valmiki, on the one hand, through his own actions as the first author of the Ramayana challenge caste hierarchies, but also, on the other, reinforce the very same system he defied? At one point in the Ramayana of Valmiki, Ram kills Shambuka, a Shudra ascetic, who, challenging the caste hierarchy—dharma—was engaged in performing penance.[2] How could Valmiki be the ultimate symbol for Shudras, and at the same time promote this kind of dharma?

Many Ramayana scholars have pointed out that Valmiki's version cannot be attributed to one author. It was a product of several centuries, beginning around the third or second century BCE and going all the way to second or third century CE.[3] Different poets added their own verses to the text, bringing with them their own interpretation of dharma. It has also been established that Valmiki himself was not the original author. The Ramayana had been recited for a few centuries before it was finally put in writing by the sage around the third or second century BCE.

It is argued that in the original text, Ram was not the divine incarnation that he was to become in the later version.[4] Other evidence suggests that in the later traditions, when Ram does begin to acquire divine attributes, it is not Vishnu but rather Indra whose incarnation he is seen as.[5] There are also, as a matter of fact, Buddhist versions of the Ramayana in which Ram is a Bodhisattva.[6] In Jain versions, Ram is a non-violent adherent of the teachings of Mahavira and it is not he who slays Ravana but his brother, Laxman.[7] However, in the beginning of the fourth century CE, under the patronage of the Gupta dynasty, the Ramayana increasingly became associated with Hinduism, thus overshadowing its other variants. Ram became an incarnation of Vishnu, the upholder of dharma, which included caste duties and hierarchy, while Sita became his obedient wife.

With the changing interpretation of Valmiki's Ramayana, there was now a need to address the issue of Valmiki's caste. A new reading was added that Valmiki was originally a Brahmin priest raised by a Shudra couple. This is also the narrative that was told to me by Bhagat Lal.

Valmiki's original caste still remains a contested issue. In the beginning of 2016, a fourteen-member committee was formed in Karnataka to determine the origins of Valmiki, after it was argued by a Kannada writer that Valmiki was a Brahmin, a claim contested by the Dalit community.[8]

To the Muslim, Christian and Hindu devotees of Valmiki, however, who gather at the Neela Gumbad Mandir, discussions of his origins or the various extrapolations into the Ramayana are not part of their everyday lived experience. Valmiki for them represents a rebellion against caste hierarchy which continues to haunt them despite conversion. United by their shared experience of untouchability, hundreds of Christians, Muslims and Hindus continue to revere Valmiki, making this little temple in the heart of Lahore a unique symbol of almost a forced religious syncretism. While today it might come across as an anomaly in an increasingly monolithic city once hailed for its metropolitan nature, it is in fact one of the last reminders of what the social fabric of the city used to be before it was ripped apart by the riots of Partition.

ACKNOWLEDGEMENTS

There are three people to whom I am particularly indebted for teaching me how to imagine Lahore in the way it is captured in the book. First on the list is Furrukh Khan, whose course 'Imagining Lahore' was one of its kind and inspired me to explore the history of the city. My writing career began with documenting stories about Lahore.

It is through the course that I discovered the writings of Majid Sheikh, a chronicler of Lahore whose weekly columns about its history in *Dawn* transformed the way I viewed the city. A collection of his articles in the book *Tales without an End* is a must-read for anyone interested in the history of the city.

Last but not the least is Iqbal Qaiser, my eternal guru, a living encyclopedia, whose mentorship is the single most important factor in my writing. I happened to discover him through Furrukh Khan's course and have clung on to him since then, desperate for the knowledge he so generously shares.

I would also like to thank the following:

Anam Zakaria, for being my anchor and an incredible companion.
Khalid Manzoor, for teaching me idealism and romance.
Nyla Khalid, for teaching me the power of passion.
Sana Shoaib, for teaching me the power of love.
Nida Umer, for her unconditional love for me.
Neelofur Zakaria, for embracing my eccentricities.
Eraj Zakaria, for his realism.

This book has also been made possible by the efforts of Kanishka
Gupta, my agent and friend, the most dynamic literary agent
in the business, and Swati Chopra, my editor. The editor is the
unsung hero of a book and without her efforts *Imagining Lahore*
would not have taken the shape it has.

NOTES

Chapter 1: A Contested City

1. Habib, 'Shahbaz the Super CM Who Heads 18 Ministries', *Pakistan Today*.
2. '"People Fed Up with 'Takht-e-Lahore'," says Imran Khan', Geo News.
3. Ahmed, 'Our Goal at the Moment Is to Mobilise the People', *The News on Sunday*.
4. There is a couplet at the structure that records the name Zebinda Begum at the end. Historians such as Syed Muhammad Latif have asserted that this was another name for Princess Zeb-un-Nissa, thus giving birth to the theory that she was the person responsible for the structure.
5. Muhammad (ed.), 'Naqoosh Lahore Number', *Idara Farogh-e-Urdu*, pp. 113–15.
6. Waris, *Tarikh Shehar Lahore*, pp. 113–15.
7. Safvi, 'Princess Zeb un Nisa or the Concealed One', Ranasafvi.com.
8. Waris, *Tarikh Shehar Lahore*, p. 89.
9. Ibid.

10. Mukherjee, *Royal Mughal Ladies and Their Contributions*, p. 156.
11. University of Alberta, 'Zeb-un-Nisa's Tomb'.
12. Asher, *Architecture of Mughal India*, p. 349.
13. Khan, 'How Not to Build a Transport System', *Dawn*.
14. Ibid.
15. Ibid.
16. Miraj, 'Shaheed and Shahdara', Dawn Blogs.
17. Miraj, 'Shaheed and Shahdara—II', Dawn Blogs.
18. Ibid.
19. Unknown, 'The True Story of Boota Singh'.
20. Qaiser, *Ujray Daran De Darshan*.
21. Ibid., p. 72.
22. Ibid., p. 158.
23. Ibid., p. 161.
24. Lal, *Tareekh-i-Lahore*, p. 233.
25. Griffin, *Punjab Chiefs*, pp. 633, 643.
26. Lal, *Tareekh-i-Lahore*, p. 232.
27. Personal visit and interview of locals.
28. Talbot and Kamran, *Lahore in the Time of the Raj*, p. 19.
29. 'Imran Khan's "Tsunami" Sweeps Lahore', *Express Tribune*.
30. Sheikh, 'Final Destruction of the Historical Minto Park', *Dawn*.
31. Ibid.
32. Ibid.
33. Mujahid, 'Lahore Resolution and the Question of Provincial Autonomy', *Business Recorder*.

Chapter 2: A City of Dissent

1. Khan and Bhatty, 'Lahore Building Collapse Kills 14', *Express Tribune*.
2. British India Revenue Department, 'Shajra Nasab Khadak'.
3. Narodin, 'Habib Jalib', *Bodhi Commons*.
4. Ibid.
5. Ibid.
6. Ibid.
7. Ibid.

8. 'Shahbaz Sharif Reciting Habib Jalib Poem (Main Nahi Manta)'.
9. Narodin, 'Habib Jalib', *Bodhi Commons*.
10. Ibid.
11. Ibid.
12. Ibid.
13. Translation of Habib Jalib's poem, 'Jaag Mere Punjab'.
14. *'Aisy Dastoor ko Mien Nahi Manta'*, Dunyanews.tv.
15. Shah, 'Sufi Shrines under Attack in Pakistan—A Chronology', *The News*.
16. Ibid.
17. Ibid.
18. Alikuzai, *A Concise History of Afghanistan in 25 Volumes*, p. 137.
19. Fauq, *Hazrat Data Ganj Bakhsh*, p. 131.
20. Shah, *Bhutto, Zia and Islam*, p. 136.
21. Awan et al., 'History of Mosque Architecture in Lahore', *Journal of Islamic Thought and Civilization*, p. 32.
22. Three PPP workers, Parvaiz Yaqoob Khokhar, Aziz Malik and Abdul Rasheed, lost their lives while others who had immolated themselves along with them in Lahore, protesting for the release of Bhutto, were saved in time. This incident is recorded in the *Pakistan Chronicle Encyclopedia*, under the date 15 September 1978.
23. Paracha, 'Bleeding Green', *Dawn*.
24. Bhutto, *Daughter of the East*, p. 322.
25. Ibid.
26. Raja, 'Villains of Habib Jalib', *The Friday Times*.
27. Wolpert, *Zulfi Bhutto of Pakistan*, pp. 305–06.
28. Ibid., p. 301.
29. Ibid., p. 280.
30. Ibid., p. 240.
31. Ibid., p. 146.
32. Lyon, *Conflict between India and Pakistan*, p. 130.
33. Wolpert, *Zulfi Bhutto of Pakistan*, p. 89.
34. Ibid., p. 267.
35. Ibid., p. 301.
36. Ibid.
37. Bhutto, *My Dearest Daughter*, Bhutto.org.
38. Qaiser, *Historical Sikh Shrines in Pakistan*, p. 286.

39. Ibid., p. 266.
40. Wolpert, *Zulfi Bhutto of Pakistan*, p. 109.

Chapter 3: To the Left, No Right

1. 'Pakistan Mosque Attacks in Lahore Kill Scores', BBC.
2. 'Why Was Salman Taseer Anti-Islamic?', Haqbaat.com.
3. Shahid, 'Addressing Constitutional Takfir', *The Friday Times*.
4. Interview with Mohammed Saeed, Sabiha Saeed and Nasir Ahmad, Lahore, 25 March 2017.
5. Gandhi, *Punjab*, p. 250.
6. Ahmad, 'A Life Sketch of the Promised Messiah', Al Islam.
7. Bentlage et al. (ed.), *Religious Dynamics under the Impact of Imperialism and Colonialism*, p. 436.
8. Ahmad, 'A Life Sketch of the Promised Messiah', Al Islam.
9. Ibid.
10. Ibid.
11. 'Revealed Sermon', Al Islam.
12. Bates, 'Race, Caste and Tribe in Central India', in *Edinburgh Papers on South Asian Studies*.
13. An example of one such community is the Nanak-Panthi Hindus—Hindus who also revere the first Sikh Guru, Guru Nanak. There is a sizeable community of Nanak-Panthi Hindus in Sindh, Pakistan.
14. Hamdani, 'Mr Jinnah's Muslim Opponents', *Pakistan Today*.
15. Ibid.
16. Ibid.
17. Shahid, 'Pakistan Movement and the Part Played by the Ahmadiyya Community', Al Islam.
18. Khan, *Facts Are Facts*, p. 40.
19. The 1954 Justice Munir Commission Report on the Anti Ahmadi Riots of Punjab in 1953.
20. Ganiel, Winkel and Monnot (eds), 'Introduction: Religion in Times of Crisis', in *Religion in Times of Crisis*, p. 139.
21. Blood (ed.), *Pakistan*, p. 217.
22. Interview with Mohammed Saeed, Sabiha Saeed and Nasir Ahmad, Lahore, 25 March 2017.

23. Meri (ed.), *Medieval Islamic Civilization*, p. 678.
24. Interview with Mohammed Saeed, Sabiha Saeed and Nasir Ahmad, Lahore, 25 March 2017.
25. Ibid.
26. Ahmad, *An Account of the Last Days and Death of Hazrat Mirza Ghulam Ahmad*, pp. 24–25.
27. Interview with Mohammed Saeed, Sabiha Saeed and Nasir Ahmad, Lahore, 25 March 2017.
28. Lal, *Tareekh-e-Lahore*, p. 179.
29. Nabha, *Encyclopedia of Sikh Literature*, p. 53.
30. Dalrymple and Anand, *Kohinoor*, p. 110.
31. Singh, *The Second Anglo-Sikh War*, pp. xv–xvi.
32. Malik, 'Political Inmates of Lahore Fort', *Pakistan Today*.
33. Taseer, 'Remembering Taseer', *The Express Tribune*.
34. Ali, 'Pakistan and the Cold War', *Dawn*.
35. Ibid.
36. Dryland, 'Faiz Ahmed Faiz and the Rawalpindi Conspiracy Case', *Journal of South Asian Literature*, p. 181.
37. T.A., 'What's Left in Pakistan?' *Economic and Political Weekly*, p. 2089.
38. Ali, 'Communists in a Muslim Land', *Modern Asian Studies*, p. 521.
39. Ibid., pp. 531–32.
40. Ibid., pp. 520–21.
41. Ibid., p. 507.
42. Ibid., p. 511.
43. Dryland, 'Faiz Ahmed Faiz and the Rawalpindi Conspiracy Case', *Journal of South Asian Literature*, p. 175.
44. Telephonic interview with Qazi Hussain Ahmad, 25 January 2011.
45. Jalal, *The Pity of Partition*, p. 133.
46. Ali, 'Communists in a Muslim Land', *Modern Asian Studies*, p. 519.
47. T.A., 'What's Left in Pakistan?', *Economic and Political Weekly*, p. 2089.
48. Ali, 'Communists in a Muslim Land', *Modern Asian Studies*, p. 529 (fn).
49. Dryland, 'Faiz Ahmed Faiz and the Rawalpindi Conspiracy Case', *Journal of South Asian Literature*, p. 182.

50. T.A., 'What's Left in Pakistan?', *Economic and Political Weekly*, p. 2089.
51. Ali, 'Pakistan and the Cold War', *Dawn*.
52. Ibid.
53. Ibid.
54. Ibid.

Chapter 4: A City Forgotten

1. Sheikh, 'Myths and Facts of the Beginnings of Lahore', *Dawn*.
2. Sheikh, 'In Search of the Origins and Age of Lahore', *Dawn*.
3. Sheikh, 'Two Ends of Ravi Road and How Our Freedom Fared', *Dawn*.
4. Brown, 'Svarāj, the Indian Ideal of Freedom', *Religious Studies*, p. 436.
5. Ibid.
6. Wolpert, *Nehru*, pp. 86–88.
7. Mikaberidze (ed.), *Atrocities, Massacres, and War Crimes*, p. 746.
8. Rana, *Chandra Shekhar Azad*, p. 26.
9. Bains, 'Lala Lajpat Rai's Idealism and Indian National Movement', *The Indian Journal of Political Science*, p. 402.
10. Jalal, *The Sole Spokesman*, p. 8.
11. Gupta, 'The Arya Samaj and Indian National Movement', *Proceedings of the Indian History Congress*, p. 722.
12. Ibid., p. 729.
13. Gandhi, 'Gandhi and Punjab', *India International Centre Quarterly*, p. 35.
14. Tuteja, 'Jallianwala Bagh', *Social Scientist*, pp. 36–37.
15. Gandhi, 'Gandhi and Punjab', *India International Centre Quarterly*, pp. 37–38.
16. Ikram, *Indian Muslims and Partition of India*, p. 207.
17. Ijaz, 'Bradlaugh Hall's Demise', *Pakistan Today*.
18. Khare, 'Indian Nationalism', *The Indian Journal of Political Science*, p. 544.
19. Ibid., p. 538.
20. Ibid., pp. 539–40.
21. Ibid., pp. 544–45.

22. Zacharias, 'The Road to Indian Autonomy', *The Review of Politics*, p. 311.
23. Singh, 'Lala Lajpat Rai', *The Indian Journal of Political Science*, p. 128.
24. Zacharias, 'The Road to Indian Autonomy', *The Review of Politics*, p. 317.
25. Wolpert, *Nehru*, p. 106.
26. Singh, 'Lala Lajpat Rai', *The Indian Journal of Political Science*, p. 129.
27. Sengupta, *Land of Two Rivers*, pp. 296–97.
28. Tuteja, 'Jallianwala Bagh', *Social Scientist*, p. 36.
29. Ibid., p. 42.
30. Collett, *The Butcher of Amritsar*, p. 263.
31. Gandhi, 'Gandhi and Punjab', *India International Centre Quarterly*, p. 34.
32. Singh, 'Lala Lajpat Rai', *The Indian Journal of Political Science*, p. 131.
33. Talbot and Kamran, *Lahore in the Time of the Raj*, p. 13.
34. Khare, 'Indian Nationalism', *The Indian Journal of Political Science*, p. 537.
35. Mittal and Habib, 'Towards Independence and Socialist Republic, Part 2', *Social Scientist*, p. 32.
36. Wolpert, *Nehru*, p. 90.
37. Ibid., p. 78.
38. Bhambhri and Bhamberi, 'Nehru and Socialist Movement in India', *The Indian Journal of Political Science*, p. 144.
39. Wolpert, *Nehru*, p. 98.
40. Ibid., pp. 90–91.
41. Ibid., p. 86.
42. Ibid., p. 107.
43. Ibid., p. 108.
44. Faletti's Hotel website.
45. Lal, 'Revolutionary Legacy of Bhagat Singh', *Economic and Political Weekly*, p. 3717.
46. Mahmud, 'Lala Lajpat Rai, Son of the Soil', Lahorenama.wordpress.com.
47. Lal, 'Revolutionary Legacy of Bhagat Singh', *Economic and Political Weekly*, p. 3717.

48. Ibid.
49. Ibid., p. 3718.
50. Bhambhri and Bhamberi, 'Nehru and Socialist Movement in India', *The Indian Journal of Political Science*, p. 144.
51. Nair, 'Bhagat Singh as "Satyagrahi"', *Modern Asian Studies*, p. 658.
52. Mittal and Habib, 'Towards Independence and Socialist Republic, Part 1', *Social Scientist*, p. 19.
53. Mittal and Habib, 'Towards Independence and Socialist Republic, Part 2', *Social Scientist*, p. 36.
54. Nair, 'Bhagat Singh as "Satyagrahi"', *Modern Asian Studies*, p. 655.
55. Dhillon, 'The Literary Face of Bhagat Singh', *The Tribune*.
56. Lal, 'Revolutionary Legacy of Bhagat Singh', *Economic and Political Weekly*, p. 3715.
57. Ibid., p. 3713.
58. Nair, 'Bhagat Singh as "Satyagrahi"', *Modern Asian Studies*, p. 655.
59. Ibid., p. 658.
60. Lal, 'Revolutionary Legacy of Bhagat Singh', *Economic and Political Weekly*, p. 3717.
61. Nair, 'Bhagat Singh as "Satyagrahi"', *Modern Asian Studies*, p. 657.
62. Ibid., pp. 657–59.
63. Lal, 'Revolutionary Legacy of Bhagat Singh', *Economic and Political Weekly*, p. 3712.
64. Nair, 'Bhagat Singh as "Satyagrahi"', *Modern Asian Studies*, p. 676.
65. Gaur, *Martyr as Bridegroom*, p. 2.
66. Lal, 'Revolutionary Legacy of Bhagat Singh', *Economic and Political Weekly*, p. 3714.
67. Ibid., p. 3712.
68. Mittal and Habib, 'Towards Independence and Socialist Republic, Part 2', *Social Scientist*, p. 32.
69. Mittal and Habib, 'Towards Independence and Socialist Republic, Part 1', *Social Scientist*, p. 26.
70. Nair, 'Bhagat Singh as "Satyagrahi"', *Modern Asian Studies*, p. 653.
71. Ibid., p. 654.
72. Ibid.
73. Ibid., p. 655.
74. Gaur, *Martyr as Bridegroom*, p. 120.

75. Agencies, 'Pakistan Puts on Hold Plan to Rename Roundabout after Bhagat Singh', *The Indian Express*.
76. Lal, 'Revolutionary Legacy of Bhagat Singh', *Economic and Political Weekly*, p. 3718.
77. Oberoi, 'Ghadar Movement and Its Anarchist Genealogy', *Economic and Political Weekly*, p. 41.
78. Ibid., p. 40.
79. Puri, 'Revolutionary Organization', *Social Scientist*, p. 55.
80. Oberoi, 'Ghadar Movement and Its Anarchist Genealogy', *Economic and Political Weekly*, p. 44.
81. Ibid., p. 40.
82. Talbot and Kamran, *Lahore in the Time of the Raj*, p. 149.
83. Ibid.
84. Puri, 'Revolutionary Organization', *Social Scientist*, p. 60.
85. Talbot and Kamran, *Lahore in the Time of the Raj*, p. 149.
86. Oberoi, 'Ghadar Movement and Its Anarchist Genealogy', *Economic and Political Weekly*, p. 42.
87. Ibid.
88. 'Ghadar Movement ke Shaheed', *Nawa Zamana*.
89. Lal, 'Revolutionary Legacy of Bhagat Singh', *Economic and Political Weekly*, p. 3713.
90. Mittal and Habib, 'Towards Independence and Socialist Republic, Part 1', *Social Scientist*, pp. 22–23.

Chapter 5: The Imperial Symbol

1. Gandhi, *Punjab*, p. 194.
2. Ibid., p. 196.
3. Alam, 'Going, Going, Gone', *The Express Tribune*.
4. Rehman, 'Changing Concepts of Garden Design in Lahore from Mughal to Contemporary Times', *Garden* History, p. 211.
5. Lahore Gymkhana website.
6. Rehman, 'Changing Concepts of Garden Design in Lahore from Mughal to Contemporary Times', *Garden* History, p. 209.
7. Sharma, 'British Policy towards Aristocracy in the Punjab', *Proceedings of the Indian History Congress*, p. 707.
8. Gandhi, *Punjab*, p. 195.

9. Ibid., p. 209.
10. Ibid., p. 208.
11. Ibid., p. 209.
12. Malik, 'The Panjab and the Indian "Mutiny"', *Islamic Studies*, p. 83.
13. Gandhi, *Punjab*, p. 223.
14. Ibid., p. 189.
15. Malik, 'The Panjab and the Indian "Mutiny"', *Islamic Studies*, p. 100.
16. Gandhi, *Punjab*, p. 218.
17. Ibid., pp. 225–26.
18. Ibid., p. 227.
19. Ibid., p. 232.
20. Ibid.
21. Malik, 'The Panjab and the Indian "Mutiny"', *Islamic Studies*, p. 92.
22. Ibid.
23. Ibid.
24. Gandhi, *Punjab*, p. 231.
25. Farooqui, '"Divide and Rule"?', *Social Scientist*, p. 50.
26. Ibid., p. 53.
27. Ibid., p. 55.
28. Barua, 'Inventing Race', *The Historian*, p. 115.
29. Farooqui, '"Divide and Rule"?', *Social Scientist*, p. 54.
30. Fair, *Fighting to the End,* p. 56.
31. Farooqui, '"Divide and Rule"?', *Social Scientist*, p. 54.
32. Ibid., p. 57.
33. World of Royalty, 'Padhania'.
34. Ibid.
35. Gandhi, *Punjab*, p. 217.
36. Sharma, 'British Policy towards Aristocracy in the Punjab', *Proceedings of the Indian History Congress*, p. 708.
37. Metcalf, 'The Influence of the Mutiny of 1857 on Land Policy in India', *The Historical Journal*, p. 159.
38. Sharma, 'British Policy towards Aristocracy in the Punjab', *Proceedings of the Indian History Congress*, p. 708.
39. Ibid., p. 709.
40. World of Royalty, 'Padhania'.

41. Ibid.
42. Ibid.
43. Ibid.
44. Glover, *Making Lahore Modern*, p. 84.
45. Ibid., p. 79.
46. Gandhi, *Punjab*, p. 240.
47. Talbot and Kamran, *Lahore in the Time of the Raj*, p. 21.
48. Ibid.
49. Glover, *Making Lahore Modern*, p. 80.
50. Ibid.
51. Ibid.
52. Ibid., p. 72.
53. Ibid.
54. Ibid., p. 76.
55. Ibid., p. 85.
56. Ibid.
57. Talbot and Kamran, *Lahore in the Time of the Raj*, p. 15.
58. Glover, *Making Lahore Modern*, p. 91.
59. Ibid., p. 90.
60. Ibid.
61. Ibid.
62. Ibid., p. 91.
63. Ibid., p. 151–52.
64. Talbot and Kamran, *Lahore in the Time of the Raj*, p. 20.
65. Glover, *Making Lahore Modern*, p. 151.
66. Ibid., p. 153.
67. Talbot and Kamran, *Lahore in the Time of the Raj*, p. 20.
68. Ibid.
69. Glover, *Making Lahore Modern*, p. 107.
70. Ibid., p. 130.
71. Talbot and Kamran, *Lahore in the Time of the Raj*, p. 23.
72. Glover, *Making Lahore Modern*, p. 149.
73. Talbot and Kamran, *Lahore in the Time of the Raj*, p. 20.
74. Qaiser, *Ujray Daran de Darshan*, p. 175.
75. 'School Outlaws Punjabi as "Foul Language"', Samaa.
76. Kumar, 'Colonial Citizen as an Educational Ideal', *Economic and Political Weekly*, p. 48.

Chapter 6: The City of Nostalgia

1. Dalrymple and Anand, *Kohinoor*, p. 188.
2. Ibid., p. 181.
3. Ibid., p. 173.
4. Ibid., p. 183.
5. Ibid., p. 185.
6. Ibid., p. 187.
7. Ibid., p. 188.
8. Singh, *The Second Anglo-Sikh War*, p. 18.
9. Dodwell (ed.), *British India, 1497-1858*, p. 548.
10. Cunningham, *A History of the Sikhs*, p. 309.
11. Singh, *The Sikhs*, p. 93.
12. Ibid., p. 103.
13. Cunningham, *A History of the Sikhs*, p. 317.
14. Bal, 'Maharaja Dalip Singh's Cis-Sutlej Territories and the Sikh War', *Proceedings of the Indian History Congress*, p. 237.
15. Ibid., p. 238.
16. Cunningham, *A History of the Sikhs*, p. 326.
17. Gandhi, *Punjab*, p. 179.
18. Ibid., p. 180.
19. Cunningham, *A History of the Sikhs*, p. 343.
20. Bal, 'British Interest in Creating the Dogra State of Jammu and Kashmir', *Proceedings of the Indian History Congress*, p. 45.
21. Singh, *The Second Anglo-Sikh War*, p. 107.
22. Ibid., p. 196.
23. Gandhi, *Punjab*, p. 186.
24. Ibid., p. 135.
25. Ibid., p. 173.
26. Dalrymple and Anand, *Kohinoor*, p. 113.
27. Gandhi, *Punjab*, p. 138.
28. Dalrymple and Anand, *Kohinoor*, p. 114.
29. Gandhi, *Punjab*, p. 138.
30. Singh, *The Sikhs*, p. 98.
31. Cunningham, *A History of the Sikhs*, p. 271.
32. Gandhi, *Punjab*, p. 174.
33. Ibid.
34. Dalrymple and Anand, *Kohinoor*, p. 115.

35. Cunningham, *A History of the Sikhs*, p. 273.
36. Dalrymple and Anand, *Kohinoor*, p. 116.
37. Cunningham, *A History of the Sikhs*, p. 292.
38. Ibid., p. 293.
39. In 2014, the smadh of Sher Singh was renovated by the Pakistan government.
40. Sheikh, 'Timeless Debate about What Mori Gate Really Is!', *Dawn*.
41. Singh, *The Sikhs*, pp. 140–41.
42. Sheikh, 'Abiding Mystery of the Roshani Gate Tragedy', *Dawn*.
43. Dalrymple and Anand, *Kohinoor*, p. 108.
44. Gandhi, *Punjab*, p. 173.
45. Dalrymple and Anand, *Kohinoor*, pp. 108–09.
46. Ibid., p. 109.
47. Singh, *The Sikhs*, p. 99.
48. Cunningham, *A History of the Sikhs*, p. 268.
49. Dalrymple and Anand, Kohinoor, p. 111.
50. Soofi, 'Mystery of Nau Nihal Singh's Death', *Dawn*.
51. Singh, *The Second Anglo-Sikh War*, p. xxi.
52. Gandhi, *Punjab*, p. 131.
53. Ibid.
54. Ibid., p. 157.
55. Rehman, 'A Mosque for All Seasons', *Dawn*.
56. Gandhi, Punjab, p. 158.
57. Tufail (ed.), 'Naqoosh Lahore Number', *Idara Farogh-e-Urdu*, pp. 161–62.
58. Banerjee and Banerji, 'Maharaja Ranjit Singh', *Proceedings of the Indian History Congress*, p. 1300.

Chapter 7: The Mughal Capital

1. Katz, 'The Identity of a Mystic', *Numen: International Review for the History of Religions*, p. 145.
2. Khalid, *Walking with Nanak*, p. 185.
3. Puri, Review of *The Mystic Prince*, *India International Centre Quarterly*, p. 149.
4. Khalid, *Walking with Nanak*, p. 209.
5. Puri, Review of *The Mystic Prince*, *India International Centre Quarterly*.

6. Kinra, 'The Persistence of Gossip', in *Writing Self, Writing Empire*, p. 245.

7. Ojha, 'Scholarship and Patronage of Learning of the Great Moghuls', *Proceedings of the Indian History Congress*, p. 193.

8. Kinra, 'The Persistence of Gossip', in *Writing Self, Writing Empire*, p. 245.

9. Ibid., p. 256.

10. Ibid., p. 257.

11. Singh, 'Darul Sultanat Lahore', p. 288.

12. Sheikh, 'The Red Stones of Dara Shikoh', *Dawn*.

13. Kinra, 'The Persistence of Gossip', in *Writing Self, Writing Empire*, p. 242.

14. Ibid., p. 247.

15. Chandra, 'Jizyah and the State in India during the 17th Century', *Journal of the Economic and Social History of the Orient*, p. 334.

16. Ibid.

17. Ibid., pp. 327, 336.

18. Ibid., p. 336.

19. Ibid., p. 325.

20. Ibid., p. 336.

21. Ojha, 'Scholarship and Patronage of Learning of the Great Moghuls', *Proceedings of the Indian History Congress*, pp. 191–92.

22. Ibid., p. 193.

23. Eaton, 'Temple Desecration and Indo-Muslim States', *Journal of Islamic Studies*, p. 296.

24. Chandra, 'Some Considerations on the Religious Policy of Aurangzeb during the Later Part of His Reign', *Proceedings of the Indian History Congress*, p. 380.

25. Brown, 'Did Aurangzeb Ban Music?', *Modern Asian Studies*, p. 115.

26. Subodh, 'Temples Rulers and Historians' Dilemma', *Proceedings of the Indian History Congress*, p. 337.

27. Brown, 'Did Aurangzeb Ban Music?', *Modern Asian Studies*, p. 115.

28. Ibid.

29. Ibid., p. 87.

30. Ibid., p. 104.

31. Ibid.

32. Ibid., p. 111.

33. Findly, *Nur Jahan*, p. 285.

34. Ibid., p. 51.
35. Ibid., p. 26.
36. Ibid., p. 33.
37. Ibid., p. 49.
38. Ibid., p. 165.
39. Ibid., p. 50.
40. Ibid., p. 165.
41. Ibid., p. 170.
42. Ibid., p. 282.
43. Ibid., p. 279.
44. Ibid., p. 283.
45. Gaur, *Martyr as Bridegroom*, p. 37.
46. Chisti, *Tehqiqat-i-Chistia*, p. 363.
47. Dogra, *Nation Keepers*, p. 36.
48. 'Dulla Bhatti', Punjabics.com.
49. YouTube, 'Story of Akbar and Dulla Bhatti 2'.
50. Gaur, *Martyr as Bridegroom*.
51. Ibid.
52. Faruqui, 'The Forgotten Prince', *Journal of the Economic and Social History of the Orient*, pp. 502–03.
53. Ibid., p. 516.
54. Ibid., p. 517.
55. Ibid., pp. 502, 507.
56. Ibid., p. 499.
57. Ibid., p. 510.
58. Gaur, *Martyr as Bridegroom*, p. 34.
59. Richards, *The Mughal Empire*, p. 187.
60. YouTube, 'Story of Akbar and Dulla Bhatti 2'.
61. Faruqui, 'The Forgotten Prince', *Journal of the Economic and Social History of the Orient*, p. 516.
62. Ibid., p. 518.

Chapter 8: Humble Origins

1. Triveda, 'Viṣṇudhvaja', *Annals of the Bhandarkar Oriental Research Institute*, p. 242.
2. Khan, 'Religious Freedom to Non-Muslims under the Delhi Sultans (Summary)', *Proceedings of the Indian History Congress*, p. 345.

3. Eaton, 'Temple Desecration and Indo-Muslim States', *Journal of Islamic Studies*, p. 293.

4. Kumar (ed.), *Demolishing Myths or Mosques and Temples?*, pp. 89–90.

5. Khalid, *In Search of Shiva*, p. 85.

6. Frembgen, *Nocturnal Music in the Land of the Sufis*, pp. 68–69.

7. Raza, 'Mahmud's Ayaz in History', *Proceedings of the Indian History Congress*, p. 286.

8. Thapar, *Somanatha*, pp. 61–66.

9. Ibid., p. 71.

10. Ibid., pp. 48–49.

11. Ibid., p. 45.

12. Ibid., p. 78–79.

13. Raza, 'Constructional Activity of the Ghaznavids', *Proceedings of the Indian History Congress*.

14. Thapar, *Somanatha*, p. 201.

15. Ibid.

16. Raza, 'Mahmud's Ayaz in History', *Proceedings of the Indian History Congress*.

17. Raza, 'Hindus under the Ghaznavids', *Proceedings of the Indian History Congress*.

18. Raza, 'Constructional Activity of the Ghaznavids', *Proceedings of the Indian History Congress*, p. 882.

19. Raza, 'Mahmud's Ayaz in History', *Proceedings of the Indian History Congress*, p. 290.

Chapter 9: A Mythological City

1. Nevile, *Lahore*, p. xii.

2. Bhattacharji, 'A Revaluation of Valmiki's "Rama"', *Social Scientist*, p. 42.

3. Ibid., p. 31.

4. Ibid., pp. 31–32.

5. Brockington, 'Religious Attitudes in Vālmīki's 'Rāmāyaṇa', *Journal of the Royal Asiatic Society*, pp. 108–09.

6. Jaiswal, 'Historical Evolution of the Ram Legend', *Social Scientist*, p. 89.
7. Ibid., p. 94.
8. Priyadarshan, 'Whose Does Valmiki Belong To?', *Forward Press*.

BIBLIOGRAPHY

Agencies. 'Pakistan Puts on Hold Plan to Rename Roundabout after Bhagat Singh.' *Indian Express*, 31 October 2012. https://indianexpress.com/article/news-archive/print/pakistan-puts-on-hold-plan-to-rename-roundabout-after-bhagat-singh/.

Ahmad, Amatul-Hadi. 'A Life Sketch of the Promised Messiah.' Al Islam, December 1996. https://www.alislam.org/library/links/00000185.html.

Ahmad, Nasir. *An Account of the Last Days and Death of Hazrat Mirza Ghulam Ahmad in Lahore with a Brief History of Ahmadiyya Buildings*. Lahore: Aftab-Ud-Din Ahmad Charitable Trust, 2006.

Ahmed, Shahzada Irfan. 'Our Goal at the Moment Is to Mobilise the People.' *News on Sunday*, 27 December 2015. http://tns.thenews.com.pk/maryam-hussain-interview-on-orange-line-project/#.WtWgvi5ubIV.

Al Islam. 'Revealed Sermon.' n.d. www.alislam.org/library/book/brief-history-ahmadiyya-muslim/revealed-sermon/.

Alam, Ahmad Rafay. 'Going, Going, Gone.' *Express Tribune*, 9 July 2010. https://tribune.com.pk/story/26767/going-going-gone/.

Ali, Kamran Asdar. 'Column: Pakistan and the Cold War.' *Dawn*, 5 January 2014. https://www.dawn.com/news/1078344.

————. 'Communists in a Muslim Land: Cultural Debates in Pakistan's Early Years.' *Modern Asian Studies* 45, no. 3 (2011): 501–34. https:// www.cambridge.org/core/journals/modern-asian-studies/article/ communists-in-a-muslim-land-cultural-debates-in-pakistans-early-years/19C70ED634031732F2D30C711B893BB3.

Alikuzai, Hamid Wahed. *A Concise History of Afghanistan in 25 Volumes*, vol. 1. Bloomington, IN: Trafford Publishing, 2013.

Asher, Catherine B. *Architecture of Mughal India*. Vol. 4 of *The New Cambridge History of India, part 1*. Cambridge: Cambridge University Press, 1992.

Awan, Muhammad Yusuf, et al. 'History of Mosque Architecture in Lahore.' *Journal of Islamic Thought and Civilization* 4, no. 2 (2014).

Bains, J.S. 'Lala Lajpat Rai's Idealism and Indian National Movement.' *Indian Journal of Political Science* 46, no. 4 (Special issue on the Indian National Congress). Meerut: Indian Political Science Association, 1985.

Bal, S.S. 'British Interest in Creating the Dogra State of Jammu and Kashmir.' *Proceedings of the Indian History Congress* 29, part 2 (1967).

————. 'Maharaja Dalip Singh's Cis-Sutlej Territories and the Sikh War.' *Proceedings of the Indian History Congress* 30 (1968).

Banerjee, N.C., and N.C. Banerji. 'Maharaja Ranjit Singh.' *Proceedings of the Indian History Congress* 3 (1939).

Barua, Pradeep. 'Inventing Race: The British and India's Martial Races.' *Historian* 58, no. 1 (1995).

Bates, Crispin. 'Race, Caste and Tribe in Central India: The Early Origins of Indian Anthropometry.' *Edinburgh Papers on South Asian Studies* 3, issue 10 (1995).

BBC. 'Pakistan Mosque Attacks in Lahore Kill Scores.' 29 May 2010. www.bbc.com/news/10181380.

Bentlage, Bjorn, et al., eds. *Religious Dynamics under the Impact of Imperialism and Colonialism: A Sourcebook*. Leiden: Brill, 2016.

Bhambhri, C.P., and C.P. Bhamberi. 'Nehru and Socialist Movement in India.' *Indian Journal of Political Science* 30, no. 2 (1969).

Bhattacharji, Sukumari. 'A Revaluation of Valmiki's "Rama".' *Social Scientist* 30, no. 1/2 (2002).

Bhutto, Benazir. *Daughter of the East: An Autobiography.* London: Pocket Books, 2008.

Bhutto, Zulfikar Ali. 'My Dearest Daughter: A Letter from the Death Cell.' Received by Benazir Bhutto, 1989. http://bhutto.org/Acrobat/Dearest_Daughter%5B1%5D.pdf.

Blood, Peter R., ed. *Pakistan: A Country Study.* Washington, D.C.: Federal Research Division, Library of Congress, 1995.

Bosworth, C.E. 'Mahmud of Ghazna in Contemporary Eyes and in Later Persian Literature.' *Iran: Journal of the British Institute of Persian Studies* 4 (1966): 85–92. https://www.tandfonline.com/doi/abs/10.1080/05786967.1966.11834702.

British India Revenue Department. 'Shajra Nasab Khadak.' *Revenue Records*, 1866.

Brockington, J.L. 'Religious Attitudes in Vālmīki's "Rāmāyaⵏa".' *Journal of the Royal Asiatic Society of Great Britain and Ireland* 2 (1976).

Brown, C. Mackenzie. 'Svarāj, the Indian Ideal of Freedom: A Political or Religious Concept.' *Religious Studies* 20, no. 3 (1984).

Brown, Katherine Butler. 'Did Aurangzeb Ban Music? Questions for the Historiography of His Reign.' *Modern Asian Studies* 41, no. 1 (2007).

Chandra, Satish. 'Jizyah and the State in India during the 17th Century.' *Journal of the Economic and Social History of the Orient* 12, no. 3 (1969).

———. 'Some Considerations on the Religious Policy of Aurangzeb during the Later Part of His Reign.' *Proceedings of the Indian History Congress* 47, no. 1 (1986).

Chishti, Noor Ahmad. *Tehqiqaat-i-Chishti.* Lahore: Punjabi Adabi Board, 1964.

Collett, Nigel. *The Butcher of Amritsar: General Reginald Dyer.* London: Hambledon Continuum, 2007.

Cunningham, J.D. *A History of the Sikhs: From the Origin of the Nation to the Battles of the Sutlej.* Lahore: Sang-e-Meel Publications, 2007.

Dalrymple, William, and Anita Anand. *Kohinoor: The Story of the World's Most Infamous Diamond.* Karachi: Oxford University Press, 2016.

Dhillon, Harish. 'The Literary Face of Bhagat Singh.' *Tribune,* 22 March 2011. http://www.tribuneindia.com/2011/20110322/edit.htm#6.

Dodwell, H.H., ed. *British India, 1497–1858.* Vol. 5 of *The Cambridge History of India,* 6 vols. Cambridge: Cambridge University Press, 1929.

Dogra, R.S.D. *Nation Keepers: Central Reserve Police Force.* New Delhi: APH Publishing Corporation, 2004.

Dryland, Estelle. 'Faiz Ahmed Faiz and the Rawalpindi Conspiracy Case.' *Journal of South Asian Literature* 27, no. 2 (1992).

Dunya News. 'Aisy Dastoor Ko Mien Nahi Manta.' 12 March 2013, dunyanews.tv/en/Pakistan/163910-Aisy-Dastoor-Ko-Mien-Nahi-Manta.

Eaton, Richard M. 'Temple Desecration and Indo-Muslim States.' *Journal of Islamic Studies* 11, no. 3 (2000).

Express Tribune. 'Imran Khan's "Tsunami" Sweeps Lahore.' 30 October 2011. tribune.com.pk/story/285058/pti-rally-in-lahore-live-updates/.

Fair, Christine C. *Fighting to the End: The Pakistan Army's Way of War.* Oxford: Oxford University Press, 2014.

Faletti's Hotel website. *Falettishotel.com.*

Farooqui, Amar. '"Divide and Rule"? Race, Military Recruitment and Society in Late Nineteenth Century Colonial India.' *Social Scientist* 43, no. 3/4 (2015).

Faruqui, Munis D. 'The Forgotten Prince: Mirza Hakim and the Formation of the Mughal Empire in India.' *Journal of the Economic and Social History of the Orient* 48, no. 4 (2005).

Fauq, Muhammad Din. *Hazrat Data Ganj Bakhsh: A Biography.* Lahore: Book Home Publishers, 2007.

Findly, Ellison Banks. *Nur Jahan: Empress of Mughal India.* New York: Oxford University Press, 1993.

Frembgen, Jurgen Wasim. *Nocturnal Music in the Land of the Sufis.* Oxford: Oxford University Press, 2012.

Gandhi, Rajmohan. 'Gandhi and Punjab.' *India International Centre Quarterly* 39, no. 1 (2012).

———. *Punjab: A History from Aurangzeb to Mountbatten.* New Delhi: Aleph Book Company, 2013.

Ganiel, Gladys, Heidemarie Winkel and Christophe Monnot, eds. 'Introduction.' In *Religion in Times of Crisis,* edited by William H. Swatos Jr. Leiden: Brill, 2014.

Gaur, I.D. *Martyr as Bridegroom: A Folk Representation of Bhagat Singh.* New Delhi: Anthem Press, 2008.

GeoTV. 'People Fed Up with "Takht-e-Lahore" Says Imran Khan.' 15 January 2017. https://www.geo.tv/latest/127416-People-fed-up-with-Takht-e-Lahore-says-Imran-Khan.

Glover, William J. *Making Lahore Modern: Constructing and Imagining a Colonial City.* Minneapolis, MN: University of Minnesota Press, 2008.

Griffin, Lepel. *Punjab Chiefs.* Translated by Bhagvan Das. Lahore: Sang-e-Meel Publications, 1993.

Gupta, Sumitra. 'The Arya Samaj and Indian National Movement.' *Proceedings of the Indian History Congress* 63 (2002).

Habib, Yasir. 'Shahbaz the Super CM Who Heads 18 Ministries.' *Pakistan Today*, 29 January 2012. https://www.pakistantoday.com.pk/2012/01/29/shahbaz-the-super-cm-who-heads-18-ministries/.

Hamdani, Yasser Latif. 'Mr Jinnah's Muslim Opponents.' *Pakistan Today*, 21 December 2013. https://www.pakistantoday.com.pk/2013/12/21/mr-jinnahs-muslim-opponents/.

Haqbaat. 'Why Was Salman Taseer Anti-Islamic?' n.d. http://haqbaat.com/why-was-salman-taseer-anti-islamic/.

Ijaz, Nadeem. 'Bradlaugh Hall's Demise.' *Pakistan Today*, 17 April 2011. https://www.pakistantoday.com.pk/2011/04/17/bradlaugh-halls-demise/.

Ikram, S.M. *Indian Muslims and Partition of India.* New Delhi: Atlantic Publishers, 1992.

Jafari, Aqeel Abbas. '15th September 1978.' In *Pakistan Chronicle Encyclopedia*, 2nd ed. Karachi: Virsa, 2011.

Jaiswal, Suvira. 'Historical Evolution of the Ram Legend.' *Social Scientist* 21, no. 3/4 (1993).

Jalal, Ayesha. *The Sole Spokesman: Jinnah, the Muslim League and the Demand for Pakistan.* Cambridge: Cambridge University Press, 1994.

———. *The Pity of Partition: Manto's Life, Times, and Work across the India–Pakistan Divide.* Karachi: Oxford University Press, 2013.

Katz, Nathan. 'The Identity of a Mystic: The Case of Sa'id Sarmad, a Jewish-Yogi-Sufi Courtier of the Mughals.' *Numen: International Review for the History of Religions* 47, no. 2 (2000).

Khalid, Haroon. *In Search of Shiva: A Study of Folk Religious Practices in Pakistan.* New Delhi: Rupa Publications, 2015.

———. *Walking with Nanak.* New Delhi: Tranquebar Press, 2016.

Khan, Abdul Wali. *Facts Are Facts: The Untold Story of India's Partition,* 2nd edn. Translated by Syeda Saiyidain Hameed. New Delhi: Vikas Publishing House, 2004.

Khan, Ahmad Fraz. 'How Not to Build a Transport System.' *Dawn,* 19 February 2017.

Khan, M. Ifzal-ur-Rahman. 'Religious Freedom to Non-Muslims under the Delhi Sultans (Summary).' *Proceedings of the Indian History Congress* 54 (1993).

Khan, Rameez, and Karamat Bhatty. 'Tragedy: Lahore Building Collapse Kills 14.' *Express Tribune,* 7 February 2012. https://tribune.com.pk/story/332741/tragedy-lahore-building-collapse-kills-14/.

Khare, Brij B. 'Indian Nationalism: The Political Origin.' *Indian Journal of Political Science* 50, no. 4 (1989).

Kinra, Rajeev. 'The Persistence of Gossip: Chandar Bhan and the Cultural Memory of Mughal Decline.' In *Writing Self, Writing Empire: Chandar Bhan Brahman and the Cultural World of the Indo-Persian State Secretary.* Oakland: University of California Press, 2015.

Kumar, Krishna. 'Colonial Citizen as an Educational Ideal.' *Economic and Political Weekly* 24, no. 5 (1989).

Kumar, Sunil, ed. *Demolishing Myths or Mosques and Temples? Readings on History and Temple Desecration in Medieval India.* New Delhi: Three Essays Collective, 2008.

Kumar, Sunil, and Ranjeeta Dutta. 'Reviewed Work(s): Demolishing Myths or Mosques and Temples? Readings on History and Temple Desecration in Medieval India.' *Social Scientist* 37, no. 11/12 (2009).

Lahore Gymkhana. 'History.' www.lahoregymkhana.pk/?page_id=2984.

Lal, Chaman. 'Revolutionary Legacy of Bhagat Singh.' *Economic and Political Weekly* 42, no. 37 (2007).

Lal, Kanhaiya. *Tareekh-i-Lahore.* Lahore: Majlis-i-taraqqi-yi adab, 1981.

Lyon, Peter. *Conflict between India and Pakistan: An Encyclopedia.* Santa Barbara: ABC-CLIO, 2008.

Mahmud, Salma. 'Lala Lajpat Rai, Son of the Soil.' *Lahorenama,* 21 October 2010, lahorenama.wordpress.com/2010/10/21/lala-lajpat-rai-son-of-the-soil/.

Malik, Farid A. 'Political Inmates of Lahore Fort.' *Pakistan Today*, 16 April 2016. https://www.pakistantoday.com.pk/2016/04/16/political-inmates-of-lahore-fort/.

Malik, Salahuddin. 'The Panjab and the Indian "Mutiny": A Reassessment.' *Islamic Studies* 15, no. 2 (1976).

Meri, Josef W., ed. *Medieval Islamic Civilization*, vol. 1. New York: Routledge, 2006.

Metcalf, Thomas R. 'The Influence of the Mutiny of 1857 on Land Policy in India.' *Historical Journal* 4, no. 2 (1961).

Mikaberidze, Alexander, ed. *Atrocities, Massacres and War Crimes: An Encyclopedia*, vol. 1. Santa Barbara: ABC-CLIO, 2013.

Miraj, Muhammad Hassan. 'Shaheed and Shahdara.' Dawn Blogs, 7 January 2013, www.dawn.com/news/777017.

———. 'Shaheed and Shahdara - II.' Dawn Blogs, 14 January 2013, https://www.dawn.com/news/778721.

Mishra, Yogendra. 'Did the Sahis Really Organize a Hindu Confederacy under Jayapala or Anandpala.' *Proceedings of the Indian History Congress* 32, (1970).

Mittal, S.K., and Irfan Habib. 'Towards Independence and Socialist Republic: Naujawan Bharat Sabha, Part 1.' *Social Scientist* 8, no. 2 (1979).

———. 'Towards Independence and Socialist Republic: Naujawan Bharat Sabha, Part 2.' *Social Scientist* 8, no. 3 (1979).

Mujahid, Sharif Al. 'Lahore Resolution and Question of Provincial Autonomy.' *Business Recorder*, 23 March 2007. http://fp.brecorder.com/2007/03/20070323542295/.

Mukherjee, Soma. *Royal Mughal Ladies and Their Contributions*. New Delhi: Gyan Publishing House, 2001.

Nabha, Kahan Singh. *Encyclopedia of Sikh Literature*, 5th edn. New Delhi: National Bookshop, 1990.

Nair, Neeti. 'Bhagat Singh as "Satyagrahi": The Limits to Non-Violence in Late Colonial India.' *Modern Asian Studies* 43, no. 3 (2009).

Narodin. 'Habib Jalib: The Poet of the People.' *Bodhi Commons*, 12 March 2013. http://li186-51.members.linode.com/article/habib-jalib-the-poet-of-the-people.

Nawa Zamana. 'Ghadar Movement ke Shaheed'. 28 October 2007.

Nevile, Pran. *Lahore: A Sentimental Journey*. New Delhi: Penguin Books, 2006.

Oberoi, Harjot. 'Ghadar Movement and Its Anarchist Genealogy.' *Economic and Political Weekly* 44, no. 50 (December 2009).

Ojha, P.N. 'Scholarship and Patronage of Learning of the Great Moghuls (1156–1707 ad).' *Proceedings of the Indian History Congress* 24 (1961).

Paracha, Nadeem F. 'Bleeding Green: The Rise and Fall of the IJT.' *Dawn*, 16 August 2012. https://www.dawn.com/news/742642/ bleeding-green-the-rise-and-fall-of-the-ijt.

Priyadarshan. 'Whose Does Valmiki Belong to?' *Forward Press*, 27 January 2016. www.forwardpress.in/2016/01/whose-does-valmiki-belong-to/.

Punjabics.com. 'Dulla Bhatti.' n.d. www.punjabics.com/Resistance/ Dulla%20Bhatti.htm.

Puri, Harish K. 'Revolutionary Organization: A Study of the Ghadar Movement.' *Social Scientist* 9, no. 2/3 (1980).

Puri, Rakshat. Review: *The Mystic Prince*. *India International Centre Quarterly* 21, no. 4 (1994).

Qaiser, Iqbal. *Historical Sikh Shrines in Pakistan*. Lahore: Punjabi History Board, 1998.

———. *Ujray Daran De Darshan*. Lahore: Pakistan Punjabi Adabi Board, 2017.

Raja, Shahzad. 'Villains of Habib Jalib.' *Friday Times*, 16 March 2012.

Rana, Bhavan Singh. *Chandra Shekhar Azad: An Immortal Revolutionary of India*. Translated by Brij Bhushan Paliwal. New Delhi: Diamond Pocket Books, 2004.

Raza, S. Jabir. 'Constructional Activity of the Ghaznavids.' *Proceedings of the Indian History Congress* 57 (1996).

———. 'Hindus under the Ghaznavids.' *Proceedings of the Indian History Congress* 71 (2010–11).

———. 'Mahmud's Ayaz in History.' *Proceedings of the Indian History Congress* 72, part 1 (2011).

Rehman, Abdul. 'Changing Concepts of Garden Design in Lahore from Mughal to Contemporary Times.' *Garden History Society* 37, no. 2 (2009).

Rehman, Sonya. 'Heritage: A Mosque for All Seasons.' *Dawn*, 6 April 2014. https://www.dawn.com/news/1098001.

Richards, John F. *Mughal Empire, Part 1*. Vol. 5 of *The New Cambridge History of India*. Cambridge: Cambridge University Press, 1995.

Safvi, Rana. 'Princess Zeb Un Nisa or the Concealed One.' Ranasafvi. com, 30 July 2016. ranasafvi.com/princess-zeb-un-nisa-or-the-concealed-one/.

Samaa TV. 'School Outlaws Punjabi as "Foul Language".' 13 October 2016. https://www.samaa.tv/pakistan/2016/10/school-outlaws-punjabi-as-foul-language/.

Sengupta, Nitish. *Land of Two Rivers: A History of Bengal from the Mahabharata to Mujib*. New Delhi: Penguin Random House, 2011.

Shah, Sabir. 'Sufi Shrines under Attack in Pakistan—a Chronology.' *The News*, 17 February 2017. https://www.thenews.com.pk/print/186913-Sufi-shrines-under-attack-in-Pakistan-a-chronology.

Shah, Syed Mujawar Hussain. *Bhutto, Zia and Islam*. Larkana: Shaheed Bhutto Publications, 2014.

Shahid, Dost Muhammad. 'Pakistan Movement and the Part Played by the Ahmadiyya Community.' Al Islam, n.d. www.alislam.org/library/articles/Pakistan-Movement-Ahmadiyya-Part2.pdf.

Shahid, Kunwar Khuldune. 'Addressing Constitutional Takfir.' *Friday Times*, 11 September 2015. http://www.thefridaytimes.com/tft/addressing-constitutional-takfir/.

Sharma, Harish C. 'British Policy towards Aristocracy in the Punjab.' *Proceedings of the Indian History Congress* 59, no. 2 (1998).

Sheikh, Majid. 'The Red Stones of Dara Shikoh.' In 'Features', *Dawn*, 20 June 2004. https://www.dawn.com/news/1066109.

———. 'Harking Back: Final Destruction of the Historical Minto Park.' *Dawn*, 13 April 2014. https://www.dawn.com/news/1099493/harking-back-final-destruction-of-the-historical-minto-park.

———. 'Harking Back: Timeless Debate about What Mori Gate Really Is.' *Dawn*, 25 May 2014. https://www.dawn.com/news/1108476.

———. 'Harking Back: Myths and Facts of the Beginnings of Lahore.' *Dawn*, 8 June 2014. https://www.dawn.com/news/1111338.

———. 'Harking Back: Abiding Mystery of the Roshani Gate Tragedy.' *Dawn*, 5 July 2015. https://www.dawn.com/news/1192448.

————. 'Harking Back: Two Ends of Ravi Road and How Our Freedom Fared.' *Dawn*, 11 September 2016. https://www.dawn.com/news/1283420.

————. 'Harking Back: In Search of the Origins and Age of Lahore.' *Dawn*, 12 November 2017. https://www.dawn.com/news/1369892.

Singh, Amarpal. *The Second Anglo-Sikh War*. Stroud: Amberley Publishing, 2016.

Singh, D.P. 'Lala Lajpat Rai: His Life, Times and Contributions to Indian Polity.' *Indian Journal of Political Science* 52, no. 1 (1991).

Singh, Khushwant. *The Sikhs*. New Delhi: HarperCollins, 2006.

Singh, Surinder. 'Darul Sultanat Lahore: The Socio-Cultural Profile of an Urban Centre, 1550–1700.' *Proceedings of the Indian History Congress* 54 (1993).

Soofi, Mushtaq. 'Punjab Notes: Mystery of Nau Nihal Singh's Death: The Story Teller's Version.' *Dawn*, 10 July 2015. https://www.dawn.com/news/1193542.

Subodh, Sanjay. 'Temples, Rulers and Historians' Dilemma: Understanding the Medieval Mind.' *Proceedings of the Indian History Congress* 62 (2001).

Swatos, William H. Jr., ed. *Religion in Times of Crisis*, vol. 24. Leiden: Brill, 2014.

T A. 'What's Left in Pakistan'. *Economic and Political Weekly* 8, no. 47 (1973).

Talbot, Ian, and Tahir Kamran. *Lahore in the Time of the Raj*. New Delhi: Penguin Random House, 2016.

Taseer, Sara. 'Remembering Taseer.' *Express Tribune*, 4 January 2018. https://tribune.com.pk/story/1599869/6-remembering-taseer/.

Thapar, Romila. *Somanatha: The Many Voices of a History*. London: Verso, 2005.

Triveda, D.S. 'Visnudhvaja.' *Annals of the Bhandarkar Oriental Research Institute* 40, no. 1/4 (1959).

Tufail, Muhammad, ed. 'Naqoosh Lahore Number.' *Idara Farogh-e-Urdu*, February 1962.

Tuteja, K.L. 'Jallianwala Bagh: A Critical Juncture in the Indian National Movement.' *Social Scientist* 25, no. 1/2 (1997).

University of Alberta website. 'Zeb-Un-Nisa's Tomb.' In 'Lahore Sites of Interest'. http://sites.ualberta.ca/~rnoor/tomb_zebunnisa.html.

Unknown. 'The True Story of Boota Singh', Blog, 4 November 2011, http://thetruestoryofbootasingh.blogspot.com/.

Waraich, Sukhmani. 'The Story behind Pakistan's Feminism of the 70s and 80s.' Vagabomb, 22 July 2015. www.vagabomb.com/The-Story-Behind-Pakistans-Feminism-Of-The-s-And-s/.

Waris, Bholanath. *Tarikh Shehar Lahore*. Lahore: Graph Publisher, 1998.

Wolpert, Stanley. *Nehru: A Tryst with Destiny*. New York: Oxford University Press, 1996.

———. *Zulfi Bhutto of Pakistan: His Life and Times*, 6th edn. Oxford: Oxford University Press, 2016.

World of Royalty. 'Padhania.' www.members.iinet.net.au/~royalty/ips/families/padhania.html.

YouTube. 'Shahbaz Sharif Reciting Habib Jalib Poem.' 25 February 2009. www.youtube.com/watch?v=33W33eZfEds.

YouTube. 'Story of Akbar and Dulla Bhatti 2.' 11 January 2010. https://www.youtube.com/watch?v=a60pNZn4NgE.

Zacharias, H.C.E. 'The Road to Indian Autonomy.' *Review of Politics* 8, no. 3 (1946).